Consciousness in Indian Philosophy

Bloomsbury Introductions to World Philosophies

Series Editor:
Monika Kirloskar-Steinbach

Assistant Series Editor:
Leah Kalmanson

Regional Editors:
Nader El-Bizri, James Madaio, Ann A. Pang-White, Takeshi Morisato,
Pascah Mungwini, Mickaella Perina, Omar Rivera and Georgina Stewart

Bloomsbury Introductions to World Philosophies delivers primers reflecting
exciting new developments in the trajectory of world philosophies. Instead
of privileging a single philosophical approach as the basis of comparison,
the series provides a platform for diverse philosophical perspectives to
accommodate the different dimensions of cross-cultural philosophizing.
While introducing thinkers, texts and themes emanating from
different world philosophies, each book, in an imaginative and
path-breaking way, makes clear how it departs from a conventional
treatment of the subject matter.

Titles in the Series:
A Practical Guide to World Philosophies, by Monika Kirloskar-Steinbach
and Leah Kalmanson
Daya Krishna and Twentieth-Century Indian Philosophy,
by Daniel Raveh
Māori Philosophy, by Georgina Tuari Stewart
Philosophy of Science and The Kyoto School, by Dean Anthony Brink
Tanabe Hajime and the Kyoto School, by Takeshi Morisato
African Philosophy, by Pascah Mungwini
The Zen Buddhist Philosophy of D. T. Suzuki, by Rossa Ó Muireartaigh
Sikh Philosophy, by Arvind-Pal Singh Mandair
The Philosophy of the Brahma-sūtra, by Aleksandar Uskokov
The Philosophy of the Yogasūtra, by Karen O'Brien-Kop
The Life and Thought of H. Odera Oruka, by Gail M. Presbey
Mexican Philosophy for the 21st Century, by Carlos Alberto Sánchez
Buddhist Ethics and the Bodhisattva Path, by Stephen Harris
Contextualizing Angela Davis, by Joy James
Environmental Equity in China and Beyond,
by Michael Nylan and Thomas Hahn

Consciousness in Indian Philosophy

Illuminating Mind, World, and Self

Matthew MacKenzie

BLOOMSBURY ACADEMIC
LONDON · NEW YORK · OXFORD · NEW DELHI · SYDNEY

BLOOMSBURY ACADEMIC
Bloomsbury Publishing Plc, 50 Bedford Square, London, WC1B 3DP, UK
Bloomsbury Publishing Inc, 1359 Broadway, New York, NY 10018, USA
Bloomsbury Publishing Ireland, 29 Earlsfort Terrace, Dublin 2, D02 AY28, Ireland

BLOOMSBURY, BLOOMSBURY ACADEMIC and the Diana logo are trademarks
of Bloomsbury Publishing Plc

First published in Great Britain 2026

Copyright © Matthew MacKenzie, 2026

Matthew MacKenzie has asserted their right under the Copyright, Designs and
Patents Act, 1988, to be identified as Author of this work.

For legal purposes the Acknowledgments on p. vi constitute an
extension of this copyright page.

Series design by Louise Dugdale
Cover image © Fuadi Alhusini / Adobe Stock

A catalogue record for this book is available from the British Library.

A catalog record for this book is available from the Library of Congress.

ISBN: HB: 978-1-3503-4299-6
PB: 978-1-3503-4300-9
ePDF: 978-1-3503-4301-6
eBook: 978-1-3503-4302-3

Series: Bloomsbury Introductions to World Philosophies

Typeset by Newgen KnowledgeWorks Pvt. Ltd., Chennai, India
Printed and bound in Great Britain

For product safety related questions contact productsafety@bloomsbury.com.

To find out more about our authors and books visit www.bloomsbury.com
and sign up for our newsletters.

Contents

Acknowledgments

I have been puzzling over the nature of consciousness, self, mind, and world for more than two decades. I have been immensely fortunate to discuss these issues and learn from many great philosophers. I would especially like to thank Arindam Chakrabarti, Evan Thompson, Mark Siderits, Christian Coseru, Dan Zahavi, Bronwyn Finnigan, Anand Vaidya, Galen Strawson, Chakravarthi Ram-Prasad, Dan Arnold, Malcolm Keating, and Laura Guerero for many helpful conversations on consciousness and Indian philosophy over the years. Thanks to Sean Smith for comments on the manuscript. Thanks also to my graduate and undergraduate students at Colorado State University who have encountered some of this material and many of these ideas in the classroom. Thanks to Monika Kirloskar-Steinbach, the editor of this series, and Colleen Coalter and the team at Bloomsbury for their unflagging support and patience. Much of this book was written during a (very appreciated!) sabbatical leave, made possible by CSU and the Department of Philosophy, and was supported in part by the Department's endowment fund. As always, my greatest thanks go to Ashby, Quinn, and Reid for their support, encouragement, and love.

Abbreviations

AK	*Abhidharmakośa* of Vasubandhu
AKBh	*Abhidharmakośabhāṣya* of Vasubandhu
BG	*Bhagavad Gītā*
BrSūBh	*Brahmasūtrabhāṣya* of Śaṅkara
BU	*Bṛhadāraṇyaka Upaniṣad*
BUBh	*Bṛhadāraṇyaka Upaniṣad Bhāṣya* of Śaṅkara
CU	*Chāndogya Upaniṣad*
CWSA	*Collected Works of Śri Aurobindo*
DS	*Dhammasaṅgaṇī*
ĪPK	*Īśvarapratyabhijñākārikā* of Utpaladeva
ĪPKV	*Īśvarapratyabhijñākārikāvṛtti* of Utpaladeva
ĪPV	*Īśvarapratyabhijñāvimarśinī* of Abhinavagupta
ĪPVV	*Īśvarapratyabhijñāvivṛtivimarśinī* of Abhinavagupta
MK	*Māṇḍūkyakārikā* of Gauḍapāda
MMK	*Mūlamadhyamakakārikā* of Nāgārjuna
MN	*Majjhima Nikāya*
NBh	*Nyāya-bhāṣya* of Vātsyāyana
NS	*Nyāya Sūtra* of Gautama
NV	*Nyāyavārttika* of Uddyotakara
PP	*Pratyakṣapariccheda* of Kumārila
PS	*Pramāṇasamuccaya* of Dignāga
PSV	*Pramāṇasamuccayavṛtti* of Dignāga
PV	*Pramāṇavarttika* of Dharmakīrti
PVin	*Pramāṇaviniścaya* of Dharmakīrti
PVT	*Pramāṇavarttikaṭīkā* of Śākyabuddhi
SN	*Saṃyutta Nikāya*
SP	*Sambandha Parīkṣā* of Dharmakīrti
ŚSV	*Śivasūtravimarśinī* of Kṣemarāja
TBh	*Tarkabhāṣā* of Mokṣākaragupta
TP	*Tattvaprādīpika* of Citsukha
Trimś	*Trimśikā* of Vasubandhu
TU	*Taittirīyā Upaniṣad*
Upad.	*Upadeśasāhasrī* of Śaṅkara
VC	*Viveka Cūḍāmaṇi* of Śaṅkara
Vimś	*Vimśatikā* of Vasubandhu
Vism	*Visuddhimagga* of Buddhaghosa

Viṃś-vṛ	*Viṃśatikāvṛtti* of Vasubandhu
YBh	*Yogabhāṣya* of Vyāsa
YcBh	*Yogācārabhūmi* of Asaṅga
YS	*Yoga Sūtra* of Patañjali

Introduction

Aims of the Book

Consciousness has been a central theme of Indian philosophy for more than 2500 years. In the Upaniṣads, sages and kings discuss the elusive light (*prakāśa*) of consciousness and its relation to one's deepest self (*ātman*) and to the fundamental ground or nature of reality (*brahman*). In early Buddhist texts, we find explorations of the complex, multivalent flow of conscious mental events within an impermanent, selfless reality. In yogic texts we find a sharp distinction between ever-shifting contents or objects and the pure light of consciousness itself. Moreover, philosophical inquiry into the nature of consciousness is closely tied to other issues in epistemology, metaphysics, ethics, and spirituality. For instance, there are sharp disagreements about the relationship between consciousness and the self. Is consciousness a fundamental capacity of the self? Is consciousness *identical* to the self? Or is the self an illusion created (in part) by the operation of an ultimately selfless consciousness? Additionally, there are important debates about consciousness and knowledge. Indian philosophers generally agreed that consciousness plays a critical role in knowledge acquisition, but there were significant disagreements concerning both the objects and the means of knowledge. Does consciousness provide direct access to a world of independent objects? Or does it facilitate knowledge indirectly through mental representations or images? And what is the relationship between consciousness and concepts or thought? Finally, what is the relationship between consciousness and the broad nature of reality? Is consciousness metaphysically fundamental? Or is it some sort of emergent property? Does it persist through time or is it merely momentary? Classical Indian philosophy is replete with rich and nuanced debates on these and related issues.

The aim of this book is to provide a comparative and critical introduction to several influential theories of consciousness developed in the Indian tradition. Primarily focused on the classical period (approximately 100 CE–1400 CE), it surveys the views of consciousness developed in the Abhidharma, Yogācāra, and Pramāṇavāda schools of Buddhism and the Nyāya, Yoga, Advaita, and Pratyabhijñā schools of Hinduism. The book covers topics such as the relationship between consciousness and self-consciousness, intentionality, the self, cognition and perception, and the unity and continuity of consciousness. It also explores the metaphysics of consciousness in relation to the self, mental causation, and spiritual liberation, as well as idealism, dualism, and materialism. The central focus of the book is on the classical Indian tradition, but it also draws on historical and contemporary Western philosophy to deepen and extend the dialogue between these traditions.

More broadly the book is a contribution to the field of global or cosmopolitan philosophy. Regarding Western philosophy, there is wide recognition that it is constituted by several distinct but interwoven historical and contemporary intellectual traditions, such as those of ancient Greece, North Africa, France, Germany, and the English-speaking countries. It incorporates and responds to several religious traditions such as Judaism, Christianity, Islam, and classical pagan traditions. And it incorporates a wide variety of methods such as conceptual analysis, transcendental phenomenology, hermeneutics, or historically influential approaches like rationalism, empiricism, or pragmatism. And yet, Western philosophy no doubt constitutes a broad and multivalent, but identifiable tradition of philosophizing.

Much the same can be said for the broad and pluralistic traditions of India, China, Africa, and more. These form distinct but by no means isolated traditions of philosophical inquiry and debate that have given rise to rich philosophical literatures. Each of these traditions is worth studying. And the existence of and interactions between these rich philosophical traditions shows that philosophy has always been a global enterprise. The aim of cosmopolitan philosophy, though, is not just to recognize the global nature of philosophy. It is to *do philosophy* in a global or cross-cultural way. At a minimum this requires familiarity with more than one philosophical tradition, including its main historical figures, texts, ideas, controversies, and methods. It also requires a commitment to doing philosophy in dialogue with multiple traditions. That is, doing philosophy in a way that goes beyond a (laudatory) recognition of its global nature and endeavors to frame and think through philosophical questions and issues informed by the perspectives afforded by more than one tradition. As Jonardon Ganeri argues, such an endeavor allows,

> a new kind of cross-cultural philosophical skill becomes available: the ability to attend to a conceptual terrain from a plurality of cultural perspectives, and to allow that act itself to deepen one's vision of the intellectual terrain. This cosmopolitan philosophical skill thus consists in an ability to sustain multiple cultural orientations,

philosophical creativity borne in the way in which inflections from each cultural perspective give shape to and infuse bicultural attention. Just as binocular vision enables one to see aspects of one's perceptual environment that are invisible to monocular sight, so multiply encultured attention enables one to grasp aspects of the conceptual terrain that go unobserved otherwise.

(Ganeri 2015, 2)

The conceptual terrain of this book is the nature of consciousness and related issues such as mind, self, and world. As I hope will be apparent in reading the following chapters, Indian thinkers develop rich, sophisticated, and rigorous philosophical accounts of these issues. By learning about their views and arguments, the reader will gain some familiarity with the Indian philosophical tradition and build the cross-cultural philosophical skill of engaging with the deep questions about consciousness from multiple perspectives.

One important upshot of this type of cross-cultural inquiry is a reconfiguration of the contemporary conceptual terrain or problem space in light of the long history of Indian debates. For much of the twentieth century in philosophy and other fields like psychology or neuroscience, the problem of consciousness was largely ignored (Strawson 2019). It was largely assumed that materialism (physicalism) had won the day and that the nature of consciousness was not a very philosophically salient concern. However, in contemporary Anglophone philosophy of mind, consciousness is very much back on the agenda (Chalmers 2010) and philosophers often approach (and introduce students to) the field through a consideration of the Western mind-body problem, or the contemporary debate between physicalism and its rivals, such as dualism, panpsychism, or strong emergentism.

Yet, in the classical Indian context, this is not the central or organizing problem. Rather, as discussed throughout this book, Indian debates are much more commonly organized around the problem of the self, both in terms of its nature and its existence. That is, arguably the main divide in this area of classical Indian philosophy is not between dualists and materialists (or idealists for that matter), but rather between those who defend the existence of the self (*ātmavādins*) and those who deny it (*anātmavādins*). Furthermore, as introduced in Chapter 1, another central controversy, which cuts across the self/no-self divide, is between self-illuminationist (*svaprakāśavāda*) and other-illuminationist (*paraprakāśavāda*) accounts of consciousness.

Regarding the self, the central question is whether mental life or experience is grounded in or organized around an enduring locus of consciousness, cognition, or agency. For all their many and important differences, the *ātmavādins* answer in the affirmative. They argue that to make sense of mental life, the coherence of experience, agency, and cognitive access to the world, one must affirm a unified self at the center of our being. In sharp contrast, Buddhist thinkers decisively reject this core commitment. They therefore must develop and defend accounts of mental life in terms of multiplicity and flux, and in terms of the causal connections between distinct, momentary particulars, rather than the unity of the self. This core difference ramifies through the rest of their thought on mind, knowledge, ethics, and more. In the contemporary context, this basic divide between models of the mind and mental life based on the self and those that reject the self is worth deeper examination. What might it mean to take the self/selfless divide as at least as, if not more fundamental than, the physicalist/non-physicalist divide? For a given model of the mind, how are its accounts of consciousness, cognition, agency, and embodiment shaped by a commitment to self or selflessness?

Regarding luminosity (*prakāśa*), as explained in Chapter 1, the fundamental idea is of consciousness as (the power of) experiential presentation. The very nature of consciousness is to illuminate, present, or make manifest. The next and crucial question is whether the basic nature of consciousness is to present that which is *other*, to present *itself*, or some combination of the two. Other-illuminationists argue that the nature of consciousness is to present that which is other. And based on this commitment, they tend to argue for a higher-order view of self-consciousness, a transparent or aspectless (*nirākāravāda*) view of awareness, an externalist view of intentionality, and a direct theory of perception. Interestingly, this applies to both the resolutely metaphysical realist, *ātmavādin* Naiyāyikas (Chapter 2) and to the resolutely non-realist, *anātmavādin* Mādhyamika Buddhists (Siderits 2020). In contrast, self-illuminationists tend to argue for a reflexive or same-order view of self-consciousness, an aspectual (*sākāravāda*) view of awareness, an internalist view of intentionality, and an indirect or phenomenalist account of perception (see Chapters 3, 6, and 7). Furthermore, as both Buddhists and Naiyāyikas have argued, the concepts of an independent persisting self and a mind-independent world of persisting objects are deeply intertwined (Chapters 2 and 5). In this way, one's views of the self and of consciousness will constrain one's view of the world and our access to and agency within it. Again, we may ask, for a given model of the mind, how are its views of self, agency, cognition, and world shaped by its commitment to other-illuminationism or self-illuminationism?

In sum, familiarity and philosophical engagement with classical Indian philosophy enriches our understanding of consciousness, our knowledge of the global history of philosophy, and sharpens the cross-cultural philosophical skill of "multiply encultured attention" that enables the reader to "grasp aspects of the conceptual terrain that go [might] unobserved otherwise"

(Ganeri 2015, 2). My goal is to advance these aims by providing a partial map of the conceptual terrain of classical Indian theories of consciousness.

This book is organized around different classical Indian philosophical schools or systems. The common term to refer to a school or system is *darśana*, from the root *dṛś*, 'to see'. *Darśana*, then, can mean a point of view, doctrine, or vision. Importantly however, a philosophical perspective is arrived at through the method of critical inquiry (*ānvīkṣikī*). So, we might say that a proper philosophical perspective (*darśana*) is one that emerges from a proper process of critical rational inquiry (*ānvīkṣikī*). The distinct philosophical schools were typically organized around a central philosophical text (usually called a *sūtra*) which laid out the core philosophical ideas of the school of thought and defended it from important objections. Additionally, there were commonly longer philosophical commentaries on the central text or texts, written by the author or subsequent thinkers associated with that school. So, for example, the *Nyāya Sūtra* is attributed to Akṣapāda Gautama, and was written sometime between the sixth century BCE and the second century CE. The text consists of several chapters on topics in logic, debate, epistemology, metaphysics, and related issues. It formed the basis for several later commentaries such as Vātsyāyana's (c450 CE) *Nyāya-bhāṣya*, which further developed and defended the Nyāya philosophical perspective.

It is common to divide classical Indian schools into so-called orthodox (*āstika*) and heterodox (*nāstika*). Here the orthodoxy in question is Vedic or Hindu—that is, *āstika* schools accept the scriptural authority of the Vedas, while *nāstika* schools do not. The six major *āstika* schools are Nyāya, Vaiśeṣika, Sāṅkhya, Yoga, Mīmāṃsā, and Vedānta. Major *nāstika* schools include Jainism, Buddhism, and Cārvāka. But despite this tidy categorization, it is important to note the great plurality of views, methods, and concerns both within and between distinct schools, thinkers, and time-periods.

Other Traditions or Schools

While this book aims to present a comparative and critical introduction to several influential classical Indian theories of consciousness, it is not a comprehensive introduction. A vast range of views and traditions have developed over the 2500-year history of Indian philosophy. To make the introduction manageable, I have had to be selective in my presentation of Indian schools. I chose schools based on direct relevance to the philosophy of consciousness, historical and philosophical influence, availability of primary and secondary literature, and fruitful comparative connections. More idiosyncratically, I chose based in part on my own interest and expertise.

Given the selectivity of the book, a few comments on schools or traditions not covered is in order.

Regarding *nāstika* (heterodox) schools or traditions, I will mention three. First is the Jain tradition which is based on the teachings of Mahāvīra (599–527 BCE). Jain philosophers defended a dualistic ontology of individual, non-physical substantial selves (*jīva*) and the "non-self" (*ajīva*) world of materiality and its organizational principles such as space, time, and motion. Further, the tradition is non-theistic. In the Jain view, the self is the enduring locus of consciousness, cognition, and agency and is subject to the bondage of karma. Thus, while its dualistic ontology is similar to the Sānkhya and Yoga views discussed in Chapter 4, Jainism differs on the issue of the agency of the self. That is, in the Jain view, the self is essentially an agent and therefore has the power and the responsibility to liberate itself from the bondage of karma. Finally, Jain philosophers defended the distinctive view of *anekāntavāda* or "non-one-sidedness" or "many-sidedness." Reality is multi-faceted and known only through multiple irreducible viewpoints (*naya*). As an adjunct to *anekāntavāda*, Jain philosophers developed a theory of conditional predication (*syādvāda*).[1]

The second school is Cārvāka (or Lokāyata), founded by the philosopher Bṛhaspati (date unknown). Cārvāka philosophers were thorough-going materialists. They argued that mind and consciousness arise from the physical body or organism, which itself arises from complex combinations of material elements. As Bṛhaspati states:

1.2　Earth, fire, air, and water are the reals.
1.3　Their combination is called the 'body', 'senses', and 'objects'.
1.4　Consciousness (*caitanya*) [is formed] out of these [elementary reals].
1.5　As the power to intoxicate [is formed] out of fermenting ingredients.
1.6　A human being (*puruṣa*) is a body qualified by consciousness.
1.7　[Thinking is] from the body alone.
1.8　Because of its presence when there is a body.[2]

As Jonardon Ganeri explains, "According to Bṛhaspati, thinking is due to the four constitutive principles of matter, just as the power to intoxicate is due to the ingredients in the wine. What we call a human body, or a sense organ, or a physical object, is just a combination (*samudāya*; an assemblage) of earth, fire, air, and water; indeed, these four kinds of matter are all there is. A person is a human body endued with thinking, and individual lives differ one from another as bubbles differ in water" (2011, 674). Given their materialism,

Cārvāka thinkers also rejected the theories of karma and rebirth, and accepted only perception (*pratyakṣa*) as a valid means of knowledge (*pramāṇa*).

The third school is Buddhist Madhyamaka (Middle Way). This school has its origin in the philosopher Nāgārjuna (c. 150–250 CE), whose major philosophical work is the *Mūlamadhyamakakārikā* (Root Verses on the Middle Way; MMK). In the MMK, Nāgārjuna's project is primarily critical, and his primary philosophical target is the notion of *svabhāva* ("own-being" or "inherent existence"). An entity has *svabhāva* when it is ontologically independent of other objects, has an intrinsic and fixed nature or essence, and can be individuated mind-independently. Importantly, then, to say that an entity is (or has) *svabhāva* is not simply to claim that it exists, but rather to specify its *mode* of existence: it is claimed to exist independently or absolutely. Mādhyamikas deny that anything could have this mode of existence and point out that the deep assumption that to be real is to be *svabhāva* inexorably leads to paradox. To say that an entity lacks *svabhāva* is just to say that the entity is empty (*śūnya*). Moreover, the emptiness of phenomena is said to be an implication of phenomena being dependently originated (*pratītyasamutpanna*) (and vice versa). As we see in MMK Chapter 24:

18. Dependent origination we declare to be emptiness.
    It [emptiness] is a dependent concept; just that is the middle path.
19. There being no *dharma* whatsoever that is not dependently
    originated,
    It follows that there is no dharma whatsoever that is non-empty.[3]

This implies that consciousness (*vijñāna*) and other mental phenomena are dependently originated and empty of inherent existence. For instance, a moment of sensory consciousness depends on its causal basis and its sensory object. More subtly, Nāgārjuna and other Madhyamaka thinkers argue that empty phenomena depend on conceptual imputation (*prajñapti*). According to Jan Westerhoff, Nāgārjuna offers a view, "in which the connection between objects [concepts] and language is based on conventions, and, more importantly, one in which there is also no preexistent, foundational division of the world 'by the joints' into a set of individuals, properties, and relations. The division of the world into things is as much convention-based as the set of [conceptual and] linguistic items we use to refer to them" (2017, 103). The upshot for philosophy of consciousness is that, according to Mādhyamikas, consciousness cannot have any kind of essence or independent existence, and our grasp of our own consciousness depends on our concepts and conventions just like any other phenomenon. On Jay Garfield's interpretation of Madhyamaka, "the fundamental cognitive illusion is to take our mental states to exist intrinsically rather than conventionally, and for our knowledge of them to be immediate, independent of conventions" (2022, 253). Indeed, he further argues that the emptiness of all phenomena implies, "We are nothing but conventionally real, interdependent beings among other beings, participants in a boundless and groundless web of dependent origination, in which nothing has any true nature, but in which everything can be understood in a matrix of interdependence" (260).[4]

Regarding the *āstika* or orthodox schools, I will mention two broad traditions. First is the tradition of Mīmāṃsā. Prābhākara Mīmāṃsā is one of the tradition's two major subschools. It was founded by Prabhākara Miśra (sixth–seventh century CE), a key interpreter of Vedic ritualism and epistemology. In the philosophy of mind and consciousness, the Prābhākara school defends the *tripuṭi-pratyakṣa* ("threefold-perception") theory of the structure of consciousness. On this view, an episode of consciousness reveals its object (*prameya*), its subject (*pramātṛ*), and the episode itself (*pramiti*). For instance, when I see a table, my perception reveals the table, the seeing, and myself as the seer. And I can articulate the perceptual content as "I am seeing a table." The other sub-school is Bhāṭṭa Mīmāṃsā, founded by Kumārila Bhaṭṭa (c. seventh century CE), was particularly focused on issues in philosophy of language and epistemology. In philosophy of mind, Kumārila was particularly critical of the theory of consciousness as self-revealing (*svataḥ prakāśa*).[5] As an alternative, he argued that what is revealed in an episode of consciousness is the object, and the consciousness and the self are revealed by subsequent cognitions in part based on the earlier consciousness of the object. In particular, it was the object *as* cognized (*jñātatā*) that supports the subsequent awareness of the cognition. For instance, it is the table *as seen* that leads to awareness that there was a seeing and seer of the table.[6]

The second orthodox tradition is Vedānta. The term *vedānta* refers to the end or highest teachings of the Vedas, the scriptural foundation of the *Brahmanical* or Hindu traditions. Their sister school, Mīmāṃsā, focused on the portion of the Vedas dealing with ritual and proper action (the *karmakāṇḍa*). Vedānta focused on the portion dealing with knowledge of the real self and ultimate reality (the *jñānakāṇḍa*), that is, the Upaniṣads. There are several sub-schools of Vedānta, including Advaita (nondualist), Viśiṣṭādvaita (qualified nondualist), and Dvaita (dualist).[7] Chapter 6 of this book covers Advaita. The Viśiṣṭādvaita philosopher, Rāmānuja (c. 1017–c. 1137), argued that it is the very nature of consciousness to present an object, and that consciousness presents itself through presenting its object. He writes in the *Śrī Bhāṣya*, "Nor is there any consciousness devoid of objects; for nothing of this kind is ever known. Moreover, the self-luminousness of consciousness has ... been proved on the ground that its essential nature consists in illumining (revealing) objects; the self-luminousness of consciousness not admitting of proof apart from its essential nature which consists in the lighting up of objects" (I.i.1). He also defended the existence of the real individual self, as against the Buddhist proponents of no-self and the Advaita proponents of a universal or non-individuated self.[8] The Dvaita philosopher, Madhva (1238–1317 CE), argues that individual selves are real and eternal. Each self has a distinct, unified domain of personal experience (*anusandhāna*) which it does not share with other selves. That is, each self experiences the world, other selves, and God from its own irreducibly unique first-person perspective. Moreover, Madhva argues against the Advaitins that the self *can* be its own object of knowledge in typical cases of self-knowledge.[9]

Again, the philosophical traditions of India are rich and varied. Further study of any of these thinkers or schools would no doubt enrich our philosophical understanding of consciousness and related issues. However, they are beyond the scope of the present work.

Overview of the Chapters

Chapter 1 "Consciousness as Luminosity" traces the origins and philosophical import of consciousness as luminosity (*prakāśa*). The metaphor of consciousness as light can be traced backed to the Upaniṣads, where both consciousness and the self are understood as akin to light in their capacity to disclose the world.[10] In later Indian philosophy luminosity takes on a more technical sense as the power of consciousness to experientially present an object or content to a subject. The chapter delineates the two broad approaches to the luminosity framework: other-luminosity (*paraprakāśatā*) and self-luminosity (*svaprakāśatā*). In the other-illuminationist view, consciousness is primarily understood as the capacity to reveal that which is other, such as a mind-independent object. In the self-illuminationist view, the distinctive feature of consciousness is that, even as it may reveal that which is other, it also reveals itself. The chapter then connects these views to the question of the existence and nature of the self. It concludes with comparative reflections on historical Western debates on the relationship between consciousness and self-consciousness, from Aristotle to Franz Brentano.

Chapter 2 "Nyāya" covers the Nyāya school's robustly realist and other-illuminationist views of consciousness and cognition. Nyāya is ontologically realist concerning self, consciousness, and world. It is epistemologically realist concerning veridical cognition of mind-independent objects and defends a direct realist theory of perception. Nyāya realism is, in turn, tightly bound up with an intentionalist and first-order analysis of consciousness. It is the very nature of consciousness to be of or about an object, and the luminosity of a cognition consists in revealing its object, not itself. That is, it illuminates that which is other than itself (its object) and requires a distinct, second-order cognition for a first-order cognition to be revealed. The chapter then explores the Nyāya argument that the diachronic unity of consciousness, grounded in an enduring self, is required for veridical cognition of an objective world. The chapter concludes with comparative reflections on the Nyāya theory in relation to the Sartrean view of intentionality, first-order representationalist theories of consciousness in analytic philosophy, and the metaphysics of substance dualism.

Chapter 3 "Abhidharma" examines analyses of consciousness developed in the Abhidharma schools of Buddhism, particularly the Sarvāstivāda, Sautrāntika, and Theravāda. These schools developed sophisticated accounts of the elements and processes of sentient experience, especially regarding the process of perception. The chapter discusses the canonical Buddhist account of the person as without self and analyzable in terms of five skandhas ("bundles" or "collections"): body (*rūpa*), affect (*vedanā*), cognition (*saṃjñā*), conditioning (*saṃskāra*), and consciousness (*vijñāna*). It will then examine the Abhidharma analysis of experience into its basic elements (*dharmas*) and the analysis of consciousness in terms of basic awareness (*citta*) and its associated mental factors (*caitta*), such as sensory contact (*sparśa*), affect (*vedanā*), cognition (*saṃjñā*), conation (*cetanā*), and attention (*manaskāra*). The resulting account understands mind and consciousness as dependently originated processes grounded in the pre-consciousness dynamics of bodily, sensory, affective, conative and cognitive events. The chapter concludes with comparative reflections on the (apparent) continuity of consciousness, reductionism about personal identity, and questions of realism and anti-realism.

Chapter 4 "Yoga" takes up the account of mind and consciousness in the Yoga school of philosophy, as set forth in the *Yoga Sūtras* of Patañjali. Drawing on the metaphysics of the older Sāṅkhya school, Yoga philosophy is based on the fundamental ontological distinction between *prakṛti* and *puruṣa*. *Prakṛti* here refers to material or natural reality in all its variegated forms. *Puruṣa* here refers to the most essential conscious, spiritual self. On this view, there is only one dynamic material reality, while there are many individual selves. *Puruṣa* and *prakṛti* are equally real, mutually distinct, and irreducible. They are, therefore, the two ultimate principles of the metaphysically dualistic system of Yoga. Unlike most forms of dualism in the West, however, Yoga views mind (*citta*) as a subtle form of *prakṛti* and therefore material. The mind is constituted by the integrated functioning of intelligence (*buddhi*), ego (*ahaṅkāra*), and other forms of mentation (*manas*). *Puruṣa*, as pure awareness, is ontologically independent from *prakṛti*, including the mind. The chapter concludes with a comparative discussion of the "hard problem" of consciousness, mental causation, and metaphysical theories of monism, dualism, and pluralism.

Chapter 5 "Yogācāra" explores the Yogācāra Buddhist account of consciousness, mainly through a discussion of Vasubandhu. According to Vasubandhu's Yogācāra, there are eight types or levels of consciousness (*citta*). There are five types of sensory consciousness (vision, hearing, and so on.) as well as a mental or inner sense (*manas*). These six constitute the manifest dimension of consciousness (*pravṛttivijñāna*). In addition, Vasubandhu posits an (ultimately delusory) self-representation (*kliṣṭamanas*) and a continuous base or background consciousness (*ālayavijñāna*). The flow of experience is explained in terms of the dynamic relations between these levels or dimensions of consciousness. Furthermore, Vasubandhu develops an account of the three natures (*trisvabhāva*) of phenomena as ultimately grounded in (selfless, dependently arising) consciousness. These analyses of consciousness and phenomena constitute a sophisticated form of Buddhist idealism that is in sharp contrast to the Advaita idealism discussed in the next chapter. The chapter concludes with comparative reflections on recent developments in cognitive science such as the "virtual world" theories developed (independently) by Thomas Metzinger and Donald Hoffman, as well as the broader issue of metaphysical idealism.

Chapter 6 "Advaita Vedānta" covers the Advaita Vedānta account of consciousness primarily as developed by Śaṅkara. According to Advaita thinkers, the nature of consciousness (*cit*) is pure self-luminous subjectivity. It is the pure witness (*sākṣin*) of any objects of consciousness. What we normally think of as the intentionality of consciousness itself actually arises from the association of pure non-intentional consciousness with certain non-conscious mental states (*vṛtti*). The *ātman*, or self as pure consciousness, is the self-luminous source of illumination for any phenomenon whatsoever, "internal" or "external," and cannot itself become an object of cognition. The chapter also explores the Advaitin account of mind, body, and world as distinct from but ultimately grounded in pure consciousness. It then turns to the problem of how the empirical subject (*jīva*) is individuated when consciousness itself is non-individuated. The chapter concludes with comparative reflections on the relationship between consciousness and intentionality, nondual awareness, and the ontological status and scope of consciousness.

Chapter 7 "Buddhist Pramāṇavāda" explores the work of Buddhist Pramāṇavādins, such as Dignāga, Dharmakīrti, and Śāntarakṣita. According to these thinkers, a typical moment of consciousness has two aspects: the object-aspect and the subject-aspect. The object-aspect presents the intentional objects (what the moment of consciousness is *as of*), while the subject-aspect presents features of the moment itself. Furthermore, every moment of consciousness is characterized by reflexive awareness (*svasaṃvedana*), the basic acquaintance of consciousness with itself. Hence, for these thinkers, consciousness is self-luminous, even as it also presents that which is (apparently) other. In this respect, the Buddhist Pramāṇavādins are like other proponents of self-luminosity, such as Yoga and Advaita. However, Buddhist self-illuminationism is articulated and defended within the context of an ontology of selfless, momentary events. The chapter concludes with some reflections on Buddhist reflexivism in relation to a phenomenological "modal model" of consciousness, the influence of Buddhist Pramāṇavāda ideas on several contemporary philosophers, and whether it might provide a minimal model of phenomenal consciousness.

Chapter 8 "Pratyabijñā" discusses the Pratyabijñā ("Recognition") school of nondual Śaivism, associated with Utpaladeva and Abhinavagupta. According to this school, the nature of consciousness is *prakāśa-vimarśa* or luminous (self-) recognition. It is the very essence of consciousness to manifest or illuminate both objects and itself. But in doing so consciousness manifests objects as objects and (necessarily) manifests itself as itself or as subject. This pre-reflective recognition of the subject in every act of illumination is central to the *vimarśa* aspect of consciousness. For the Pratyabijñā school, this has several important implications. First, it implies that consciousness as subjectivity is radically non-objectifiable. Second, it implies that consciousness is essentially dynamic. Third, it implies the diachronic unity of this dynamic subjectivity. The self is neither a false construction, as in Buddhism, nor a pure, static witness, as in Advaita. Rather it is free, creative, dynamic subjectivity. Furthermore, as a form of nondualism, the Pratyabijñā school argues that each individual self is not ontologically distinct from the free, creative, and self-luminous universal consciousness (*Śiva*). The chapter concludes with a comparative reflection on nondual Śaivism in relation to contemporary forms panpsychism and cosmopsychism, as well as three forms of metaphysical monism.

Finally, the conclusion traces some of the developments in Indian philosophy after the classical period, including the thought of Śrīharṣa and Gaṅgeśa. The conclusion ends with a discussion of two important figures from the early twentieth-century Indian Renaissance, Sri Aurobindo and Krishnachandra Bhattacharyya. Both thinkers made significant contributions to the philosophy of consciousness and developed truly global forms of philosophy.

Notes

1 For more on Jain philosophy see (Balcerowicz 2017), (Matilal 2012), (Shah 2000), and (Gorisse 2024).
2 (Bhattacharya 2002, 612)
3 Translation by (Siderits and Katsura 2013).
4 For more on Madhyamaka philosophy see (Siderits and Katsura 2013), (Siderits 2015), (Siderits 2020), (Garfield 2006), (Garfield 2015), (MacKenzie 2021), (MacKenzie 2022), (Westerhoff 2009), and (Westerhoff 2024).
5 See Chapter 1, sections 1.3–4 for further discussion.
6 For more on Mīmāṃsā see (Taber 1990), (Taber 2012), (Arnold 2008), (Watson 2020), and (Keating 2022).
7 Others include Bhedābheda (difference and non-difference), Śuddhādvaita (pure nondualism), and Acintyabhedābheda (inconceivable difference and non-difference).
8 For more on Rāmānuja and Viśiṣṭādvaita see (Rāmānuja 1890), (Bhatt 2023), and (Bartley 2013).
9 For more on Madhva and Dvaita see (Sarma 2003) and (Sharma 2000).
10 For instance, see *Bṛhadāraṇyaka Upaniṣad* (4.3.5) and *Chāndogya Upaniṣad* (3.14.3–4).

1

Consciousness as Luminosity

1.1 Origins

The textual origins of Indian philosophy, including reflection on the nature of consciousness, can be in part traced back to the Upaniṣads. These texts, likely composed between 800 and 400 BCE, reflect a deep and broad range of spiritual and philosophical concerns. The Upaniṣads respond to and expound upon many of the central ideas and themes in the earlier Vedas, but we can also see the development of new ideas and themes. Moreover, the Upaniṣads are primarily dialogues—between family members, kings and sages, forest-dwelling seekers, even between gods and demons.[1] It is through these conversations and debates that we see the emergence of many of the broad themes that characterize later Indian philosophy.

Perhaps the most central theme of the Upaniṣads is the quest for knowledge of the deepest nature of things. The world presents a huge variety of forms, but what is the underlying source and nature of the world? Can it be known? The term for the deepest nature and source of all things is *brahman*, from the root *bṛh* related to "grow" and "great," the deepest source and highest principle of all things. In the *Taittirīyā Upaniṣad*, Bhṛgu asks his father Varuṇa:

> "Sir, teach me brahman." And Varuna told him this: "Food, lifebreath, sight, hearing, mind, speech." He further said: "That from which these beings are born; on which, once born, they live; and into which they pass upon death—seek to perceive that! That is brahman!" ... "Seek to perceive brahman by means of austerity. Brahman is austerity."
>
> (TU 3.5.1)

Here we see *brahman* understood as the originating and sustaining cause of the world as well as that which receives beings upon death. And this reality can be known by rigorous practice of austerity leading to spiritual purification. Elsewhere in the Upaniṣads knowledge of *brahman* is compared to understanding the nature of clay from one lump of clay or the nature of gold from one nugget (CU 6.1.4–6). Here *brahman* is understood as the fundamental material cause of reality, known through examination of the shared nature of its forms. In another passage, *brahman* is likened to salt dissolved in water (CU 6.12.1–4). It is the unseen but all-pervading essence of things, that can be known through a direct taste (or direct experience).

A second and closely related theme of the Upaniṣads is the quest for knowledge of the self, our own deepest nature. Is there a fundamental core or essence of each individual? If so, can it be known? The Sanskrit term for the deepest core or nature of the individual is *ātman* (self), originally meaning "breath." We will discuss the *ātman* more fully in the next section. For now, it is important to note the key features of the *ātman*. First, it is the essence of the person, knowledge of which is necessary for spiritual liberation (*mokṣa*). Second, it is the vital principle enlivening the body, but which transcends the body. That is, it is immaterial, distinct from the body, and it survives the death of the body. Third, it is deeply connected to consciousness and the nature of the person as a subject of experience. The quest for knowledge of *ātman* is the search for the "self which is free from evil, ageless, deathless, sorrowless, without hunger, without thirst, of true desire, of true resolve. The one who has found and knows the self attains all worlds and all desires" (CU 8.7.1).

Unlike the Upaniṣadic thinkers, Siddhattha Gotama (c. 563–c. 483 BCE), the historical Buddha or "awakened one," eschewed the search for a single root or source of existence and a single eternal self. Instead, the Buddha's quest for liberation from suffering was based on an insight into the impermanent (*anicca*), selfless (*anattā*), and unsatisfactory (*dukkha*) nature of all things that arise from causes and conditions (*saṅkhārā*).[2] In place of *brahman* as the unified ground of being, the Buddha understood the world in terms of the dependent origination of events (*paṭiccasamuppāda*). Phenomena in the world arise in dependence on prior phenomena and in turn give rise to subsequent phenomena. These patterns of dependence are regular and, with sufficient insight, can be understood. As we see in the early Buddhist text,[3] the *Saṃyutta Nikāya*:

> When this exists, that comes to be. With the arising (*uppada*) of this, that arises. When this does not exist, that does not come to be. With the cessation (*nirodha*) of this, that ceases.
>
> (SN 12.61)

According to the Buddhist account, the world is not really a collection of stable, enduring objects or *things*. Rather, it is a fluid and interconnected network of events and processes, arising and ceasing in regular patterns of dependence. Grasping after or clinging to such phenomena, likened to foam on the surface of water, leads only to frustration and dissatisfaction (*dukkha*). Yet, by understanding how this *dukkha* arises and continues, the wise person may ultimately remove its causes and conditions and attain the spiritual freedom of *nibbāna*. Indeed, this understanding is so central that the Buddha's disciple Sāriputta proclaimed "one who sees dependent origination sees the *dhamma* [the truth taught by the Buddha]; one who sees the *dhamma* sees dependent origination" (MN 28).

On the Buddhist view, human persons are no exception to this understanding of reality as impermanent and dependently originated. In place of a persisting self or innermost essence (*ātman*), the Buddha and his followers understand persons in terms of an interconnected flow of mental and physical events and processes. As discussed in the next section, the Buddhists understand persons and other sentient beings in terms of five aggregates (*khandas*), or groupings of interconnected phenomena. The five *khandas* are material form (*rūpa*), feeling (*vedanā*), perception (*saññā*), conditioning (*saṅkhāra*), and consciousness (*viññaṇa*). The person, then, is an interconnected system of impermanent and dependently originated mental and physical phenomena, not a fixed and enduring self. Indeed, the Buddha states unequivocally, "It cannot happen that a person possessing right view could treat anything as self—there is no such possibility" (MN 115.12).

1.2 Self and No-Self

In the *Bṛhadāraṇyaka Upaniṣad*, we find a dialogue between the brahmin Bālāki and the king Ajātaśatru. Bālāki declares that he must teach the king about the nature of *brahman*, for which the king offers him a thousand cows. Bālāki then proceeds to declare that he worships *brahman* as the person (*puruṣa*) in the sun. Ajātaśatru replies, "Do not talk to me about him. I worship him as the topmost, the head and king of all beings. Whoever worships him as such becomes the topmost, the head and king of all beings" (BU 2.1.2). Upon hearing this rebuke, the brahmin goes on to say he worships *brahman* in the moon, lighting, fire, mirror, and so on. Each time he is similarly rebuked, until he falls silent. He then asks the king to be his teacher. Ajātaśatru then leads Bālāki to a sleeping man, whom he gently awakens. The king asks,

17. 'When he fell asleep, the person made of knowledge, by knowledge taking his knowledge with him, lay down in the space within the heart. When the person takes these to himself, he is said to be asleep: the breath is taken, the eye is taken, the ear is taken, the mind is taken.

18. 'When in dreams he moves about, these are his worlds. He seems to become a great king, or a great Brāhmana, or to move high and low. Just as a great king, taking his subjects with him, moves about at will in his own country, so he, taking his senses (prāna) with him, moves about at will in his own body.'

20. 'As a spider moves up along its thread, as small sparks fly up from a fire, so all breaths, all worlds, all gods, all beings come up out of the self. Its inner meaning (upaniṣad) is "the truth of the truth": the breaths are the truth, and it is the truth of them.

Here the king reveals a core teaching of Upaniṣads: to find the deepest nature of reality, one must find the deepest nature of the self. And that deep nature is found when the senses and other manifest functions of the person have withdrawn as in deep sleep. There, in the "space in the heart," is the source of the myriad forms of experience emerging like sparks from a fire.

In another dialogue in the *Bṛhadāraṇyaka Upaniṣad*, King Janaka asks the sage Yājñavalkya, "Yājñavalkya, what is the source of light for a person here?" In response, Yājñavalkya mentions the external sources of illumination, such as the sun, moon, and fire, as well as the illumination provided by a voice in the darkness. The King then asks,

"But when both the sun and the moon have set, the fire has died out, and the voice is stilled, Yājñavalkya, what then is the source of light for a person here?"

"The self (*ātman*) is then his source of light [*svayaṃjyoti*]. It is by the light of the self that a person sits down, goes about, does his work, and returns."

"Which self is that?"

"It is this person—the one that consists of perception among the vital functions (*prāṇa*), the one that is the inner light within the heart."

(BU 4.3.6)

Here we see the self-understood as an inner light that makes possible the activities and awareness of the person. The self, like a light, reveals the world to the subject and allows her to act within it. Yet just a light is distinct from the objects it illuminates, the light of the self is distinct from that which it reveals. As Yājñavalkya proclaims, "You can't see the seer who does the seeing; you can't hear the hearer who does the hearing; you can't think of the thinker who does the thinking; and you can't perceive the perceiver who does the perceiving. The self within all is this self of yours. All else besides this is grief!" (BU 3.5.1). The idea here is that, because the *ātman* is the inner subject of all experience, it cannot be grasped in the same way as the objects and activities of experience. In this sense, the *ātman* is elusive—it is presupposed in all mental processes such as perceiving or thinking, but it is not revealed as just one more object for those processes (Ganeri 2007).

Of course, this elusiveness does not stop Upaniṣadic thinkers seeking, discussing, and debating the nature of the self. What emerges from these inquiries is a conception of the *ātman* as a persisting subject of experience, conscious, a unity, an owner, an agent, and as deeply implicated in the very nature of reality.[4] Upaniṣadic seekers, then, were quite clear that the true self is not the same as and is quite a bit more elusive than the ordinary flesh and blood human being. Indeed, one common diagnosis for our supposed bondage to the interminable round of birth and death (*saṃsāra*) is that we suffer from a deep case of mistaken identity. We human beings identify with the body and mind, with their desires and aversions, their limitations and infirmities. Yet, the Upaniṣads teach, the real self is the immaterial *ātman*. As the sage Prajāpati says to the god Indra, "Oh, Indra, this body is truly mortal. It is bound by death. Yet, it is the seat of the self which is deathless and bodiless. The embodied self is subject to pleasure and pain. There is no escape from pleasure and pain for the embodied. But they do not touch the one who is bodiless" (CU 8.12.1). Here we see the important evaluative dimension of philosophical inquiry into the nature of the self. The body, and by extension, the embodied individual is subject to death and pain, whereas the true self is deathless, bodiless, and not subject to pleasure and pain.

This distinction between the *ātman* and the living individual (*jīva*) or person (*pudgala*) is also important for understanding the Buddhist view of no-self (*anattā, anātman*). Buddhist thinkers deny the very existence of *ātman* and give a distinctive account of the person (or other kinds of sentient beings). As mentioned in the previous section, the standard Buddhist account of the person is in terms of the five *skandhas* of (in Sanskrit) material form (*rūpa*), feeling (*vedanā*), perception (*saṃjñā*), conditioning (*saṃskāra*), and consciousness (*vijñāna*). Further, the working assumption, based on observation, is that all the empirically or experientially available aspects of the person fall within these groupings. On the Buddhist view, we consistently misapprehend the *skandhas* as being or belonging to a persisting self.

There are two important early Buddhist arguments against the self: the argument from control and the argument from impermanence. We see both arguments deployed in the *Anattalakkhaṇa Sutta* ("The Characteristic of Nonself"). The Buddha states:

"Bhikkhus [monks], form is nonself. For if, bhikkhus, form were self, this form would not lead to affliction, and it would be possible to have it of form: 'Let my form be thus; let my form not be thus.' But because form is nonself, form leads to affliction, and it is not possible to have it of form: 'Let my form be thus; let my form not be thus.'

"Feeling is nonself.... ... Perception is nonself.... Volitional formations are nonself.... Consciousness is nonself. For if, bhikkhus, consciousness were self, this consciousness would not lead to affliction, and it would be possible to have it of consciousness: 'Let my consciousness be thus; let my consciousness not be thus.' But because consciousness is nonself, consciousness leads to affliction, and it is not possible to have it of consciousness: 'Let my consciousness be thus; let my consciousness not be thus.'

(SN 22.59)

As we have seen in the context of the Upaniṣads, the true self is supposed to be "deathless," not "subject to pleasure and pain," and (in many views) the locus of agency (*antaryāmin*, "the inner controller"). Here the Buddha inquires whether anything in our experience (namely, the five *skandhas*) could answer to the last two properties. Are the body or any of the mental *skandhas* free of affliction and under complete self-control? If not, then none of the *skandhas* can be the self. And, the Buddha observes, the five *skandhas* are very much liable to affliction and not under complete control.

Turning to the argument from impermanence, the Buddha asks:

"What do you think, bhikkhus, is form permanent or impermanent?"— "Impermanent, venerable sir."—"Is what is impermanent suffering or happiness?"—"Suffering, venerable sir."—"Is what is impermanent, suffering, and subject to change fit to be regarded thus: 'This is mine, this I am, this is my self'?"—"No, venerable sir."

"Is feeling permanent or impermanent? ... Is perception permanent or impermanent? ... Are volitional formations permanent or impermanent? ... Is consciousness permanent or impermanent?"— "Impermanent, venerable sir."—"Is what is impermanent suffering or happiness?"— "Suffering, venerable sir."—"Is what is impermanent, suffering, and subject to change fit to be regarded thus: 'This is mine, this I am, this is my self'?"—"No, venerable sir."

"Therefore, bhikkhus, any kind of form whatsoever, whether past, future, or present, internal or external, gross or subtle, inferior or superior, far or near, all form should be seen as it really is with correct wisdom thus: 'This is not mine, this I am not, this is not my self.'

(SN 22.59)

Again, since the true self must be "deathless" or permanent, the Buddha asks whether there is anything in our experience of the person that is permanent. Finding none, the conclusion is that none of the five *skandhas* could be the self. Of course, it remains open to the proponent of the self to argue that it exists over and above the *skandhas*. However, Buddhist philosophers developed powerful epistemological and phenomenological arguments against this move (Smith 2021). So, like in the Upaniṣads, on the Buddhist view we mistakenly identify with the changing body and mind as if they were the self. But here the root error is believing that *anything* could be the self.

This divide between proponents (*ātmavādins*) and opponents (*anātmavādins*) of a persisting self is at the roots of Indian thinking about the nature of mind, consciousness, agency, and more. As we survey the various theories of consciousness developed in the Indian tradition, we will see that the view of the self and the view of no-self continues to be one of the most fundamental philosophical issues in Indian thought.

1.3 Self-Luminosity

In the dialogue between Yājñavalkya and Janaka we see "the self" characterized as an inner light within the heart and as *svayaṃjyoti*, "self-shining" or "self-luminous." This idea that the self is the inner light links it directly to consciousness. The self is the locus of consciousness or just is consciousness itself. But what does it mean to say that consciousness (and so the self) is like light (*prakāśa*)? Like a light, consciousness has (or is) the capacity to shine forth (*prakāśate*) and illuminate (*prakāśayati*) its object. It "lights up" or reveals the world for the subject. Indeed, just as without illumination no objects could be visible, without the light of consciousness, no object could be experienced. The world would be in darkness (*jagadāndhyaprasanga*). Thus, luminosity comes to denote the capacity to disclose, present, or make manifest. Furthermore, it is a fundamental conviction of Brahmanical thinkers from the Upaniṣads onwards, that only the non-physical self can be luminous in this way (Berger 2015). The body, of course, has external senses and the mind has an internal sense (*manas*), and these are necessary for cognitive access to the world. But on this view, without the light of the conscious self the operations of the outer and inner senses would go on 'in the dark', utterly unconscious.

Over time, the notion of consciousness as luminosity (*prakāśatā*) transforms from an evocative metaphor to a technical concept in Indian philosophy. It is the unique capacity to make experientially present any object or content of consciousness. Yet while Indian philosophers generally agreed that luminosity is the distinctive mark of consciousness, they disagreed about the proper analysis of luminosity. Here the fundamental divide is between understanding consciousness as self-luminous (*svaprakāśa*) or as other-luminous (*paraprakāśa*). For proponents of other-illumination, the distinctive mark of consciousness is that it reveals that which is *other* (its object). The function of a lamp, to extend the analogy, is to illuminate objects in the world. For proponents of self-illumination, the distinctive mark of consciousness is that whatever else it may present, it reveals *itself*. A lamp, they point out, does not need a second lamp for its light to be revealed. In shining, the light reveals itself as it also reveals objects.

It is important to point out at the outset that debates about the luminosity of consciousness cut across some of the other important distinctions and divides we will discuss in coming chapters. The self- versus other-luminosity distinction is widespread in Indian debates and there are proponents of each type of view to be found in Brahmanical (Hindu) and non-Brahmanical (Buddhist, Jain, and so forth) thinkers and traditions. For instance, the Brahmanical Nyāya thinker Uddyotakara (sixth century CE) as well as the Buddhist Madhyamaka Candrakīrti (600–650 CE) argued for other-luminosity. In contrast, both the Brahmanical Advaita Vedāntin Śaṅkara (eighth century CE) and the Buddhist Dignāga (480–540 CE) argued for self-luminosity. Moreover, this distinction cuts across the self/no-self divide in Indian philosophy. That is, we find proponents of self-luminosity who accept the existence self and others who reject it, and likewise for proponents of other-luminosity. As we will see, though, debates about luminosity are closely connected to issues of intentionality, subjectivity, self-awareness, and the self.

One way to understand self-luminosity is in terms of awareness of awareness. The idea here—which we also see going back to Aristotle in the West (Caston 2002)—is that whenever the subject has an experience of some particular object, she is also aware of that very experiencing. In seeing a tree, she is aware of the tree *and* aware of the seeing. And it is in virtue of this awareness of awareness that the seeing is *conscious*. That is, if the subject were not at all aware of her seeing, she would not be *consciously* seeing at all. The contemporary philosopher of mind, Michelle Montague, calls this the *awareness of awareness thesis*: "Conscious awareness always involves—constitutively involves—some sort of awareness of that very awareness" (Montague 2016, 41). David Rosenthal has defended a similar idea, which he calls the *transitivity principle*: A subject is in a conscious state just in case she is (in an appropriate way) aware of the state or of being in that state (Rosenthal 1997). As we will see in Chapter 7, for instance, Buddhist philosophers such as Dignāga, Dharmakīrti, and Śāntarakṣita argue that awareness of awareness or reflexive awareness (*svasaṃvedana*) is a necessary feature of each moment of consciousness.

Another way to understand self-luminosity is in terms of subjectivity. Physical light can reveal objects in the sense of making them visible. But to what or to whom are the visible objects revealed? Terms like 'reveal', 'appear', 'experience' seem to imply that *to which* things appear or are revealed, and so forth. That is, they seem to presuppose that there is a *subject* to which objects are revealed. As we will discuss in Chapter 6, Advaita Vedānta philosophers argued that all conscious cognition of objects presupposes a unified conscious subject they sometimes called witness-consciousness (*sākṣin*) (Gupta 1998). On this view, witness-consciousness is the ultimate subject to which all inner and outer phenomena are given. Because it is what makes possible any awareness of objects, they argue, it cannot itself be revealed as an object. And yet, we also cannot coherently doubt whether we are conscious. In this sense, witness-consciousness is self-luminous. It is present to itself as subject or subjectivity, but never as object.[5]

Throughout this book, we will see several arguments for and against the idea that consciousness is self-luminous. Here I will discuss two connected considerations in favor of self-luminosity that repeatedly appear in Indian debates.[6] The first consideration concerns the immediacy with which we seem to be aware of our own consciousness. The Buddhist philosopher Dharmakīrti states, "Just as an illuminating light is considered to be the illuminator of itself, because of its nature, just so, awareness is aware of itself" (PV 3.329). On this view, it is the very nature of consciousness to be present to itself. In this sense, being in a conscious state implies that the subject is in some (appropriate) way aware of the state.[7] And when one is in a conscious state, one doesn't need to *do* anything—such as actively introspect or infer—to be aware that one is conscious. Just *being* conscious is enough. Likewise, the Advaita Vedānta philosopher Citsukha (thirteenth century CE) says that consciousness is *aparokṣa* ("unhidden" or "immediately present") and *abādhita* ("indubitable") (TP 2.1.16). That consciousness is *aparokṣa* means that conscious experiences are not like sticks and stones, that can exist whether or not any subject is aware of them. Rather, to have a conscious experience entails that one lives through it subjectively. Experiences, on this view, have what John Searle (Searle 2000) calls a first-person ontology. They only exist as lived through by the subject. That consciousness is *abādhita* means that its existence cannot be doubted. We may be wrong about the contents of consciousness or even its metaphysical nature, but not that it exists.[8] As we will see throughout this book, all of these claims can be and have been challenged in Indian debates about consciousness. The point here is that proponents of self-luminosity repeatedly appeal to the (purported) distinctive and immediate presence of consciousness to itself (or to the self).

The second consideration concerns the problem of regress (*anavasthiti*). There are two steps to generating a vicious regress. First is the idea that a conscious state is one the subject must (in some way) be aware of. For instance, as we'll see in Chapter 7, the Buddhist philosopher Dharmakīrti argues that a cognition of an object can only make the subject conscious of the object if the cognition itself is cognized (PV in 1.54cd). More concretely, in order for me to *consciously* see a tree, I must in some way be aware of my seeing of the tree. Otherwise, I would only have an *unconscious* perception of the tree. This view implies Montague's awareness of awareness thesis. But what is the relation between the first-order cognition of the tree and the second-order cognition of the cognition? Are they independent cognitions? If so, then we have the second step to generating the vicious regress. If the first-order cognition C1 requires a separate second-order cognition C2, then what about C2? For C2 to make the subject aware of *its* object (C1), it would need to be cognized by C3, and so on. Buddhist proponents of self-luminosity try to block the regress by denying the second step. That is, they argue that C1 and C2 are not separate and that conscious cognitions are reflexive or self-cognizing (*svasaṃvedana*) (Kellner 2011). However, one might also block the regress by denying the first step. That is, as Nyāya thinkers argued, one may reject the claim that C1 requires C2 to reveal its object. On this type of view, C1's being a consciousness state does not depend on C2, but rather is explained in terms of features of C1 itself.

To sum up, the luminosity of consciousness indicates the basic capacity to experientially disclose, present, or make manifest. It is then a further question what can be manifest and how. Advocates of self-luminosity argue that consciousness is distinctively or uniquely self-manifesting or self-presenting. Whatever else consciousness may reveal, such as physical objects or the contents of thoughts, it always also presents *itself*. While an object may be hidden from awareness as if in a dark room, consciousness is not hidden from itself. Like a lamp, it reveals itself as it illuminates what was in darkness. Further, just as the lamp does not need a second lamp to reveal its presence, so consciousness does not need a second consciousness for it to be revealed.

1.4 Other-Luminosity

In contrast to the view of self-luminosity, proponents of other-luminosity (*paraprakāśavādins*) argue that the basic luminosity of consciousness consists in its capacity to present that which is *other* than the act or moment of awareness itself. As Nyāya philosophers put it, the distinctive mark of consciousness is *svābhāvika viṣayapravaṇatvam*, the quality of being of an object, or what contemporary philosophers call intentionality. And since other-directed intentionality is the very nature of awareness, awareness of awareness requires two distinct acts or moments of cognition.

One important version of *paraprakāśavāda* comes from the Nyāya tradition.[9] As we'll see in Chapter 2, for Nyāya thinkers, consciousness is a fundamental quality or capacity of the immaterial self. It is cognitive and it takes a (distinct) object, it is *saviṣāyaka* (with-an-object). Further, a common Nyāya view of intentionality is that a conscious cognition reveals its object without the mediation of conscious mental images or representations (*ākāra*). In this way, consciousness is like a transparent window through which objects in the world can be viewed. On this Nyāya view, then, when one has a perception of a tree, one is in a conscious state with the content <there is a tree>. The first-order cognition derives its content from the worldly object it discloses, and it makes no reference to either the cognition itself or its subject. The term for a first-order cognition in this context is *vyavasāya*. It presents the tree in a particular way (in terms of color, shape, and so on), but this is ultimately a function of the properties of the tree. But in what sense is this cognition conscious? It is conscious in that it makes its subject aware of the object. When one has a perception of a tree, that perception makes one conscious *of the tree*. On this view, one need not be aware of the cognition in any way for it to make one conscious of its object. More formally, we can call this the *independence condition*: the presence of a conscious mental state does not depend on the subject's being aware of that state (or aware of being in it).

How, then, do we come to be aware of our conscious states, when we are? According to the Nyāya philosopher Gaṅgeśa (fourteenth century CE), our first-order cognitions (*vyavasāya, pratyaya*) are cognized by a subsequent, higher-order cognition (*anuvyavasāya*, literally "after-cognition") or apperception. In the typical case of perception, a first-order cognition triggers a second-order cognition that takes the first-order cognition as its intentional object. While the *vyavasāya* and the *anuvyavasāya* are distinct cognitions, their content is intimately related. When a perception with the content <there is a tree> is apperceived, the content of the apperception will be <I perceive a tree>. The *direct* object of the meta-cognition (cognition of a cognition) is the first-order cognition, while the *indirect* objects of the meta-cognition are the first-order cognition's object (the tree) and the self. Finally, Nyāya thinkers hold that the meta-cognition is direct and infallible—we cannot be mistaken in this basic form of meta-cognition (Phillips 2014).

Another important version of other-luminosity is found in the Bhāṭṭa Mīmāṃsa tradition. The Mīmāṃsā philosopher Kumārila Bhaṭṭa (seventh century CE), like Nyāya thinkers, holds that cognitions are other-luminous in that their function is to reveal a distinct object (PP). However, Nyāya holds a first-order view of consciousness in that an object-directed first-order cognition is sufficient for the subject to be in a fully conscious cognitive state. That is, a first-order cognition yields a personal-level conscious state, such as seeing a tree. In contrast, for Kumārila there is a two-stage process leading to full-blown person-level conscious states (Ram-Prasad 2016). In the first stage, one has a perceptual state that presents an independent object. In the second stage, one has a meta-cognition that makes available on the person-level the object of the first cognition. Further, it is important to note here that the meta-cognition here is directed at the *object* of the first-order cognition, not the cognition itself. But in this case, the meta-cognition grasps the object *as cognized* (*jñānatā*) and from there existence of the first-order cognition is (implicitly) inferred. So, when a person sees a tree, this leads to another cognition that registers the tree as seen, allowing the person to be aware of the tree and her seeing it. At this stage of the cognitive process, the person can be aware that "I am seeing the tree." On this picture, full person-level consciousness of the tree involves awareness of the tree, the seeing, and the subject, but there is no one cognition that is self-luminous (Watson 2020). Furthermore, even the first-order cognition is luminous and is a form of low-level consciousness.

Again, we will encounter other more specific and technical arguments for other-luminosity in subsequent chapters. For now, I want to discuss two considerations in favor of other-luminosity. The first consideration comes down to skepticism or outright rejection of the kind of reflexivity proposed in self-luminosity theories. Just as an eye does not see itself, a knife does not cut itself, and a finger does not point at itself, so an awareness is not directed at itself. More technically, the idea is that, on the standard account, 'aware of' is a transitive, irreflexive relation. Just as we say that 'Devadatta chops wood,' we also say 'Devadatta sees wood' and not 'Devadatta sees his seeing wood.' In this context Mark Siderits has argued that there was a wide-spread anti-reflexivity principle in Indian philosophy (Siderits 2015, 46). This shifts the burden to the proponents of self-luminosity to spell out this relation of reflexivity or self-presentation.

The second consideration concerns the relation between causality and cognition. For many Indian thinkers, the relation between a cognition and its object is causal.[10] When a person with functioning senses and in proper lighting conditions, and so forth, encounters a tree, the tree may cause her to be in the perceptual state of seeing it. But, at least on one prominent view (namely, *satkāryavāda*), causation occurs between distinct things. As the Buddhist philosopher Saṃghabhadra puts it, causal "factors do not have the function of production with regard to themselves" (Hu 2022). Just as no event is self-caused, so no cognition is self-cognizing. Thus, cognition of cognition too must be the result of some kind of causal relation between distinct cognitions.

In summary, the luminosity of consciousness consists in its capacity to present its object. Like a knife that cuts other things but not itself, awareness makes the subject aware of other things but not itself. This does not rule out self-awareness either in the sense of awareness of awareness or awareness of the self (if there is one). It is just that, for the other-illuminationists, these modes of awareness are explained in terms of how distinct other-directed cognitions relate to one another or the self, but not in terms of any particular cognition somehow cognizing itself.

1.5 Comparative Connections

The question of the connection between awareness and self-awareness has a long history in the West as well. It is not possible to offer a comprehensive survey here, so a few signposts must suffice. Aristotle, for instance, believed that there was a close (perhaps necessary) connection between perceptual awareness and a kind of self-awareness (Caston 2002). In the *Nichomachean Ethics* (9.9) he writes,

> The person seeing perceives that he is seeing, the person hearing [perceives] that he is hearing, the person walking [perceives] that he is walking, and similarly in other cases there is something that perceives that we are in activity, so that we will perceive that we perceive and think that we think.

Yet, as he argues in *De Anima* (425b12–a17),

> Since we perceive that we see and hear, it must either be by sight that one perceives that one sees or by another [sense]. But in that case there will be the same [sense] for sight and the colour which is the subject for sight. So that either there will be two senses for the same thing or [the sense itself] will be the one for itself. Again, if the sense concerned with sight were indeed different from sight, either there will be an infinite regress or there will be some [sense] which is concerned with itself; so that we had best admit this of the first in the series.

Noteworthy here is that Aristotle, like some Indian philosophers we have discussed, posits a tight connection between awareness and awareness of awareness, is puzzled by the nature of that connection, and realizes the possibility of an infinite regress.

In the broadly Platonic tradition, we find an even more basic mode of self-awareness that does not depend on awareness of other things, but is rather the mind's inherent presence to itself (Matthews 1992). And Avicenna (Ibn Sīnā), in his flying man thought experiment, holds that a man floating in a void, without sensory or bodily awareness, would nevertheless be self-aware (Kaukua 2015). In early modern writers such as Descartes, Locke, and Berkeley, we again find the idea that there is an intimate connection between awareness and self-awareness. For instance, Descartes' *cogito* implies that all awareness of other things involves both awareness of that awareness and awareness of oneself as the subject (Descartes 1641). For his part, Locke asserts that "In every Act of Sensation, Reasoning, or Thinking, we are conscious to ourselves of our own Being" (IV.ix.3) (Locke 1689). In sharp contrast, Hume (1739) famously denies any introspective perception of self:

> there are some philosophers, who imagine we are every moment intimately conscious of what we call our self [...] For my part when I enter most intimately into what I call *myself*, I always stumble on some particular perception or other, of heat or cold, light or shade, love or hatred, pain or pleasure. I never can catch *myself* at any time without a perception, and never can observe anything but the perception. (bk.1, ch.4, §6)
>
> (bk.1, ch.4, §6)

Kant (1781) agrees with Hume that there is no awareness of the self as an object of introspection. However, he argues that there must be a form of self-awareness, transcendental apperception, that unifies the various contents of the mind as one's own. Yet this self-awareness is strictly formal and does not go beyond this unification of experience (Kitcher 2011). These concerns with the nature and relationship between consciousness, self-consciousness, and the subject continue to occupy post-Kantian thinkers such as Fichte, Hegel, and Schopenhauer.

Another important signpost is the philosopher Franz Brentano. Brentano is perhaps best known for his reintroduction of the concept of intentionality in modern Western philosophy. In his *Psychology from an Empirical Standpoint*, he writes:

> Every mental phenomenon is characterized by what the Scholastics of the Middle Ages called the intentional (or mental) inexistence of

an object, and what we might call, though not wholly unambiguously, reference to a content, direction towards an object (which is not to be understood here as meaning a thing), or immanent objectivity. Every mental phenomenon includes something as object within itself, although they do not all do so in the same way.

(Brentano 1874, 92)

For Brentano, mental phenomena are *about* or *directed* toward an object or content, and this feature is a distinctive mark of *mental* phenomena. Indeed, he asserts, "This intentional in-existence is characteristic exclusively of mental phenomena. No physical phenomenon exhibits anything like it" (1874, 93). The details of Brentano's view need not concern us here, but there are two things worth noting. First, there is an important similarity between Brentano's notion of intentionality and the idea of luminosity in Indian philosophy. Both emphasize the distinctive capacity of the conscious mind to present, reveal, or disclose objects, events, thoughts, and so forth. Further, the notion of intentionality here is quite consonant with the concept of cognition (*jñāna*) as that which takes an object (*viṣayatā*). Second, Brentano's search for the distinctive marks of the mental as mental (he ultimately identifies six, including intentionality), is similar to later Indian thinkers' search for the nature (*prakṛti*) or unique mark (*svalakṣaṇa*) of consciousness, either in its other-luminosity or its self-luminosity.

Brentano further argues that mental phenomena are perceived by an inner consciousness, whereas physical phenomena can only be perceived by outer perception. This inner consciousness not only accompanies all mental acts, but is an integral part of them.

The presentation of the sound and the presentation of the presentation of the sound form one single mental phenomenon; it is only by considering it in its relation to two different objects, one of which is a physical phenomenon and the other a mental phenomenon, that we divide it conceptually into two presentations. In the same mental phenomenon in which the sound is present to our minds we simultaneously apprehend the mental phenomenon itself. What is more, we apprehend it in accordance with its dual nature insofar as it has the sound as content within it, and insofar as it has itself as content at the same time.

(Brentano 1874, 132–33)

Brentano, then, is grappling with several of the same issues as our Indian philosophers: the nature of cognition, the distinctive nature of the mind, the relationship between awareness and self-awareness, and whether and how anything could be self-presenting. Finally, it is important to note that Brentano is a historical precursor of both the modern phenomenological and analytic styles of philosophy that have been influential since the twentieth century and about which we will see more in coming chapters.

To conclude this section, I will present some sharpened characterizations of key ideas:

Luminosity (prakāśatā): The capacity of consciousness to present, reveal, or manifest some object, content, or quality to some subject.

Other-luminosity (paraprakāśatā): The nature of consciousness is to present that which is distinct from the revealing (state, moment, and so forth) consciousness, paradigmatically objects in the world.

Self-luminosity (svaprakāśatā): The nature of consciousness is to present itself, whether or not it presents distinct objects, contents, or qualities.

The Transitivity Thesis: For any mental state M of a subject S (at a time t), M is conscious (at t) only if S is aware of M (at t).

The Independence Thesis: The presence of any given mental state, M, in a subject S, is independent of S being introspectively conscious of M.

Each of these ideas will be important for describing and understanding the theories of consciousness in the coming chapters.

1.6 Questions

1. As discussed in section 1.1, what are some important differences between the Upaniṣadic and Buddhist thinkers regarding reality and the self?
2. What is the luminosity of consciousness? Can you think of an example of a state of consciousness that was not luminous?
3. In your own words, distinguish between the other-luminosity view and the self-luminosity view. Which view is more plausible and why?
4. What is the *transitivity thesis*? Can you think of a good counterexample to this thesis?

Notes

1 Indeed, the term 'upaniṣad' can mean 'to sit down near' (*upa* 'by, near' + *ni-ṣad* 'sit down'), as when a student sits before a teacher to receive knowledge.

2 In this discussion of early Buddhism I am using Pāli terms, such as *nibbāna* (nirvana). Later Buddhist thinkers typically wrote in Sanskrit, and I will use Sanskrit terms when discussing them.

3 Buddhism emerged as a distinct tradition during the same time that the later Upaniṣads were taking shape. As we will see, Buddhism as a textual, religious, and philosophical tradition is not grounded in the Upaniṣads, but rather the teachings of the Buddha as passed down in the Nikāyas (early discourses) and subsequent texts.

4 These are paradigmatic features of the *ātman*, but different thinkers or texts may not agree with each aspect listed here.

5 Citsukha defines self-luminosity as "fitness for being immediately known without being an object of any cognition" (TP 2.1.16).

6 And Western debates, for that matter. For a comparative survey see (MacKenzie 2007).

7 Of course, as a proponent of the no-self view, Dharmakīrti will ultimately dispense with the idea of a distinct subject of experience, reducing the subject to a series of moments of reflexive awareness.

8 Similarly, the Buddhist philosopher Mokṣākaragupta (1050–1292) in his *Tarkabhāṣā* asserts, "reflexive awareness is called indeterminate knowledge free from fictional constructs and unerring, because its nature consists in the direct intuition of the nature of itself" (TBh 6.2).

9 It is important to keep in mind that terms like 'Nyāya' name broad textual traditions and philosophical tendencies, not rigidly defined or dogmatic schools of thought. For simplicity, I will sometimes talk about a 'Nyāya view' or a 'Yogācāra view' of some topic, but it should be kept in mind that there was a great deal of variation and controversy within these traditions or "schools of thought."

10 Of course, they do not argue that it is *merely* causal. A cognition has an object, it is *viṣayatā*, not just a cause. But the occurrence of the cognition is still underpinned by causal relations.

Further Reading

Bodhi, Bhikkhu. 2005. *In the Buddha's Words: An Anthology of Discourses from the Pali Canon.* Wisdom Publications.

Ganeri, Jonardon. 2007. *The Concealed Art of the Soul: Theories of the Self and Practices of Truth in Indian Ethics and Epistemology.* 1st edition. Clarendon Press.

MacKenzie, Matthew D. 2007. "The Illumination of Consciousness: Approaches to Self-Awareness in the Indian and Western Traditions." *Philosophy East and West* 57 (1): 40–62.

Ram-Prasad, Chakravarthi. 2016. *Indian Philosophy and the Consequences of Knowledge: Themes in Ethics, Metaphysics and Soteriology*. 1st edition. Routledge.
Roebuck, Valerie, trans. 2004. *The Upanishads*. Penguin UK.

2

Nyāya

2.1 The Nyāya School

In the previous chapter we discussed the origins of Indian philosophy in the Upaniṣads, having its roots in the Vedic tradition, as well as early Buddhism, which rejected the authority of the Vedas. It is important to note that the Upaniṣadic and early Buddhist thinkers were part of a very diverse and dynamic intellectual and spiritual culture on the sub-continent. Other important traditions include Jainism and the skeptical and materialist school of Cārvāka. Over a period from about the fifth century BCE to the fourth or fifth century CE, we see the development of distinct philosophical schools or systems, often called *darśana-s* ("perspective," "point of view"). These systems were often organized around a foundational text called a *sūtra* ("thread") that contained, in highly condensed form, the core ideas and doctrines of the school. These texts were then elaborated in prose commentaries called *bhāṣya-s*, which included not just exposition of the root *sūtra* but also innovative philosophical and argumentative work in their own right. Later scholars have organized these various philosophical tendencies and systems into a list of distinct schools. So-called "orthodox" (*āstika*) schools are in some important way rooted in and continued the cultural and philosophical tradition of the Vedas, and are what we today would broadly call "Hindu" schools. These six schools are Sāṃkhya, Yoga, Nyāya, Vaiśeṣika, Mīmāṃsā, and Vedānta. So-called "heterodox" (*nāstika*) schools in some important way reject the authority of the Vedas and prominently include the Buddhist, Jaina, and Cārvāka traditions.

The term *nyāya* means "right reasoning" and the Nyāya school has its roots in the earlier traditions of *ānvīkṣikī* ("critical, rational inquiry") and *vāda-śāstra* ("rules of debate and proper reasoning"). Not surprisingly then, the main concerns of the Nyāya school are epistemology, logic, and metaphysics. However, thinkers in this tradition also made important contributions to the philosophy of language, mind, religion, and other areas. The foundational text of this school is the *Nyāyasūtra* by Akṣapāda Gautama (c. 200 CE). Other important texts include Vātsyāyana's commentary, the *Nyāyabhāṣya* (5th cent. CE), Uddyotakara's *Nyāyavārtikka* (sixth century CE), and Jayanta Bhaṭṭa's *Nyāyamañjarī* (ninth–tenth century CE). By the fourteenth century

CE, the school had developed into a distinctively new phase and came to be divided into old Nyāya and new Nyāya (Navya-Nyāya). The most significant work of new Nyāya is Gaṅgeśa's *Tattvacintāmaṇi* (fourteenth century CE).

In the opening verses of the *Nyāya-sūtra* Gautama makes an explicit connection between proper reasoning, debate, and the attainment of the highest good.

> 1.1.1 Knowledge sources, objects of knowledge, doubt, motive, example, accepted position, inferential components, suppositional reasoning, certainty, debate for the truth, disputation, destructive debate, pseudo-provers, equivocation, misleading objections, and clinchers: from knowledge of these, there is attainment of the supreme good.
> 1.1.2 When pain, rebirth, activity, vice, and wrong understanding have been dispelled in reverse order, there is final beatitude (*apavarga*).

Here the critical first step to the highest good (*apavarga, mokṣa* "spiritual freedom") is to dispel misunderstanding (*mithyājñāna*). This requires rational, philosophical reflection on knowledge, the objects of knowledge, and the valid means of knowledge. It also requires the recognition and avoidance of errors of reasoning and unreliable means of knowledge.

For Nyāya an episode of knowledge (*pramā*) is a veridical cognition (*jñāna*) produced through a reliable means of knowledge (*pramāṇa*, "knowledge-source"). Nyāya epistemology concerns the enumeration and analysis of the proper knowledge sources (*pramāṇas*) and the proper objects of knowledge (*prameyas*). The school recognizes four basic knowledge sources: perception (*pratyakṣa*), inference (*anumāna*), analogy (*upamāna*), and verbal testimony (*śabda*). Among the proper objects of knowledge are the various everyday entities in the external world, universals, as well as the immaterial self (*ātman*) and God (*īśvara*). Moreover, the Naiyāyikas (members of the Nyāya school) are staunchly realist and anti-skeptical in both epistemology and metaphysics. They affirm and defend the view that the external world and its objects and properties are independently real and knowable. They defend the reality of the immaterial self and the existence of God. They also hold the view that our means of knowledge are presumptively veridical, innocent until proven guilty as it were. More specifically, the default assumption is that the standard means of knowledge produce veridical cognitions. This default assumption is supported in two ways. The first is based on the pragmatic point that, as Vātsyāyana argues, cognitions that lead to successful practice are likely (but not necessarily) veridical. The second is based on the conceptual point that doubt only makes sense in a certain context and against the background of generally valid knowledge. One is lead to reasonable doubt for instance when two perceptions conflict, when there is disagreement between individuals, or when two distinct sources of information conflict. In these types of cases, doubt is reasonable and must be addressed through further critical inquiry. However, in Nyāya there is no room for global skeptical doubts of the kind that lead to, for example, skepticism about the external world or other minds.

In summary, the Nyāya tradition defends a robust form of realism in both epistemology and metaphysics. The world consists in a plurality of real, independent individuals (*dravya*, "substance") that have real properties and fall under real natural kinds or universals. Among the real things in the world are enduring, immaterial selves that are the locus of various capacities, including consciousness, cognition, and agency. Furthermore, Nyāya thinkers develop a version of the argument from design to support a general form of theism. In epistemology, they argue that human beings have reliable, but by no means infallible, access to reality through distinct knowledge sources such as perception and inference. We are rationally entitled to trust the deliverances of these sources unless there is positive reason to doubt them. Finally, for Nyāya the proper use of reason to gain knowledge of reality is a necessary condition of achieving the highest human good. As we will see in the coming sections, these background commitments fundamentally shape Nyāya philosophy of mind and consciousness.

2.2 Other-Luminosity

For Nyāya the paradigm case of knowledge is an occurrent state of cognitive awareness (*jñāna*) which is directed at an object in the external world and produced through a reliable knowledge source. Take perception (*pratyakṣa*) for example. The *Nyāya-sūtra* defines it as follows:

> 1.1.4: Perceptual knowledge arises from a connection of sense faculty and object, does not depend on language, is inerrant, and is definitive.

For example, when I encounter a tree under the appropriate conditions—proper lighting, working senses, directed attention, and so forth—I am caused to be in a perceptual state of seeing the tree. That cognition is properly related to its object by being caused by a real tree in my environment, as well as functioning sense organs, and the like. The cognition takes the tree and its visible properties as its intentional object. It is a perception *of* a large white and gold aspen. Moreover, seeing a tree does not depend on or require knowing or thinking the word "tree."[1] And when I am in the state of perceiving the tree, it is the real tree in the world that I'm seeing, not some intermediary mental image. Finally, when the perceptual process works properly, according to Nyāya, I am in a state of perceptual knowledge of a determinate object (the tree). Indeed, in this view, a process that yields a mistaken cognition is not really perception at all, but a pseudo-perception.[2] In short, Nyāya defends a robustly direct realist view of perception.

On the Nyāya view, the basic function of a cognition is to reveal an object (*artha-prakāśanam*) and it does so through proper causal contact between the object and the cognizer. This implies that the cognition and its object, as cause and effect, are distinct. Thus, the basic function of a cognition is to reveal that which is *other*, it is other-illuminating. Additionally, the cognition reveals its object transparently or directly, without the need for a mediating mental image (*ākāra*). When this cognitive process works as it should, then, the cognition makes the subject aware of the object and does so without the subject needing to be aware of the cognition itself. In this way, as mentioned in the last chapter, Nyāya is committed to the independence thesis when it comes to standard forms of cognitive awareness. Recall that the independence thesis states: The presence of any given mental state, M, in a subject S, is independent of S being introspectively conscious of M.

Now, in current philosophy of mind and cognitive science, there is a distinction between *conscious* and *unconscious* mental states. This distinction is not without controversy and there is no consensus on exactly how to draw this distinction. Nevertheless, philosophers and others studying the mind generally agree that there are unconscious mental states, such as various stages of perceptual processing leading to the occurrence of a conscious perception. In the context of classical Indian philosophy of mind, one does not generally find a sharp distinction between conscious and unconscious mental states (Dreyfus and Thompson 2007). Rather, it would perhaps be more accurate to posit a distinction between (more or less) subliminal and supraliminal states of mind. And what marks the difference is availability to introspection. A mental state that is easily available to introspection, such as one's current visual perception, is supraliminal. In contrast, a state that would be difficult (perhaps even impossible) to introspect would be subliminal, such as a very fast flash of an image or a very weak sound.

This is important in our discussion of Nyāya because these thinkers hold the independence thesis and also that non-introspected mental states can be conscious. That is, they accept the independence thesis and deny the transitivity thesis. On this view, a subject S, can be in a *conscious* mental state M, without S being aware of M or that she is in M. In contemporary terms, Naiyāyikas hold a first-order view of consciousness. What makes a mental state conscious is independent of the subject's awareness of that state. So, what makes a state conscious? In keeping with their strict view of other-luminosity, Naiyāyikas argue that consciousness consists in revealing a distinct object to the subject, or what contemporary philosophers call *intentionality*. Roughly, my perception of the tree is conscious just in so far as it reveals the tree to me. In addition, a typical case of conscious perception will be available for other mental operations such as introspection, verbal report ("Look, a tree!"), inference, as well as actions.

To sum up, the Nyāya school defends a resolutely realist, intentionalist, and first-order view of consciousness. It is realist in three relevant respects. First, Nyāya is fully ontologically realist about consciousness. Consciousness is a real, unique, and irreducible capacity of the self. Second, Nyāya is epistemologically realist in that veridical episodes of conscious cognition disclose real, mind-independent objects and properties in the word. Third, the school defends a direct realist account of perception in that veridical episodes of perception reveal mind-independent physical objects, without the intermediary of conscious mental images or representations (*ākāra*). Nyāya realism is, in turn, tightly bound up with their intentionalist analysis of consciousness. It is the very nature of consciousness to be of or about an object (*svābhāvika viṣayapravaṇatvam*). Episodes of conscious cognition are individuated by their object, and the intentional object of cognition is (in the standard case) an object in the world, not any kind of mental intermediary. Thus, intentionality is the mark of the mental and the intrinsic intentionality of consciousness is understood in externalist terms. Moreover, since consciousness is transparent (*nirākāra*, "without image/ aspect"), the phenomenal features of a conscious state are grounded in (and perhaps reducible to) the way the object is presented through the state. Finally, Nyāya defended a first-order view of consciousness. The luminosity of a cognition consists in it revealing its object (*arthaprakāśobuddhi*), not itself. That is, it illuminates that which is other than itself (its object) and requires a distinct, second-order cognition for a first-order cognition to be revealed.

2.3 Apperception

According to the Nyāya school, perception is the basic *pramāṇa* because it is directly connected to its object and because other knowledge sources such as inference and verbal testimony depend on perceptual input. However, the full uptake and integration of perception depends on the faculty of *manas*, often translated as "mind" but here referring to an inner sense organ or faculty.[3] *Manas* plays several important functions in Nyāya philosophy of mind. First, it is the cognitive faculty of the self that connects to the sense organs, which in turn connect to the external object. Second, the *manas* integrates the input from the different senses into a single perceptual field. Third, it includes the faculty of selective attention, which makes possible the voluntary focus on different parts of the perceptual field. Fourth, it is the faculty responsible for the retrieval and occurrent presentation of memories. Fifth, it is the faculty of apperception, introspection, and other forms of meta-cognition. That is, through *manas* the self can become aware of its own mental states, including perception, desire, and volition.

In the last section I pointed out that Naiyāyikas defend a first-order view of consciousness. A mental state can be conscious even when the subject is not aware of the state. Yet, this is not to deny that the subject can be and often is aware of her own states. According to Nyāya, our first-order cognitions (*vyavasāya*) are cognized by a higher-order cognition (*anuvyavasāya*, "after-cognition") or apperception. In the typical case of perception, a first-order cognition triggers a second-order cognition that takes the first-order cognition as its intentional object. Whereas the first-order perception is a function of the outer senses, the second-order cognition is a function of the *manas*, here understood as the inner sense.

There are several features of this view worth noting. First, apperception is thought to be an automatic causal process. It is causal in that, in minds like ours, the occurrence of a first-order conscious perception triggers an apperceptive meta-cognition. Second, *anuvyavasāya* as automatic meta-cognition should be distinguished from voluntary reflective introspection. While we do typically apperceive our basic perceptions, we do not usually go around introspecting our cognitions. Third, while the *vyavasāya* and the *anuvyavasāya* are distinct cognitions, their content is intimately related. When a perception with the content <there is a tree> is apperceived, the content of the apperception will be <I perceive a tree>. In the case of the perception, the perceptual *object* is the tree, whereas as the conceptually-formed (*savikalpa*) content of the perception is <there is a tree>. In the case of the apperception, the direct object of the meta-cognition is the first-order cognition, while the indirect objects of the meta-cognition are the first-order cognition's object (the tree) and the self. Further, the content of the apperception is <I perceive a tree>. Fourth, apperception is a form of *perception* (*pratyakṣa*) and so is direct and non-inferential. As we will see below, this has important implications for the epistemic security of apperception.[4]

With these four points in mind, let us examine some of the Nyāya arguments for this view. As I have emphasized throughout this chapter, the Nyāya account of cognition is grounded in, though not reducible to, causation. We come to know by our causal commerce with objects of knowledge. Additionally, Naiyāyikas, like the Buddhists, defend the *asatkaryavāda* account of causation. This is the view (*vāda*) that the effect does not pre-exist (*a-sat*) in the cause (*karya*).[5] In other words, cause and effect are distinct and in the typical case, cause precedes effect. Applied to cognition, this entails that a cognition and its object are distinct—the tree and my perception of it are distinct and quite different things. One is a physical object and the other, according to Nyāya, is a mental state of the immaterial self. Applied to apperception, then, the first-order cognition as the object is both causally connected to the meta-cognition and also distinct from it. Furthermore, on this view, causation is irreflexive. Nothing can cause itself. Therefore, no cognition could be self-cognizing.

Now since the relationship between perception and apperception is causal and contingent, Nyāya thinkers point to cases where, arguably, there is perception without apperception. For instance, one might see a small blue pot just as a loud noise captures one's attention. In this case, one can argue that one is aware of the blue pot but not aware that one is aware of it. This is because the causal process by which one would apperceive the visual cognition is interrupted by the loud noise. In contemporary terms we might say that one's top-down attention is captured by the audial modality. Similarly, one might have a first order perception but then be knocked unconscious before it can trigger an apperception. Finally, one might become so focused on or absorbed in an object that there is no apperception at all. In such a case, it is not unnatural to say that one 'loses oneself' in the object or activity. That is, there is awareness without any awareness of awareness.

These two lines of argument emphasize the distinctness and contingent relation between perception and apperception. But can that be the whole story? There seems to be something distinctive about my awareness of my own conscious mental life, my perceptions, pains, and thoughts. On the Nyāya account, two distinctive features of our awareness of our own mental lives are its immediacy and its self-refence. Regarding immediacy, recall that apperception is a form of (inner) perception. As a form of perception, it is immediate in two ways. First, it is non-inferential. Second, it does not rely on any intermediary mental image (*ākāra*). Hence it is the most epistemically secure form of cognition. Further, as the later Navya Nyāya philosopher Gaṅgeśa argues, because apperception does not rely on a material sense organ, it is not vulnerable to errors caused by poor vision or the like. When a first-order cognition is apperceived, the subject gains certain knowledge of the *content* of the cognition, but not its *truth*. For example, I might come to know that I'm having a visual experience as of a blue pot, even if I later find out that the pot is not actually blue but only looked blue due to unusual lighting. In this way, the subject has secure knowledge of her own mental states, even when those mental states themselves do not offer secure knowledge of the world.

Regarding self-reference, the important point is that first-order and second-order cognitions have distinct types of objects and contents. The content of a first-order perception of a white and gold tree would be <there is a white and gold tree>.[6] The content of the cognition is a function of the mind-independent object and its properties. The content of a second-order apperception of that perception would be <I see a white and gold tree>. Here the direct object of the apperception is another cognition (seeing). There are two indirect objects: the object of the earlier perception (the tree) and the self as the subject of cognition. So, the perception of the tree is only about the tree, but the apperception of the perception also refers to the self (<I see …>). In this way, apperceptive cognition serves to integrate first-order cognitions into the first-person perspective of the subject. The apperceived state is now one that the subject can report being in, it is laid down in memory, and it is available for inference and other cognitive operations. Furthermore, because apperception is supposed to be infallible, the subject cannot be mistaken about the occurrence of the state, its content, or its subject. In short, while apperception need not always occur, when it does it provides secure knowledge.

Finally, it is important to recognize the connection between the other-luminosity and transparency of cognition and Nyāya's overall commitment to metaphysical and epistemological realism. As we have seen, according to the Nyāya theory, it is the very nature of consciousness to be of or about an object (*svābhāvika viṣayapravaṇatvam*). The capacity for consciousness allows us to be in direct epistemic contact with a mind-independent world. The conscious mind is not a self-enclosed domain, but rather an open mode of cognitive access to the world. From this perspective, attempting to understand consciousness in terms of self-luminosity is fundamentally backwards—it mistakenly treats what is essentially world-directed as if it were essentially self-directed. Additionally, Naiyāyikas argue that consciousness is *nirākāra* or without intermediary mental images or phenomenal forms (*ākāra*). Like a transparent window in an otherwise opaque wall, consciousness provides a view of the world beyond it. Importantly, this view of consciousness as formless or transparent does not rule out its having contentful intentional structure (*viṣayatā*). Rather, the point is that this form of intentionality is direct and presentational as opposed to the indirect and *re*-presentational account given by proponents of *sākāravada* (the view that consciousness has mental images or phenomenal forms). To extend the example, the content of consciousness is like the external scene that can be viewed through the window. In contrast, proponents of *sākāravada* argue that conscious content is a function of internal images or phenomenal forms, which then (by way of the appropriate causal and functional links) serve to represent external objects. On this view, there is no transparent window, but rather something like a video screen whose displayed images represent other objects. It may seem to us that we are looking at the external objects directly but in fact we are directly aware of images internal to the screen itself. Naiyāyikas argue that the combination of self-luminosity and *sākāravada* is recipe for skepticism about the external world and even subjective idealism, the metaphysical view that there are really only minds and their internal contents. As we will see in Chapter 5, this is a result embraced by some Buddhist thinkers.

2.4 Self and World

Nyāya is robustly realist about the self (*ātman*). On their view, the self is an individual, enduring, unitary, non-physical locus of consciousness and agency. It is the central organizing principle of cognition and the condition of the possibility of both world-knowledge and self-knowledge. In the *Nyāya-sūtra* (1.1.9) the self is identified as a proper object of cognition (*prameya*). How is it known? Nyāya philosophers hold to the idea of *pramāṇasamplava*, the availability of a single object to distinct pramāṇas. So, for instance, Uddyotakara argues that the self is known through perception, inference (*anumāna*), and verbal testimony (*śabda*). Commenting on the *Nyāya-sūtra*, he writes:

> Thus, in this manner, first of all, the self is directly perceived (*pratyakṣa*) because of being the domain of 'I'-cognition (*ahaṃpratyaya*). It has been explained under NS 1.1.10 how the self is also cognized (*upalabhyate*) through inference (*anumāna*). In addition, verbal testi mony (*āgama*), too, is just that through which the self is cognized.
>
> (NV on NS 3.1.1 (705))

Regarding inferential knowledge of the self, we see in the *Nyāya-sūtra* and Vātsyāyana's commentary (NBh):

> 1.1.10: Inferential marks for the self are desire, aversion, effort, pleasure, pain, and knowledge.
>
> Vātsyāyana [16.5–20]: From sensory contact with a certain type of object, pleasure arises and is experienced by a self. Observing another object of the same type, the person desires to have it. The desire to have, "This is the kind of thing I experienced before"—on the part of a single observer seeing multiple objects of the same type and recognizing them as such—is an inferential mark for the self. For, such a desire would

not be possible if there existed only a series of distinct cognitions each with its own fixed content, just as it would not be possible with a body different from one's own.

Here the self can be known because it can be reliably inferred from the characteristic mental activities of desire, aversion, and the like. We have introspective access to various mental activities—including hedonic and affective activities—that are integrated at a time and over time. From this we infer that there is a single enduring subject or locus of these activities, which is the self.

Moreover, Uddyotakara argues:

> These items, desire and the rest, are qualities (*guṇa*), and qualities demand things other than themselves in which to reside. This is the reasoned position ... (Thus) a self can be proved by means of an eliminative argument: because desire and the rest are impermanent, they are not self-supporting. Another reason they depend on things other than themselves is that they are effects. They are like color and other material qualities, which depend upon the substances in which they inhere. Furthermore, these are not qualities belonging to the body, since they do not inhere in material substances. And material substances being ruled out, we identify these as qualities of a self, a psychological substance. Thus, a self is proved.
>
> (NV 64.12-18)

The idea here is that mental states like pains, desires, or thoughts are not like material objects such as sticks and stones. They do not exist independently. One does not trip over a stray pain or thought in one's path as one might do with a stick or stone. Rather, mental states are like colors or other qualities that inhere in or are dependent on some entity. They are *adjectival* on a substance (*dravya*).[7] Just as dent on a surface is a feature of the surface, so mental states are features of a particular subject or self. And just as the movement of a tree branch is the activity of that particular branch, so mental activities such as thinking and perceiving are activities of a particular subject or self.

Now, one might grant that mental states and activities must be the states and activities *of* some particular substance or entity. Nyāya thinkers, though, make a further claim. Mental states and activities belong to the self as an immaterial substance that is ontologically distinct from the body. That is, they are substance dualists. But why not hold that these states and activities belong to a particular body or organism? Or, perhaps, they belong to one part of the body, such as the brain? Naiyāyikas offer a variety of arguments for substance dualism. Here we'll consider only one line of argument, which we can call the *distinct properties argument*. Gautama (NS 3.2.53) argues that consciousness is not a quality of the body because "it is utterly dissimilar to bodily qualities." As Vātsyāyana elaborates:

> For this too, consciousness is not a quality of the body, viz., because of utter dissimilarity from bodily qualities. Bodily qualities are of two types: (1) imperceptible, such as weight, and (2) [externally] perceptible, such as color, etc. But consciousness is of a different type. It is not imperceptible, for it is internally perceptible; nor is it [externally] perceptible, for it is grasped by the inner sense. Therefore, [it] is the quality of a different substance.
>
> (NBh 3.2.53)

According to Vātsyāyana, qualities of the body like color or shape are externally observable, while properties like weight are measurable, but not externally observable (through the senses). Is consciousness like these qualities? Arguably, it is not externally perceptible. For instance, there is no observable glow of consciousness that we can perceive in another person.[8] And even when another person appears to be awake and alert, it seems we only *infer* that she is conscious based on her observable behavior. Perhaps in reality she is a robot or a zombie and, despite her behavior, she is not really conscious at all. What about the brain? In the normal case, that's not perceivable either, but surely the brain counts as belonging to the body! Yet the brain *is* perceivable, such as in brain surgery. However, in such circumstances, we don't find consciousness as an observable property of the brain, like its color, shape, or temperature.

So perhaps consciousness is like weight, not perceptible but measurable. While we cannot do so today, it seems in principle possible that neuroscientists will discover the neural correlates of consciousness in the brain, allowing them to reliably infer the presence of consciousness based on observable brain activity. The Nyāya dualist, though, does not need to deny that consciousness could be inferred based on distinct observable properties, such as certain patterns of electrical activity in the brain. Rather, the argument is that a bodily property like weight is imperceptible, but measurable. Consciousness, in contrast, is not imperceptible. Conscious states are perceptible by the subject who has them. A neuroscientist may infer that I am in pain based on measuring certain of my brain states. But I can be aware that I am in pain much more directly, through introspection or apperception of my own hedonic state. I *feel* the pain and don't need to infer its presence from a brain scan. So, according to this line of argument, the quality of consciousness is quite unlike the standard material properties of the body. The later Nyāya philosopher Uddyotakara develops a similar argument. He points out that material properties of the body are (in principle) perceptible by oneself and others (*ātmaparātmapratyakṣa*), whereas consciousness is only perceptible by oneself. Thus, consciousness is not a material property of the body. It is therefore a property of a different type of substance, namely the self.

The distinct properties argument aims to establish that the properties of consciousness are ontologically distinct from material properties. And since properties must inhere in a substance, these mental properties must inhere in a non-material substance—the self.

Another important argument for the reality of the self concerns the unity of the self at a time and over time, both of which are denied by Buddhist philosophers. Regarding the unity and persistence of the self over time, Nyāya philosophers argue that mental capacities such as memory and recognition (*pratisandhāna*) presuppose the existence of an enduring self (Chadha 2013).

Vātsyāyana [NBh16.5–20] argues:

> From sensory contact with a certain type of object, pleasure arises and is experienced by a self. Observing another object of the same type, the person desires to have it. The desire to have, "This is the kind of thing I experienced before"—on the part of a single observer seeing multiple objects of the same type and recognizing them as such—is an inferential mark for the self. For, such a desire would not be possible if there existed only a series of distinct cognitions each with its own fixed content, just as it would not be possible with a body different from one's own.

When I see the full cup of hot coffee on my desk, I may desire to drink some because I enjoy coffee. Vātsyāyana's argument is that there must be an enduring subject to account for this. *I* must have had coffee before and enjoyed it. *I* must now see the coffee and recognize it as something pleasurable, thereby forming a desire for what *I* have previously enjoyed. A series of distinct mental events won't do. Somewhere at some time a coffee-enjoying occurred. Somewhere at some time a coffee-seeing occurred. Somewhere at some time a coffee-desiring occurred. On this line of argument, these occurrences don't add up to *my* desiring coffee on the basis of *my* recognition of coffee as pleasurable to *me*. As Vātsyāyana says:

> Proponents of the view that there is no self would admit that a series of distinct cognitions, each with its own fixed content, could not recognize previous experiences generated in connection with bodies other than

one's own. Similarly (in the absence of an enduring self), distinct cognitions with content restricted by connection with one's own body could not be the basis of recognition, because the two scenarios are fundamentally the same.

(NBh 16.10-20)

Furthermore, he argues that:

It is well known that remembering belongs to the one who had some precise earlier experience, a single creature. One does not remember something experienced by another or something he himself has never experienced before. In the same way, it is well known that for all sorts of creatures one does not remember the things found in another's experiences. Proponents of the "no-self" view cannot account for either of these occurrences. In contrast, matters as we have presented them, namely, that there is a self, accords well with the phenomena described.

That is, one only remembers what one has experienced before and one does *not* remember what another has experienced. Yet, if there is no persisting self, how can these facts be accommodated? In Chapters 3 and 7, we'll discuss some important Buddhist responses to this challenge.

Regarding the unity of the self at a time, Nyāya thinkers appeal to the synthesis or integration of the different senses (Chakrabarti 1992). NS 3.1.1 states: "Because one grasps the same object through sight and touch, there is a self that is distinct from the body and sense organs." In his commentary Vātsyāyana argues [NBh 135.14–136.4]:

Some particular object is grasped by sight; the same object is also grasped by touch: "That very thing which I saw with my eyes I am now feeling through my sense of touch," and "That very thing which I felt through my sense of touch I am now seeing with my eyes." The two instances of mental content that are each directed towards one and the same object have—in being comprehended—a single subject.

In everyday life we take for granted that we can see and touch (or hear and smell, etc.) the same object. If this everyday experience is accurate, this presupposes that there are objects that are both visible and tangible. It also presupposes that one can *integrate* information from vision and touch, so that one is aware of the same object through both senses. Further, on the Nyāya view, it also requires a single subject who is aware of the object through both senses. That is, it must be the same *I* that both sees and feels the tree, for instance. And this entails, they argue, that there is a unitary self that is the subject of this integrated awareness.

Imagine that one person sees the tree and another feels it. It is the same tree in both cases, but there is no integration of seeing and feeling in a single awareness. For there to be a single integrated awareness, it seems there needs to be a single subject as well; a single knower who knows the tree through both seeing and touch. Furthermore, one can go beyond merely seeing and feeling the tree and can reflectively *recognize* (*pratyabhijñā*) that the tree one is feeling is the same as the tree one is seeing. Just as one can recognize that the tree one sees today is the same as the tree one saw a week ago, one can recognize the same tree through different senses. And in both cases, the argument goes, there must be a single subject of the various states.

Additionally, notice this view entails that, to be aware of enduring objects in the world, there must be an enduring subject as well. If seeings and touchings are separate states with their own isolated content, then we don't have an integrated cognition of one and the same object that is both visible and tangible. Likewise, if cognitions at different times are separate, then we don't have the kinds of temporally integrated cognition we call memory and recognition. On the Nyāya view, there must be a single subject of multiple states at a time and over time for there to be integrated awareness of objects in the world at a time and over time. A stable, enduring self and a stable, enduring world are correlative in our cognitive experience. Realism about the self and realism about the world go hand in hand (Chakrabarti 2019). As we'll see in later chapters, several of Nyāya's Buddhist opponents agree with this point. However, they argue the proper conclusion is that *both* the stable self *and* the stable world of objects are in fact mere constructions.

2.5 Comparative Connections

The Nyāya tradition offers many avenues for fruitful cross-cultural philosophical work in metaphysics, epistemology, philosophy of language, philosophy of religion and more. Here I will focus on three comparative connections: 1) transparency and intentionality, 2) first-order and higher-order views of consciousness, and 3) substance dualism.

As discussed in sections 2.2 and 2.3, Nyāya thinkers argued for both the other-luminosity (*paraprakāśatā*) and the formlessness (*nirākāratā*) of consciousness. First, the fundamental function of consciousness is to reveal that which is other than the conscious act, paradigmatically a mind-independent object. Second, an act of consciousness reveals its object without the need for any further mental intermediary, such as a distinct phenomenal form or mental image (*ākāra*). In contemporary terms, their view is that consciousness is characterized by an intrinsic intentionality (object-directedness or "aboutness") and transparency.

This line of thinking is strikingly like one developed by the French phenomenologist, Jean-Paul Sartre. In the introduction to *Being and Nothingness*, he writes, "All consciousness, Husserl has shown, is consciousness *of* something. This means that there is no consciousness that is not a positing of a transcendent object, or if you prefer, that consciousness has no 'content'" (Sartre 1993, 11). Following Mark Rowlands (2013) we can identify two important theses here. The first is the *intentionality thesis* that all consciousness is consciousness *of* something. The second is the *no content thesis* that any object of consciousness is outside consciousness. What Sartre means by "positing of a transcendent object" is precisely that an act of consciousness is intentionally directed (posits) an object that is distinct from (transcends) that act of consciousness. Moreover, Sartre thinks that the intentionality thesis entails the no content thesis. As he remarks, "All consciousness is positional in that it transcends itself in order to reach an object, and it exhausts itself in this same positing" (Sartre 1993, 11).

The view that all consciousness is intentional is widespread but by no means universal in either Indian or Western philosophy. In contrast, the idea that consciousness is strictly formless or contentless is much less common. Indeed, a common way to analyze intentionality is precisely in terms of content or form, understood as internal to consciousness. On that analysis, intentionality entails content. Unfortunately, Sartre does not give much in the way of explicit argument for the no content thesis. In contrast, Nyāya thinkers developed interesting anti-skeptical and anti-idealist arguments (section 2.3 of this chapter) for their combination of other-luminosity and formlessness that, I think, deserve the attention of contemporary philosophers.

Another fruitful comparative connection concerns first-order and higher-order views of consciousness. The distinction between these two (families of) approaches to consciousness has to do with the *transitivity thesis* and the *independence thesis* introduced in Chapter 1. Recall:

- **The Transitivity Thesis:** For any mental state M of a subject S (at a time t), M is conscious (at t) only if S is aware of M (at t).
- **The Independence Thesis:** The presence of any given mental state, M, in a subject S, is independent of S being introspectively conscious of M.

Proponents of higher-order views of consciousness accept the transitivity thesis. On this view, for a mental state to be conscious, the subject of the state must be aware of it (in the right way). So, higher-order cognition of the first-order state is a necessary condition of the first-order state's being conscious. Furthermore, some higher-order theorists go further and argue that the (right kind of) higher-order state is what *makes* the first-order state conscious. The higher-order state is both necessary and sufficient. Furthermore, higher-order theorists are split between those who think the higher-order cognition is something like a *thought* and those who think it is something like an inner *perception* (Rosenthal 2009).

In sharp contrast to the higher-order view, proponents of first-order theories of consciousness reject the transitivity thesis. Indeed, they accept a stronger form of the independence thesis:

- **The Independence Thesis***: The presence of any given *conscious* mental state, M, in a subject S, is independent of S being introspectively conscious of M.

Whatever it is that makes a mental state conscious, it does not involve a higher-order cognition of the first-order state.[9] This view is well-captured by Fred Dretske:

> There are, to be sure, states in (or of) us without which we would not be conscious of trees and pianos. We call these states experiences. Since these experiences make us conscious of things ... the states themselves can be described as conscious. But we must be careful not to conclude from this that because the states are conscious, we must, perforce, be conscious of them.
>
> (Dretske 1997, 100)

According to the first-order theory, then, one can have a fully conscious visual perception of an object, without being at all conscious of that perception. One is conscious of the perceptual *object*, not the perception or perceptual state itself. So, what makes the perceptual state *conscious* rather than *unconscious*? One common answer given by first-order theorists appeals to the mode of representation or way the state cognizes its object. For example, Michael Tye defends what he calls the PANIC theory of conscious cognition (Tye 1999). A cognition or mental representation is conscious just in case it is *poised, abstract, non-conceptual,* and has *intentional content*. There are important similarities and differences between this view and the Nyāya view. However, the important idea here is that the difference between an unconscious and a conscious state is that the latter is appropriately *poised* or available for further mental operations such as belief and desire, while the former is not. This is an essentially *functional* account of what makes a state conscious—that is, it is in terms of the role the state plays in the larger cognitive economy.

On the Nyāya account, a conscious cognition plays the role of informing or making the subject aware of its object. Further, the first-order conscious state (*vyavasāya*) is thereby *available* for apperception (*anuvyavasāya*). In this way, the Nyāya view is similar to contemporary first-order views of consciousness. However, there are two important differences. First, while the first-order state does not need to be apperceived to be conscious, it is not yet fully *poised* or *available* to further cognitive operations unless it is apperceived. The Nyāya view, then, combines aspects of both first-order and higher-order perception views of consciousness. Second, contemporary theories of consciousness are often trying to explain the difference between conscious and unconscious mental states and processes. However, as we discussed in Chapter 1, this isn't how Indian philosophers thought about consciousness. For Naiyāyikas, consciousness is not really a merely functional property ('being *poised*') that might or might not attach to certain mental states. Rather, it is a basic and irreducible capacity of the self. Hence, what makes a particular state conscious is that it is the result of the exercise of this basic capacity. What makes that state properly *integrated* into the self's overall mental life is its functional availability for other mental operations. We can connect these two points, I think, by seeing that a particular first-order state that is conscious but not apperceived is a *subliminal* state. It's conscious, but not fully integrated or available for belief, desire, or memory. These are subtle distinctions, perhaps, but certainly worth further philosophical and empirical investigation.

The final comparative connection has to do with the distinct properties argument. According to this argument, mental properties are radically unlike material properties (e.g. color, weight, etc.). For instance, conscious mental properties are not publicly observable, but they are privately observable by their subject through apperception or introspection. There is, on this account, a deep epistemic asymmetry between mental and physical properties. Further, Naiyāyikas argue that radically distinct properties (*guṇas*) require distinct types of substance (*dravya*). Therefore, mental properties must inhere in a non-physical substance, the self.

In contemporary philosophy of mind, some philosophers argue that mental properties are distinct from and irreducible to physical properties. For instance, non-reductive physicalists argue that mental properties are irreducible to physical properties, but nonetheless metaphysically depend on them in a way that preserves physicalism (Stoljar 2022). Other philosophers go further. Property dualists argue that mental and physical properties are metaphysically distinct and so physicalism is false. Mental and physical properties may be related by laws of nature, but there is nothing contradictory about them being related differently or not at all (Robinson 2020).[10] The view that mental properties are different and irreducible is well-expressed by John Searle. He writes, "consciousness has a first-person ontology; that is, it only exists as experienced by some human or animal, and therefore, it cannot be reduced to something that has a third-person ontology, something that exists independently of experiences" (Searle 2000, 60). In other words, physical properties have a third-person ontology, while (conscious) mental properties have a first-person ontology.

Yet even those philosophers who admit that mental properties are irreducible tend to accept that they are properties of a *physical* thing, namely some human or animal. But how could a physical substance also have non-physical concrete properties?[11] One worry raised by contemporary substance dualists is that standard material objects seem to have vague identities in a way that subjects (if there are any) seem not to. As Dean Zimmerman argues:

> Garden variety materialism identifies me with one of the garden variety candidates, a thing that already has a place in our commonsense conception of the world. Such an object will have relatively natural boundaries, such as those of an organism, or a brain, or even a single hemisphere of a brain. But animals and their organs belong on a spectrum that includes bushes, branches, clouds, mountains, rivers, tidal waves, and all manner of fuzzy entities. All such familiar material objects exhibit vagueness or indeterminacy in their spatial and temporal boundaries. And the strategies rightly implemented to resolve the puzzles posed by vague objects do not seem so satisfactory when applied to *oneself*.
>
> (Zimmerman 2010, 137)

So, what's the problem? Given the synchronic and diachronic unity of consciousness, and the assumption that mental properties inhere in a physical object, Zimmerman argues that:

> No cell or molecule or atom in the brain is distinguished in a way that would suggest that it is a better candidate than any of its rivals for being conscious; there seems no precise physical entity in the vicinity that fundamental laws could pick out in virtue of some special physical status, either intrinsic (for example, a special type of particle, atom, or molecule) or extrinsic (for example, a special place in my brain where only one particle, atom, or molecule could be located).
>
> (Zimmerman 2010, 145)

According to this line of argument, then, not only are mental and physical *properties* quite different, but the *locus* of those properties seems quite different as well. My mental life has a kind of internal unity that my body lacks. My kidney could be transferred into the body of another, and the atoms that make up my body now have likely been parts of many other living beings at one time or another. In contrast, my current pain or sensation of red cannot be transferred to the mind of another or be recycled into another living thing. On this view, these states belong to me *as a subject*. Substance dualists therefore propose that irreducible mental properties are best understood as aspects of an irreducible mental substance.

2.6 Questions

1. What is the Nyāya view of other-luminosity? How is it related to their philosophical realism?
2. What is the relationship between perception and apperception in Nyāya? Do Naiyāyikas accept the *transitivity thesis*?
3. What is the nature of the self in Nyāya?
4. Nyāya thinkers argue that realism about the external world and realism about the self go hand in hand. Is this argument persuasive?

Notes

1 The proper interpretation of this condition is debated within Nyāya. The standard Nyāya view is that normal perception deploys concepts (it is *savikalpa*) but that these concepts need not depend on linguistic cognition as part of the perceptual state. So, for instance, perceptual recognition of a tree does not require thinking the word "tree."

2 This view of perception as inerrant is quite controversial and Nyāya thinkers developed sophisticated accounts of cognitive error in order to deal with illusions, hallucinations, and the like.

3 Indeed, the Sanskrit term *manas* is cognate with the Latin *mens* from which we derive "mental," etc.

4 See the perception chapter (*pratyakṣa-khaṇḍa*) of Gaṅgeśa's *Tattvacintāmaṇi* for an extensive discussion of these issues.

5 The alternative view is *satkaryavāda*, the view that the effect is implicit or latent in the cause.

6   This linguistic gloss is not meant to imply that the perceptual state has linguistic content or that the perceiver must think that thought. In Nyāya, a standard perceptual state involves concepts but does not depend on language. See Chadha (2024) for a good overview.

7   Here the term *dravya* (substance) refers to an individual entity that has various properties, such as a stone or an animal.

8   But see (Ganeri 2018) and (Zahavi 2014) for important challenges to this line of thought.

9   Here I am referring to both voluntary introspection and apperception.

10 So, a property dualist can accept the possibility of philosophical zombies—beings that outwardly act just like human beings, but have no inner conscious life.

11 One might think that merely formal or abstract properties (e.g. mathematical features) of a physical object are non-physical. But qualitative features of mental states like phenomenal colors or pains are not abstract in this way.

Further Reading

Chakrabarti, Arindam. 2019. *Realisms Interlinked: Objects, Subjects, and Other Subjects*. Bloomsbury Publishing.

Chakrabarti, Kisor Kumar. 2024. *Classical Indian Philosophy of Mind: A Nyāya Dualist Tradition*. Motilal Banarsidass Publishing House.

Dasti, Matthew R. 2023. *Vātsyāyana's Commentary on the Nyāya-Sūtra: A Guide*. Oxford University Press.

Phillips, Stephen. 2014. *Epistemology in Classical India*. 1st edition. Routledge.

Phillips, Stephen H., and N. S. Ramanuja Tatacharya, trans. 2004. *Epistemology of Perception: Gaṅgeśa's Tattvacintāmani*. Bilingual edition. American Institute of Buddhist Studies.

3

Abhidharma

3.1 The Abhidharma Schools

As introduced in Chapter 1, Buddhist philosophy has its origins in the teachings of Siddhattha Gotama (c. 563–c. 483 BCE), honorifically known as Śākyamuni Buddha. The central focus of the Buddha's teachings was the "noble quest" for *nirvāṇa*, the liberation from suffering and the cycles of rebirth. His teachings are preserved in the *Nikāyas* and *Āgamas*, or collections of early Buddhist discourses. In general, the Buddha's teachings have a colloquial and pragmatic cast. However, over the course of his teaching career, he developed deep and sophisticated core teachings regarding the self, mind, world, knowledge, and ethics. In particular, the Buddha taught that liberation from suffering (*duḥkha*) requires an accurate understanding of the regular causal patterns of mind and world that give rise to and perpetuate this suffering. These causal patterns are understood in terms of dependent co-arising (*pratītyasamutpāda*). In the early Buddhist view, then, the world is not seen as a collection of stable *things*, but rather an interconnected network of fluid and impermanent phenomena. And the sentient being or person is understood in the same way. Unlike the Brahmanical thinkers, the Buddha rejected the existence of the self, namely, the stable, enduring locus of mental life.

Within the first centuries after the death of the Buddha his movement had spread throughout the Indian subcontinent. Over that time, several distinct teaching lineages and schools of interpretation and thought emerged within the disparate monastic communities. These lineages had the great responsibility to preserve and pass on the teachings of the Buddha, his *dharma*, which had developed over his more than forty-year career. These efforts to organize, interpret, and systematically reflect on the *dharma* came to be called *abhidharma* ("about or concerning (*abhi*) the teachings (*dharma*)"). Abhidharma, then, becomes both a genre of Buddhist literature and a set of analytical and expository methods concerning the early Buddhist canon. A key feature of the emerging Abhidharma method is the extensive use of lists or matrices (*mātṛkā*) to organize various topics, points of doctrine, or other aspects of the teaching. For example, we find discussion of the five aggregates, the six senses, the twelvefold chain of dependent arising, the twelve sense bases, and more. Another key feature is the use of extended analysis and argumentation concerning points of doctrine. This aspect of the Abhidharma includes both points of interpretation of the texts as well as discussion and debate regarding the entailments or philosophical implications of specific Buddhist ideas. And as these discussions developed over time, we see the emergence of reflective, systematic, and technical presentations of Buddhist thought. That is, we see in Abhidharma the development of systematic Buddhist *philosophy*. Historically, there were several distinct schools within the broad category of Abhidharma. However, there are only two schools with extant, complete canonical collections: Theravāda and Sarvāstivāda. The Theravāda tradition gained prominence in Sri Lanka and Southeast Asia, while the Sarvāstivāda school became dominant in northern India.

A central element of Abhidharma thought is the careful, reflective analysis of sentient experience using the various methods and tools developed in the Buddhist tradition. So, rather than analyzing sentient experience in terms of distinct substances (namely, stable individual entities) and their properties and relations, Abhidharma thinkers analyzed experience in terms of distinct mental and physical phenomena arising and ceasing depending upon various causes and conditions. Sentient experience is seen as a flow of interconnected phenomena, not the states or activities of an enduring entity like a substantial self. Further, these analyses are both categorically and temporally fine-grained. Abhidharma thinkers developed extensive typologies of mental and physical phenomena. For instance, drawing on early Buddhist analyses, we find 108 distinct types of *vedanā* ("feeling") (SN 36.6). A particular feeling may be bodily or psychological; pleasant or unpleasant; associated with one of six sensory modes; associated with various background psychological events; or distinguished in terms of past, present, and future. Temporally, the analyses are fine-grained in that the mental and physical phenomena are considered both discrete and short-lived. Indeed, as we will see below, Abhidharma thinkers see basic phenomena as momentary, and the processes of sentient experience therefore change from moment to moment.

These basic moments of sentient experience are called *dharmas*. Again, they are not substances or enduring *things*, but rather discrete causally conditioned events or occurrences.[1] At this point, however, we face an important interpretive divide in our approach to Abhidharma. In one approach, Abhidharma offers both a disciplined and reflective account of the nature of experience (a phenomenology) *and* an account of how things really are (a metaphysics). As Noa Ronkin explains:

> Ultimately, *dharmas* are all that there is: all experiential events are understood as arising from the interaction of *dharmas* ... The

Abhidharma exegesis thus attempts to provide an exhaustive account of every possible type of experience—every type of occurrence that may possibly present itself in one's consciousness—in terms of its constituent *dharmas*. This enterprise involves breaking down the objects of ordinary perception into their constituent, discrete *dharmas* and clarifying their relations of causal conditioning. The overarching inquiry subsuming both the analysis of *dharmas* into multiple categories and their synthesis into a unified structure by means of their manifold relationships of causal conditioning is referred to as the "*dharma* theory."

(Ronkin 2022)

Here *dharma* theory is deployed as a rigorous analysis of experience and as an ontology or catalogue of the basic constituents of reality. This interpretation fits well with the Sarvāstivāda and Sautrāntika schools of Abhidharma as developed by Vasubandhu (among others). It is also how Abhidharma seems to have been understood by its critics, both Buddhist and non-Buddhist.

However, as contemporary scholars Maria Heim and Chakravarthi Ram-Prasad have argued, this interpretation does not fit the work of the great Theravāda Abhidhamma philosopher, Buddhaghosa. On their view, Buddhaghosa is,

anti-metaphysical in the sense that … he follows the Buddha's teaching that one should not hold "views" (the sixty-two that the Buddha criticized), and offers a process to therapeutize the practitioner away from such commitments. At the same time, and consonant with this, since his thoroughgoing phenomenological methodology means his project is given over to the contemplation of an analysis of experience, he offers nothing positive or negative on what an ontology might be that was consistent with his phenomenological methodology (as perhaps later writers in his tradition developed).

(Heim and Ram-Prasad 2018, 1088)

Buddhaghosa's approach to Abhidhamma, they argue, is *strictly* phenomenological and he deploys Abhidhamma categories in a fluid and contextual way, rather than as a fixed analysis of the real constituents of experience or reality. In the remainder of this section, I will focus on the first approach to Abhidharma, but I will return to the strictly phenomenological approach to Theravāda Abhidhamma in section 3.4.

Let us unpack some of the core ideas developed in the Abhidharma, keeping in mind that there were different tendencies and strong disagreements within this broad approach to Buddhist thought. The first core idea is the momentariness of all conditioned *dharmas*. In the context of early Buddhism, we find the view that all dependently arisen phenomena are impermanent (*anicca* (Pali), *anitya* (Sanskrit)), without self (*anattā*, *anātman*), and unsatisfactory (*dukkha*, *duḥkha*). In other words, anything that arises from causes and conditions—which is very nearly everything we could experience—must also pass away. Within the rigorous Abhidharma approach, this emphasis on causal conditions and impermanence develops into the view that conditioned *dharmas* are momentary (*kṣanika*) (AKBh 193.2–8). Here a moment (*khana*, *kṣana*) is a very brief, basic unit of time, likened to an atom or a syllable. In the northern Sarvāstivāda tradition, a moment is in fact the smallest temporal unit. Thus, physical and mental *dharmas* exist for the shortest possible length of time, like instantaneous flashes. In the southern Theravāda tradition, a moment is a very brief interval, but it is not considered the smallest temporal unit. Further, different types of *dharmas* (mental and physical) may last for different lengths of time. In both traditions, though, the basic idea is that what we naively take to be stable, enduring objects are in fact a causal series of momentary events. What appears to us the same over time is in fact radically impermanent.

The second core idea is the reducibility of complex phenomena to the basic *dharmas* posited in *dharma* theory (AKBh 6.4). In ordinary experience, we seem to be aware of many complex, enduring entities such as inanimate physical objects, living organisms, and people. Yet, according to the Abhidharma approach, these complex things can be exhaustively analyzed into physical and mental *dharmas* arising and ceasing each moment based on their causes and conditions. What appears to be a stable whole made of parts is, upon further analysis, an aggregation or colocation of fleeting events. What appears to endure through time, in fact changes every moment, with new *dharmas* replacing old *dharmas* with incredible rapidity. Moreover, since Ābhidharmikas hold that their *dharma* theory can in principle account for all the phenomena of sentient experience, they are engaged in an ambitious reductionist project. That is, they aim to account for the whole range of complex phenomena in terms of a simpler set of phenomena and the causal regularities between them.

The third and closely related core idea of Abhidharma is that *dharmas* are to be understood in terms of their intrinsic nature (*sabbhāva*, *svabhāva*). As stated in the Theravāda *Visuddhimagga* "*dhamma* means but intrinsic nature" (*Vism* VIII 246). The idea of intrinsic nature here is directly linked to the Abhidharma as a project of categorizing the various factors of experience. In the Sarvāstivāda Abhidharma, for instance, there are 75 basic types of *dharma* (AKBh 2.1–8). Each distinct type of *dharma*, then, has a distinct intrinsic nature in virtue of which it is that basic type. For example, the intrinsic nature of a *dharma* of earth is solidity, while the intrinsic nature of a fire *dharma* is heat. Indeed, on the Abhidharma view, the material elements (earth, water, fire, and the like) are not really substantial things like permanent atoms. Rather, they are more accurately analyzed as instances of solidity, heat, and so forth. Likewise, mental *dharmas* are understood in terms of their intrinsic nature (*svabhāva*) or distinctive quality (*lakṣaṇa*). For instance, a particular moment of sensory experience would be understood and categorized in terms of its distinctive sensory quality (such as color or taste). Yet, while Abhidharma thinkers argue that each *dharma* falls under a single kind based on its intrinsic nature, they also maintain that these *dharmas* arise causally and in turn have their own causal efficacy. The overall picture of the world is of a causal flux of momentary qualities, with no underlying or enduring substances.

Finally, as we'll see in the coming sections of this chapter, these core ideas of the Abhidharma inform their understanding of the central Buddhist ideas such as no-self, the five aggregates, and dependent origination. They also drive philosophical innovations such as reductive analysis, the notion of two truths (or two levels of truth), and models of the mind and consciousness based on the core Abhidharma ideas.

3.2 Consciousness and Mental Factors

The Theravāda Abhidhamma identifies 82 distinct types of *dhammas*. This list includes 28 types of material *dhammas* (*rūpa*), the unconditioned *dharma* of *nibbāna*, and 53 types of mental *dhammas* (Vism 3.14). Similarly, the Sarvāstivāda Abhidharma identifies 75 types of dharmas. There are 11 types of physical dharmas, three types of unconditioned dharmas, 14 dharmas "dissociated from consciousness," and 47 mental dharmas. Our focus in this section is on the mental dharmas. In this regard, we find a similar model in both Abhidharma traditions. The central or most important mental dharma is *citta* or consciousness. As consciousness, it falls within the aggregate of *vijñāna* (consciousness, awareness) in the five *skandha* analysis of the person mentioned in Chapter 1 and discussed further in section 3.4 below. As a basic dharma, *citta* is a moment of awareness (*saṃvitti*) directed at particular object. The paradigm case is a moment of perceptual awareness. For example, in a moment of visual awareness one might see a particular combination of color and shape. Yet, a moment of awareness does not occur in isolation. It is, of course, caused by sensory contact with the world, but it is also accompanied by several distinct mental factors called *caitta* or *cetasika*. As we'll see in more detail shortly, these mental factors are distinct dharmas and have distinct functions in the overall flow of sentient experience. On the Abhidharma view, each moment of sentient experience is understood as a dependently originated assemblage or ensemble of mental dharmas, understood on the basic model of *citta* and associated *caittas*. And each moment causally emerges from the prior moment and gives rise to the subsequent moment, forming an episodic continuum (*santāna*) of consciousness.

Let's begin with the basic *citta dharma*. As just mentioned, a *citta* is a moment of mind or consciousness. Its fundamental function is to present (or illuminate) an object, here understood as anything that can show up as a distinct target of awareness. Indeed, Vasubandhu defines *citta* as "bare apprehension of its object" (AKBh 1.30). The basic category of *citta* is then divided into six types corresponding to the standard six senses in Indian philosophy: visual, auditory, tactile, olfactory, gustatory, and the inner or mental sense (*manas*). These different types of sensory consciousness are distinguished in terms of their connection to different sensory systems, objects, and contents. A moment of visual awareness, for example, is connected to the visual system, apprehends visual objects, and presents color and shape. Despite these differences, however, each moment of *citta* may be characterized as luminous (*prakāśa*) and cognitive (*saṃvit*). That is, a moment of consciousness presents an object and does so in a cognitively relevant or informative way. In contemporary terms we might say that it is the nature of consciousness to be both phenomenal (involving experiential qualities) and intentional (directed to or about something). The visual awareness of the tree presents a particular pattern of color and shape and does so in a way that is relevant to other cognitive operations and for action. Furthermore, since every moment of consciousness is luminous and cognizant regardless of its object, it is sometimes characterized as 'clear' (*prabhāsvara*). Consciousness is like a clear mirror that reflects whatever is placed in front of it without being "stained" by what it reflects. In this way some Abhidharma thinkers identified the continuously present nature of each moment of consciousness as distinct from the ever-shifting particular contents of consciousness.

The various *caittas* or mental factors represent distinct mental functions associated with a basic moment of consciousness. The Theravāda Abhidhamma (DS) identifies 52 distinct mental factors, while the Sarvāstivāda identifies 46 (AKBh 2.1–8). Vasubandhu explains the difference between *citta* and the *caittas* as follows: "Cognition or awareness apprehends the thing itself, and just that; mental factors or dharmas associated with cognition such as sensation, etc., apprehend special characteristics, special conditions" (AKBh 1.30). Abhidharma thinkers further distinguish the omnipresent and the variable mental factors. In Vasubandhu's *Abhidharmakośa* we find ten omnipresent factors: sensory contact, feeling, perception, desire, intention or volition, attention, mindfulness, decision, wisdom, and concentration. Buddhaghosa identifies seven: contact, feeling, perception, volition, concentration, attention, and the life faculty.

Take our prior example of a moment of visual awareness. The moment of awareness has a sensory element based on the operation of the visual system, which is the factor of sensory contact (*sparśa*). It involves the perceptual discernment (*saṃjñā*) of an object, such as a cup of coffee. This factor concerns the basic capacity to distinguish the object from others in the experience. If one's visual experience is just a blur or one's audial experience is just indistinct noise, one has not perceptually discerned a specific object. It is important to note, however, that this capacity need not involve conceptual or linguistic identification of the object. The moment of visual awareness is attentionally (*manasikāra*) focused on the object. The degree of attention can certainly vary, but here a minimal degree of attention accompanies all conscious experience. The moment is felt (*vedanā*) as pleasant, unpleasant, or neutral. Indeed, it is an important and distinctive aspect of the Abhidharma view that all moments of experience have an affective element. Following on this affective factor, the object is experienced as desirable, aversive, or indifferent. Finally, the moment of experience is shaped by a basic intention or motivational factor (*cetanā*). Thus, one may be inclined toward or against the object depending on whether one experiences as pleasant and desirable or unpleasant and aversive.

In this model, we may think of the moment of *citta* as the bare presentation of the object, while the various *caittas* specify the distinctive modes of experiential engagement with the object. Of course, *how* the sensory, attentional, affective, and other aspects of experience show up can vary a great deal. The key point is that these factors condition each moment of sentient experience. Thus, what may seem like a simple and wholly transparent experience of an object in fact has a complex experiential texture of sensory, affective, cognitive, conative, and other factors. These typically operate below the level of introspective awareness, but according to Abhidharma thinkers, they can in principle be discerned and properly categorized. Furthermore, it is important to recall that the Abhidharma mode of analysis is basically reductive. In discerning the different *dharmas* involved in a single episode of sentient experience, one is also in a sense dissolving the complex experience into discrete elements. That is, what we ordinarily take to be a single, unified moment of conscious experience is analyzed into the basic awareness (*citta*) and its associated mental factors (*caitta*). The experience is therefore an aggregate or ensemble of mental *dharmas*, arising and functioning together but having no substantial unity.

3.3 Perception and Cognition

Abhidharma thinkers took sensory perception as the paradigm case of sentient experience. And like many Indian thinkers, they also took perception to be the fundamental mode of cognitive access to the world, the basic *pramāṇa*. Following early Buddhist accounts of perception, Ābhidharmikas distinguished between the sense base (*āyatana*), the sense system (*indriya*), and the sense consciousness (*vijñāna*). For example, the visual system operates in the domain (or base) of visible qualities like color and shape, whereas the auditory system has sound as its sensory domain. It is by way of causal contact (*sparśa*) between a functioning sensory system and the sensory domain that there arises a moment of sensory consciousness. As we saw in the previous section, the moment of sensory consciousness (the *citta*) presents the sensory object and is accompanied by various mental factors, yielding the overall perceptual experience. Each phase of the perceptual process is analyzed into momentary *dharmas* and their causal-functional connections. This basic picture is shared by the different Abhidharma schools, but there are quite important differences in their overall accounts of perception.

In the Theravāda Abhidhamma, we find an important distinction between perception related to the five senses (*pañcadvāra*) and that related to the sixth inner or mental sense (*manodvāra*). On this account, each sensory system is said to have a sense "door" (*dvāra*) which we can understand as the field of sensory receptivity or sensitivity. For example, if one is in a quiet room and an audible sound arises, it will automatically be picked up by one's hearing. In the terms of the Theravāda view of perception, it will present at the auditory sense door. Yet mere sensory detection is just the first stage in a complex sensory process. Following Buddhaghosa, we can say that the perceptual process has three basic stages (Ganeri 2017): the reception of an object (*sampaṭicchana*), the investigation of that object (*santīraṇa*), and the determination (*votthapana*) of that object. In the reception stage we first have sensory detection and then the mind adverts or turns toward the sensation. This stage is like what we now call "bottom-up" attention, as when the sudden noise grabs your attention. Once the mind has turned to the sensation, the sensory object is minimally perceived. In the investigation stage, the bare perception gives rise to basic discrimination and further sensory processing of the object. So, in hearing the sound in the room one might start to distinguish the sound from the sonic background and discern further features such as pitch or distance. In the determining stage, the object is identified and certain responses are elicited. One might recognize the sound as a voice from outside the room. Once the object has been identified it triggers wholesome or unwholesome reactions—perhaps the happy recognition of a child's laugh or the mild annoyance of a disturbed quiet. What emerges in this three-stage process is a determinate perception of a voice at a distance, including certain affective and conative responses to the perceived object. After this process, the object is retained in consciousness as a continuing object of perception and as available for higher cognitive operations such as thought, which occur through the mind "door." And all of this is said to take place mostly subliminally and within the span of a few moments.[2]

So far, we have discussed what we might call the micro-structure of the perceptual process. And the Sarvāstivāda Abhidharma develops its own similar account of the perceptual process. However, for the remainder of this section I want to take up a fundamental difference between Abhidharma schools regarding the nature of the *object* of perception (*ālambana*). For Theravāda and Sarvāstivāda thinkers, the object of perception—at least in the case of the five external senses—is a material object or event that is independent of the perceptual process itself. When one hears a voice, it is the sound event in the environment that one hears. When one sees a coin, it is the physical object that is seen. In short, both Theravāda and Sarvāstivāda endorse forms of direct perceptual realism.

In contrast, the Abhidharma school of Sautrāntika defend a form of indirect realism or classical representationalism. On this view, while perception arises from causal contact between external objects or events and the sensory system, the *ālambana* or immediate object of perception is in fact a mental image (*ākāra*). The Sautrāntikas defend this view based on a few interconnected commitments. First, they hold that all *dharmas* are momentary. They therefore reject the Theravada view that *rūpa dharmas* last longer than mental *dharmas*. And they also reject the Sarvāstivāda view that past and future dharmas exist in an inactive form.[3] For Sautrāntikas, all *dharmas* exist only in the present moment. Second, they hold that cause precedes effect and so deny the Sarvāstivāda view that some causation is simultaneous. The implication of these two views is that the cause of perception has ceased to exist by the time the perception has arisen. Third, they hold that the cognitive object (*ālambana*) or content of the perception is simultaneous with perception. That is, all moments of consciousness present a cognitive object and, in the case of perception, that object is *in the present*. Given these three views, the Sautrāntikas conclude that the cognitive object of perception cannot be the same as the external cause of perception. Rather, it is a mental image or phenomenal form (*ākāra*) that is caused by and appropriately resembles its prior external cause. Hence, the perceiver is directly aware of a mental or perceptual image and indirectly aware of the external object.

Note the contrast between this Sautrāntika view and the Nyāya view discussed in the last chapter. Recall that Naiyāyikas defend a view of consciousness as formless (*nirākāra*) or transparent. Consciousness is like a clear window. It is precisely because it has no form of its own that it can present external objects. In contrast, in the Sautrāntika view consciousness is like a polished mirror. It takes on or reflects the form of objects held up to it. But the reflection is not the object and cannot exist apart from the mirror, even if it resembles the reflected object. So, on this view, consciousness is 'with form' (*sākāra*). Indeed, as later Buddhist proponents of this view such as Yaśomitra argued, it is precisely because (moments) of consciousness can take on different phenomenal forms that we can have awareness of the world (Kellner 2014). An insentient (*jaḍa*) material object cannot produce or take on a mental or phenomenal image. Only a moment of consciousness (*citta, vijñāna*) can be a contentful awareness of anything. And *which* content it presents is a function of its cause and its capacity to take on a particular phenomenal form.

Furthermore, note that the Theravāda and Sarvāstivāda schools treat consciousness as by nature other-directed or *paraprakāśa*. The core feature of a moment of experience is the *citta dharma*, which is a bare awareness of the distinct object. The co-arising mental factors further engage and determine the object, but they too are fundamentally other-directed. Mental dharmas themselves can become objects of awareness when they are perceived by the *manas* or inner sense. But the manas, like the outer senses, is distinct from its object and yields a higher order perception of mental dharmas within the stream of consciousness (*citta santāna*). In contrast, on the Sautrāntika view, what is grasped in perception is itself a mental image produced by the perceiving mind. It is experienced *as if* it is an independent external object, but this is not strictly true. Therefore, in perception, the cognizer is immediately or directly aware of their own mental images and mediately or indirectly aware of external objects. And as we'll see in detail in Chapter 7, this type of view leads to a distinctively Buddhist theory of consciousness as self-illuminating or *svaprakāśa*.

Finally, it is important to note that Abhidharma thinkers distinguish between perception (*pratyakṣa*) and various forms of mental proliferation (*prapañca*). In ordinary perceptual experience, one not only perceives an object, but one does so in the context of various associations, expectations, appraisals, and so forth. These mental associations are, on the Abhidharma view, fabrications (*prapañca*) or mental constructions that, while perhaps pragmatically useful, may not accurately reflect the content of perception. Indeed, it is due to mental proliferation that we construct an experiential world of stable, enduring objects cognized by a stable enduring subject. And we also experience these objects in terms of our deeply entrenched desires and aversions. Yet, if the Ābhidharmikas are correct that all *dharmas* are in fact momentary, then the experiential world constructed through the interplay between perception and mental proliferation is ultimately a distortion of what is immediately given in perception.

3.4 Selflessness

In Buddhist thought, all phenomena that arise from causes and conditions have three features or marks: impermanence (*anitya*), selflessness (*anātman*), and unsatisfactoriness (*duḥkha*). And this analysis certainly applies to humans and other sentient beings. From a Buddhist point of view, a fundamental truth about us is that we are selfless and impermanent, so that our deeply entrenched habits of desire and aversion are based on false assumptions about ourselves as well as the world. We take ourselves and the world to be stable and enduring when both are in fact impermanent and without substance.

First and foremost, the doctrine of no-self (*anātmavāda*) is a rejection of the *ātman*, the enduring substantial self. On this view, the 'self' (*ātman*) is not just another term for the empirical person (*pudgala, jīva*), but is rather the substantial, essential core of the person—the core self whose existence grounds the identity of the person at a time and over time. As we see throughout this book, this robust view of the self is not an invention of the Buddhists. Rather, it has its early roots in the Upaniṣads and the Sāṃkhya school of philosophy and is maintained in one form or another by the major Brahmanical and Jain traditions.

Rejecting the existence of the substantial self, the Buddhists argue the existence of a person (*pudgala*) just consists on the existence of the five *skandhas* (bundles, aggregates, or collections) organized in the right way. The five *skandhas* are:

1. *Rūpa*: the body or corporeality
2. *Vedanā*: hedonic valence or affect
3. *Saṃjñā*: perception and cognition
4. *Saṃskāra*: conditioning and volition
5. *Vijñāna*: consciousness.

These five *skandhas* are not to be taken as independent things but instead are seen as interdependent aspects of a causally and functionally integrated mental and physical (*nāma-rūpa*) system or process (*skandhasantāna*: an "aggregate-stream" or "bundle-continuum").

The *rūpa-skandha* (material form) refers to the corporeal aspect of the human being, including the organizational structure of the person as an organism. The *vedanā-skandha* denotes affective dimensions of the person and their experience (pleasant, unpleasant, or neutral). The *saṃjñā-skandha* denotes the more fully cognitive faculty of perception, including the ability to identify and re-identify objects of experience. The operation of this capacity depends on sensory contact (*sparśa*) with the environment. Next, the *saṃskāra-skandha* (conditioning) includes the various dispositions, capacities, and formations—such as sensorimotor skills, memories, habits, emotional dispositions, volitions, and cognitive schemas—that both enable and constrain the person and their experiences. This category also includes our basic conative impulses—attraction, repulsion, and indifference—which are in turn closely tied to our feelings and the affective modalities (*vedanā*) of experience. Finally, the *vijñāna-skandha* denotes consciousness, particularly associated with discrete moments of sensory consciousness.[4]

In the standard Buddhist analysis, the person is not an entity that can exist independently of the five *skandhas*. Take away the complex, impermanent, changing *skandhas* and we are not left with a constant, substantial self; we are left with nothing. Moreover, the (supposed) identity of a person over time consists in the appropriate degree of continuity and connectedness of the *skandhas*—that is, it is a matter of there being a causally and functionally integrated series or stream of *skandhas*.

Having briefly sketched the theory of no-self, let us examine two lines of argument against the existence of the self (*ātman*): the *criterial* argument and the *epistemic* argument.[5] First, it is argued that none of the *skandhas* individually, nor the whole complex of *skandhas* could be the self—namely, the independent, substantial, enduring, inner controller and owner of the *skandhas*. Upon examination, none of the five *skandhas* meets these criteria of selfhood.[6] The various mental phenomena (*nāma-skandha*) are simply too transitory, too mutable to constitute the stable, enduring essence of the person. Moreover, mental phenomena are revealed in experience as a stream (*santāna*) or flow, rather than as a substance or object. The body is perhaps more stable, but the fundamental problem is the same: like any complex phenomenon, the body is in perpetual flux. How should we specify the persistence-conditions of the body? One might attempt to identify the body's unique ontological boundary or some essential part of the body that explains its persistence. But neither of these strategies looks particularly viable. The physical boundaries of the body are vague and even if one could find the essential part of the body, it is doubtful that this essential part could meet the other criteria of selfhood. Thus, it appears that none of the *skandhas* individually, neither mental factors nor the body, could be the substantial enduring self.

What, then, of the *skandhas* taken together, the *nāma-rūpa* or psycho-physical complex? Could this be the self? One problem with this response is that the psycho-physical complex is the empirical person, whereas the self is being posited as the essence of the person which grounds and explains the persistence of the person. The empirical person, like the individual *skandhas*, is in flux and therefore its endurance is equally problematic. Therefore, to simply identify the self with the person as a whole would be to conflate the *explanans* with the *explanandum*. Secondly, the relationship between a whole and its parts is problematic and the Buddhists deny that a complex could be the *independent* owner and controller of its parts. Therefore, the substantial, essential self is not found among the *skandhas* individually or collectively.

Of course, proponents of the self (*ātmavādins*) would *agree* that the core self can't be found among the shifting and changing phenomena of the body and mind. Instead, the self is thought to be the non-material substance that underpins mental life, as in Nyāya, or the non-objectifiable subject to which all experiential objects appear, as in Advaita Vedānta. In either case, defenders of the self reject the Buddhist assumption that if there were a self, it would be found among the *skandhas* individually or collectively.

The second, and later, line of argument builds on the first but also takes up the possibility that the self may not be observed in the *skandhas*, but established through inference. According to Vasubandhu (AKBh 9.1.2), we must apprehend the self either through direct acquaintance or through inference. But he thinks we do not apprehend the self through either means. Therefore, we have no epistemic warrant for the existence of the *ātman*. The self is not a direct object of the five external senses or introspection. And while human beings typically have a *sense* of self, it does not follow from this that the sense of self provides direct acquaintance with an enduring, substantial self. Moreover, while it is certainly possible for "the self" to be an object of thought, again it does not follow that the self exists.

So, if the self is not known through direct acquaintance, then perhaps it is known through inference. Vasubandhu examines a valid inference of the existence of the unobservable sense faculties and then asserts that there is no such valid inference of the existence of the unobservable self. In the case of the sense faculties, there is some reasonable way to tell whether the sense faculties are present or absent (for example, in the case of the blind person versus the sighted person). Can the same be said for the *ātman*? One might, for example, posit the existence of distinct substantial selves to individuate persons A and B. But because the substantial self is supposed to retain its identity independently of the ever-changing stream of mental and physical events associated with A and B, how are we to establish anything about these posited selves? As it stands, the empirical evidence—for example, distinct bodies, various uses of names and 'I'—is consistent with both the presence and the absence of the posited self, as well as a single shared self or a new substantial self each moment. Hence, the inference to the existence of the *ātman* looks weak. Vasubandhu's assertion here is not decisive, but the underlying argumentative strategy is to shift the burden of proof onto the proponent of the substantial self. Is there inferential warrant for positing an enduring substantial self or can the phenomena (for example, memory) be accounted for in terms of the systematic relations between various mental and physical events and processes? The Buddhists, of course, opt for the latter approach on grounds of epistemic and ontological parsimony. We are, they argue, *selfless persons* (*pudgalanairātmyā*).

There is broad agreement among different Buddhist schools on this basic account of persons as impermanent and selfless. However, the Abhidharma schools such as Sarvāstivāda and Sautrāntika develop and defend these Buddhist views in a more philosophically rigorous and radical form. There are three important Abhidharma innovations that I will take up in the remainder of this section: momentariness, part-whole reductionism, and the theory of two truths.

First, as discussed in the previous section, Abhidharma thinkers such as Vasubandhu argue that conditioned phenomena are not just impermanent, but momentary. On this view, the basic phenomena are *dharmas*, understood as simple events. They arise causally from prior events, but as basic, their place in the causal flow cannot be analyzed in terms of simpler events. Now, given that all conditioned *dharmas* are impermanent, we can ask whether their inevitable cessation is caused by something else or is intrinsic. Is it the nature of *dharmas* to cease, or is it just that they are (always) caused to cease? Vasubandhu argues that it is the very nature of *dharmas* to cease. On his Sautrāntika view, causation occurs between real and distinct *dharmas*. However, in the case of causing cessation, the effect would be non-existence or an absence. But an absence is not a real and distinct *dharma*, it is nothing.[7] Vasubandhu therefore concludes that cessation must be intrinsic. It is the nature of *dharmas* to self-destruct. Further, since dharmas are simple events, their nature must be occurrent whenever they exist. Unlike a substance, a *dharma* can't have latent properties that become manifest over time. So, the intrinsic impermanence of a *dharma* must be manifest at the time of its existence. And this leads to the surprising conclusion that a *dharma* must cease as soon as it occurs. In other words, it is momentary.

The second important philosophical innovation is strong part-whole reductionism. On this Abhidharma view, what appear to us as really existing wholes made up of parts are in fact mere aggregates of their simple parts. As Vasubandhu writes in the *Abhidharmakośa*, "An entity, the cognition of which does not arise when it is broken and, mentally divided, is conventionally existent like a pot. Ultimate existence is otherwise" (AK 6.4). Everyday entities such as pots and people are not ontologically basic (*dravyasat*), but rather are reducible to aggregations of basic entities. On this view, the seemingly objective, mind-independent unity of everyday composite objects is illusory—these entities have only a secondary, conceptual existence (*prajñaptisat*).

This view constitutes a type of anti-realism about everyday composite entities, including persons. Such entities may be pragmatically or conventionally real (*saṃvṛtisat*), but they are not ultimately real (*paramārthasat*). The being of these entities is fully accounted for in terms of more basic entities; they are fully analytically and ontologically decomposable. Thus, they have a merely derived nature (*parabhāva*), rather than their own irreducible intrinsic nature (*svabhāva*). Further, conventionally real entities must be epiphenomenal because if they were to have their own causal powers, they would not be completely reducible. Hence, according to the Abhidharmas, all causation is microcausation—that is, real causation occurs only between simple, momentary *dharmas*. Further, the genuine causal powers of these entities are determined by their intrinsic natures. Notice, then, that this two-tiered ontology rests on a radical dichotomy between the entities with a purely extrinsic nature (*parabhāva*) and those with a purely intrinsic nature (*svabhāva*).

The third philosophical innovation complements the ontological distinction between ultimate and conventional reality. On the Abhidharma view, conventional truths (*saṃvṛtisatya*) are those truths that quantify over reducible or conventionally real (*saṃvṛtisat*) entities, whereas ultimate truths (*paramārthasatya*) only quantify over irreducible or ultimately real (*paramārthasat*) entities. When using conventional discourse, one is not ontologically committed to anything but the entities mentioned in the ultimate discourse, even if conventional discourse is not analytically reducible to ultimate discourse. Further, the discourse of ultimate truth is the Abhidharma's "philosophically favored discourse"—that is, the discourse in terms of which all other discourses are ultimately to be explained.

With these three innovations in place, we can now get a better sense of the Ābhidharmika's reductionist alternative to belief in an enduring self. As Mark Siderits aptly summarizes the reductionist view:

> The continued existence of a person must then be said to consist in a causal series of sets of suitably arranged psychophysical elements: these body parts only exist for a while but cause similar successor parts to arise; this feeling only exists for a while but causes a successor desire, and so

> on. Buddhist Reductionists hold, then, that the existence of a person just consists in the occurrence of a causal series of psychophysical elements.
>
> (Siderits 2016, 265)

The continued existence of a person is not due to the continued existence of a self. Rather it is due to the causal connections between momentary mental and physical *dharmas*. There is no unified thing at the center of the person and no persisting thing to ground their identity over time. Furthermore, the Ābhidharmikas are in the end anti-realists about the person as a whole and the continued existence of the person. It is conventionally appropriate to talk about persons, actions, and so on, but ultimately there are no complex or enduring entities. Conventionally, we are selfless persons, but ultimately there is only a causal flux of *dharmas*.

Now, as mentioned in section 3.1, Buddhaghosa's strictly phenomenological approach to the Theravāda Abhidhamma differs from the ontological approach just discussed. According to Heim (2018) and Ram-Prasad (2022), Buddhaghosa develops a type of contemplative phenomenology that deploys Abhidhamma categories as aids to reflective attention and discernment. Here the goal is not to come to the correct metaphysical picture, but to undo the tendency to 'resort to views' that distort experience and to develop the capacity for clear or purified seeing, or "eyes to see." As Buddhaghosa quotes the Buddha: "And how, monks, do those with eyes see? Here, monks, a monk sees what has become as become. Having seen what has become as become, he reaches disenchantment, dispassion, and cessation for what has become. In this way, monks, those with eyes see" (Vism XVIII.30).[8]

In this phenomenological method, the practitioner reflectively attends to and explores the various and deeply interconnected mental (*nāma*) and bodily (*rūpa*) phenomena (*dhamma*). And for Buddhaghosa the distinction between *nāma* and *rūpa*, like the joint category *nāmarūpa*, is analytical not ontological. They point to two broad types of phenomena—those with and without form—that are factors in two dimensions of experience. For instance, Buddhaghosa identifies the various elemental forms (earth, water, and so forth.) as follows:

> Having adverted to the four elements in this way, the characteristic, etc. should be attended to thus: "What are the characteristic, function, manifestation of the earth elemental?" The earth elemental has the characteristic of hardness. Its function is to act as a foundation. It is manifested as receptivity. The water elemental has the characteristic of flowing. Its function is to spread. It is manifested as accumulating.
>
> (Vism XI.93)

Here even those *rūpa dhammas* that in other contexts we may understand as basic material building blocks are treated by Buddhaghosa in terms of their function and manifestation in experience. Other *rūpa dhammas* such as the senses (touch, smell, sight, and so forth), the sensory phenomena (odor, color, and so on), and various aspects of the living body are primarily understood in terms of sensitivity (*pasāda*) or "the receptivity of bodily awareness" (Heim and Ram-Prasad 2018).

Buddhagosa treats the phenomena in the *nāma* category in similarly experiential and functional terms. For instance, regarding the phenomena of cognition (*viññāṇa*) he states:

> The mind component has the characteristic of taking cognizance of the visible, etc. [the data of the sense organs], immediately after visual cognition, etc., itself. The component of mental cognition, with the operation of investigation, has the characteristic of taking cognizance of the six [types of] objects (i.e., including the mental).
>
> (Vism XIV.97)

Here he distinguishes two functions of cognition. The first is *manas* or the "mind component" which has as its basic function cognitive receptivity or uptake of sensory phenomena, such as visible form. The second is *manoviññāṇa* or "mental cognition" which has as its basic function investigation of the cognitive objects of outer and inner sense.

There is much more that could be said about Buddhaghosa's approach to Abhidhamma. For my purpose in this section, the key point is that Budhaghosa arrives at an account of selflessness through fine-grained phenomenological analysis, rather than through reductive ontological analysis as we find in an Abhidharma thinker like Vasubandhu. He writes:

> Thus, one should define, in a double way, name and form in all phenomena of the three realms, the eight components, the twelve actualities, the five aggregates, as if one were splitting the top of the double palmyra fan or slicing open a box with a knife. One concludes that there is only name and form and nothing beyond them such as a being, person, deity, or Brahmā.
>
> (Vism XVIII.24)

For Buddhaghosa, rigorous attention to and contemplation of the phenomena of experience reveals the unified subject to be unnecessary. There is only the selfless dynamics of *nāma* and *rūpa*.

3.5 Comparative Connections

Abhidharma thought offers a rigorous and radical challenge to our common ways of thinking about mind, self, and reality. Not surprisingly, there is an extensive literature in comparative philosophy engaging with Buddhist thought, including Abhidharma. In this section I will discuss three comparative connections that are particularly relevant for the philosophy of consciousness.

The first connection concerns the (apparent) continuity of consciousness. As Abhidharma philosophers will admit, it certainly *seems* to us that our consciousness is continuous over time. In normal waking experience, it seems that I am conscious continuously for many hours, even as my attention may jump from one thing to another much more frequently. Contrast this with the experience of losing consciousness (say, from falling asleep or being knocked out) and regaining consciousness later. Here we have a gap in the continuity of consciousness and an awareness of the gap afterwards. Yet, if the Abhidharma reductionist view of consciousness as momentary is right, the apparent continuity of consciousness may be *merely* apparent. Just as we don't notice certain rapid changes in our perceptual environment, so we don't normally notice the rapid change in our stream of consciousness. Indeed, what we take to be a continuous stream is in fact a series of discrete moments.

Of course, defenders of the self in India and the West would respond to this issue by pointing out the need to posit a persisting self or subject to account for our experience of continuous consciousness. However, like their Western cousins the empiricists, Abhidharma thinkers resist the move to posit enduring substances or entities behind or beneath the flow of experience. In this respect, they continue a broadly empiricist sensibility going back to the early Buddhist discourses:

> "Monks, I will teach you the All. Listen & pay close attention. I will speak."
>
> "As you say, lord," the monks responded.
>
> The Blessed One said, "What is the All? Simply the eye & forms, ear & sounds, nose & aromas, tongue & flavors, body & tactile sensations, intellect & ideas. This, monks, is called the All. Anyone who would say, 'Repudiating this All, I will describe another,' if questioned on what exactly might be the grounds for his statement, would be unable to explain, and furthermore, would be put to grief. Why? Because it lies beyond range."

(SN 35.23)

Comparative philosophers have long pointed out the important similarities between Abhidharma and Western empiricism. For instance, David Hume (1739) famously states:

> For my part, when I enter most intimately into what I call myself, I always stumble on some particular perception or other, of heat or cold, light or shade, love or hatred, pain or pleasure. I never can catch myself at any time without a perception, and never can observe anything but the perception … I may venture to affirm … that [persons] are nothing but a bundle or collection of different perceptions, which succeed each other with an inconceivable rapidity, and are in perpetual flux and movement.
>
> (T 1.4.6.3)

Again, the seemingly smooth or continuous flow of conscious experience is really a misapprehension. The reality of our basic experience here is rapid succession and flux, but our higher-order expectations and beliefs about, coupled with the difficulty of close attention to, the flow of experience creates the false idea of the continuous experience of a persisting self.

More recently contemporary philosopher of mind, Galen Strawson, has also challenged our sense of the continuity of consciousness. On Strawson's view, our experience is "a gappy series of eruptions of consciousness out of non-consciousness" (Strawson 2017, 73). However, Strawson's account differs from Abhidharma reductionism in two important ways. First, while experience is gappy rather than continuous, Strawson does not take the "eruptions of consciousness" to be strictly momentary. Rather, he argues that we do have (usually short-lived) temporal stretches of experience followed by (usually unnoticed) lapses into unconsciousness. Second, Strawson argues that experience entails a subject. But this subject is not separable from experience and exists only as long as the stretch of experience it unifies. He writes:

> The total experiential field involves many things—rich interoceptive (somatosensory) and exteroceptive sensation, mood-and-affect-tone, deep conceptual animation, and so on. It has, standardly, a particular focus, and more or less dim peripheral areas, and is, overall, extraordinarily complex in content. But it is for all that a unity… simply in being, indeed, a total experiential field; or equivalently, simply in being the content of the experience of a single subject at that moment. The unity or singleness of the (thin) subject of the total experiential field in the living moment of experience and the unity or singleness of the total experiential field are aspects of the same thing.
>
> (Strawson 2017, 179)

For Strawson, the 'pulses' or 'eruptions' of consciousness from unconsciousness are unified as thin subjects or a unified field of experience. As we've seen, Abhidharma philosophers would take issue with the commitment to any notion of a unified subject of experience. But, interestingly, Theravāda Abhidhamma thinkers such as Buddhaghosa would also take issue with Strawson's "gappy" view of consciousness.

Theravāda Abhidhamma posits a type of consciousness called *bhavaṅga citta* or "life-continuum consciousness." As Sean Smith has recently argued, *bhavaṅga citta* is a "primal sentient consciousness, a passive form of basal awareness that individuates sentient beings as the type of being that they are" (Smith 2020, 458). It is "a subliminal mental event that functions to sustain the causal continuity of the stream of consciousness when more ordinary sensory-cognitive events become dormant." On this view, below the level of our normal waking episodes of perception, feeling, thought, and the like, there are moments of primal sentience (*bhavaṅga citta*) that fill the gap between these episodes. Moreover, in deep sleep for example, these moments of *bhavaṅga* form an uninterrupted continuum of subliminal sentience. So, despite their commitment to the momentariness of mental events, the flow of consciousness may not be as gappy as Strawson believes.

Returning to the issue of the self, a central controversy throughout Indian philosophy is whether mental life or experience is grounded in or organized around an enduring locus of consciousness, cognition, or agency. For all their many and important differences, the *ātmavādins* answer in the affirmative. To make sense of mental life, the coherence of experience, agency, and cognitive access to the world, one must affirm a unified self at the center of our being. In sharp contrast, Buddhist thinkers decisively reject this core commitment. They therefore must develop and defend accounts of mental life in terms of multiplicity and flux, in terms of the causal connections between distinct, momentary particulars rather than the unity of the self.

Abhidharma thinkers developed a distinctive set of tools for defending this selfless account of experience and mental life. In place of a unified subject, they argue for tight causal and functional connections between discrete, momentary events. In addition, Abhidharma reductionists such as Vasubandhu argue for eliminativism about selves and a novel form of reductionism about persons. In contemporary philosophical discussions of personal identity, skepticism about an enduring substantial self is common. Yet even philosophers who reject the existence of the self may vigorously defend the reality of persons. For example, the most well-known proponent of reductionism about persons, Derek Parfit, argues, "on the Reductionist View, each person's existence just involves the existence of a brain and body, the doing of certain deeds, the thinking of certain thoughts, the occurrence of certain experiences, and so on" (1987, 211). And facts about persons and their existence at a time and over time are nothing over and above certain more particular (and impersonal) mental and physical facts. Yet, he insists: "On this Reductionist View, persons do exist. But they exist only in the way nations exist. Persons, are not, as we mistakenly believe, fundamental. This view is in this sense more impersonal" (1987, 445).

More specifically, Parfit calls his own view "constitutive reductionism" in contrast to what he calls "hyper-reductionist" views. He holds: "A person's existence just consists in the existence of a body, and the occurrence of a series of thoughts, experiences, and other mental and physical events." But also: "A person is an entity that has a body, and has thoughts and other experiences. On this view, though a person is distinct from that person's body, and from any series of thoughts and experiences, the person's existence just *consists* in them" (1987, 471). And this entails: "Though persons are distinct from their bodies, and from any series of mental events, they are not independent or separately existing entities" (Ibid.).

Persons exist, but only in the way nations do, not fundamentally. How are we to understand this position? The Ābhidharmika account of two truths gives us a way to make sense of reductionism. In the Abhidharma reductionist framework, a whole made up of parts, such as a table or a person, is conventionally real (*saṃvṛtti sat*), but not ultimately real (*paramārtha sat*). 'Person' is a useful conceptual designation that we apply to certain aggregates of mental and physical events that have the right sorts of causal and functional connections. This conceptual designation has its use within certain modes of conceptualizing, in the context of certain practices, and relative to certain human interests. And within the context of that conceptual scheme, persons are *not* identical to a particular momentary collection of mental and physical events. Rather, the person is the one who has thoughts or performs actions. These are conventional truths. Yet, persons are not ultimately real. Only the momentary *dharmas* that ground the conventional reality of persons are ultimately real.

So, from an Abhidharma perspective, there are two mistakes to avoid when it comes to understanding persons. The first mistake is to assume that if the existence of the person is distinct from the body and series of experiences, then it is a separately existing entity such as the *ātman* or the Cartesian ego. On the Abhidharma view, there is no such independent entity. The second mistake is to assume that if the existence of the person just consists in the existence of a body and a series of mental states, then we must do away with the concept 'person' as such. On the Abhidharma view, persons are conventionally real (as are, for example, nations and the US dollar) and there are (conventional) truths and falsehoods about them.

At this point, though, a difficult question arises. Are conventionally real things real (do they exist) in the same sense as ultimately real things? Here one might adopt a pluralist stance and say that there are different ways of being real or modes of existing. On this view, *dharmas* are real, but so are persons, rainforests, nations, and novels. *Dharmas* are ultimately real because they are fundamental and exist independently of our concepts, interests, and practices. Novels don't exist that way, but they exist, nonetheless. On the other hand, one might adopt a monist stance and say that genuine existence—being *really* real—is ultimate existence. On this view, we can give a philosophically anti-realist account of our conventional talk about persons, nations, and novels. The idea here is to explain the coherence and utility of talk about conventional entities while giving up any commitment to their genuine existence. These approaches raise a host of interesting issues at the intersection of ontology, philosophy of language, and philosophy of mind. Abhidharma thinkers have much to contribute to the on-going investigation of these issues.

3.6 Questions

1. What is the Abhidharma doctrine of momentariness and how is it related to the doctrine of no-self?
2. How do Abhidharma thinkers understand consciousness (*citta*) and its relation to the mental factors (*caitta*)?
3. What are the two views of perception developed by Abhidharma thinkers? Which is more plausible?
4. How do Abhidharma thinkers differ from Nyāya thinkers on the issue of the self? Which view do you find more convincing and why?

Notes

1 Unless otherwise noted, in what follows I will just use "*dharmas*" rather than "conditioned *dharmas*."
2 This account just scratches the surface of a Buddhaghosa rich account of the processes of perception but see (Ganeri 2017) especially Chapters 7–10 for a fuller treatment.
3 On this aspect of Sarvāstivāda see, for example, (Bastow 1995) and (Maas 2020).

4 Thus, for instance, a moment of visual consciousness (*vijñāna*) may be conditioned by latent dispositions (*saṃskāras*) and in turn condition a moment of pleasant feeling (*vedanā*).
5 The next few paragraphs draw from (MacKenzie 2022).
6 The classic version of the criterial argument occurs in *Saṃyutta Nikāya* 3.66–68.
7 The ontological status of absences, negations, and so forth. is contested in Indian philosophy. For instance, the Vaiśeṣika school included absence or non-existence (*abhāva*) as one of its basic ontological categories (*padārtha*).
8 The translations from Vism in this section are from Heim and Ram-Prasad (2018).

Further Reading

Buddhaghosa. 1991. *The Path of Purification: Visuddhimagga*. Buddhist Publications Society.

Chadha, Monima. 2023. *Selfless Minds: A Contemporary Perspective on Vasubandhu's Metaphysics*. Oxford University Press.

Ganeri, Jonardon. 2017. *Attention, Not Self*. Oxford University Press.

Goodman, Charles. 2009. "Vasubandhu's Abhidharmakósa: The Critique of the Soul." In *Buddhist Philosophy: Essential Readings*, edited by William Edelglass and Jay L. Garfield. Oxford University Press.

La Vallee Poussin, Louis de. 2014. *Abhidharmakośabhāṣyam of Vasubandhu*. Translated by Leo M. Pruden. Jain Pub Co.

4

Yoga

4.1 The Yoga School

The word 'yoga' (from the Sanskrit root *yuj*, 'to join') had a variety of meanings in the ancient Indian tradition. It may mean simply 'conjoin' or 'yoke' as with a chariot. However, by the time of the Upaniṣads, the term had a more specific spiritual and philosophical meaning. In that context 'yoga' referred to contemplative and ascetic techniques or practices. Specifically, 'yoga' was the spiritual discipline leading to knowledge of the true nature of the self (*ātmatattva*) and thereby spiritual freedom (*mokṣa*). This notion of yoga is also found throughout the epics, principally the *Mahābhārata* and *Rāmāyaṇa*. For instance, in the *Bhagavad Gītā*, a sub-section of the *Mahābhārata*, yoga refers to several distinct paths to spiritual liberation, such as *karma-yoga* (the path of action) (BG 2.47) or *bhakti-yoga* (the path of devotion) (BG 12.2). Of course, in the contemporary world, 'yoga' most often refers to the various postural techniques related to the tradition of *haṭha* yoga. These systems developed later and their relationship to earlier forms of yoga is a complex matter (Singleton 2010).

In addition to these meanings, Yoga (capitalized in English) is one the six orthodox (*astika*) Hindu schools of philosophy. Its primary text is Patañjali's *Yoga Sūtras* (c. 200 CE), which consists of 196 aphorisms (*sūtras*) on the view and path of Yoga. This text is not the origin of the Yoga school, but rather draws on earlier traditions and sources. The tradition takes the text as an authoritative presentation of the Yoga philosophy. The primary concern of the Yoga school of philosophy is yoga as contemplative meditative techniques deployed in service of attaining a soteriological goal, such as liberation or union with divinity. Indeed, Patañjali famously defines yoga as the "stilling of the modifications of mind" (*citta vṛtti nirodha*), a state which is a precondition of spiritual liberation (*kaivalya*). Thus Yoga, like Buddhism, is not just a systematic philosophical view, it is also a soteriological philosophy and practice.

Drawing on the metaphysics of the older Sāṅkhya school,[1] Yoga philosophy is based on the fundamental ontological distinction between *prakṛti* and *puruṣa*. *Prakṛti* here refers to material or natural reality in all its variegated forms. *Puruṣa* here refers to the most essential conscious, spiritual self—what most other Hindu schools refer to as *ātman*. On this view, there is only one dynamic material reality, while there are many individual selves. *Puruṣa* and *prakṛti* are equally real, mutually distinct, and irreducible. They are, therefore, the two ultimate principles of the metaphysically dualistic systems of Sāṅkhya and Yoga. It is important to note, however, that the dualism of the Sāṅkhya and Yoga schools is in certain respects quite different from forms of mind-matter dualism in the West. In the most familiar Western forms of dualism the ontological dualism is between body and matter, on one hand, and the mind, on the other. In this type of dualism, the mind is identified with the self or soul, and it is an immaterial substance metaphysically distinct from the body as a material substance. In contrast, according to the Sāṅkhya and Yoga view, mind (*citta*) is a subtle form of *prakṛti* and therefore material. What we call the mind is constituted by the integrated functioning of intelligence (*buddhi*), ego (*ahaṅkāra*), and other forms of mentation (*manas*). These are capacities and functions of a living sentient being, conceived as a complex material system. Thus, perhaps surprisingly, Yoga has a non-reductive physicalist theory of mind. *Puruṣa*, as pure awareness,[2] is ontologically independent from *prakṛti*, including the mind. Hence, the fundamental dualism here is between mind and body, on one hand, and pure consciousness, on the other.

The soteriological goal of Yoga is the liberatory recognition of *puruṣa* in its pristine and eternal independence (*kaivalya*) from *prakṛti*. The bound individual is embroiled in the world and falsely identifies with the body-mind as her true nature. The practice of yoga, then, involves techniques allowing for direct recognition of one's true nature as *puruṣa* and subsequent liberation from bondage to the world. Liberation in Yoga necessarily involves a transcendence of the ego or false sense of self and a recognition of one's true nature or self as pure awareness.

The path to this soteriological goal consists of the eight limbs (*aṣṭāṅga*) of yoga. The eight limbs are: moral restraint (*yama*), moral observance (*niyama*), posture (*āsana*), breath control (*prāṇāyāma*), sensory withdrawal (*pratyāhāra*), concentration (*dhāraṇā*), meditation (*dhyāna*), and contemplative absorption (*samādhi*). There is no need to go into great detail here concerning each limb. However, two points are worth noting. First, yoga is an explicitly holistic and integrated path of development or self-cultivation (Phillips 2009). Careful attention to the body, breath, senses, and mind are required to achieve liberation from spiritual bondage. In this way, rigorous cultivation of body and mind can serve as the vehicle for the recognition of oneself as pure consciousness. Second, moral restraint (*yama*) and moral observance (*niyama*)—that is ethical self-cultivation—is at the foundation of the path.[3] Thus, the cultivation of virtue is a necessary condition of self-realization.

4.2 Stilling the Modifications

As Patañjali puts it in the first chapter of the *Yoga Sūtras*:

I.2 Yoga is the stilling of the modifications of mind.
I.3 When that is accomplished, the seer abides in its own nature.
I.4 Otherwise, there is identification with the modifications [of mind].[4]

Here we see yoga defined as *citta vṛtti nirodha*: as the stilling (*nirodha*) of the modifications (*vṛtti*) of the mind (*citta*). The conscious mind (*citta*) is normally active and agitated, manifesting a wide variety of mental states or mental modifications (*vṛttis*) from one moment to the next. These can include intentional or object-directed states like perception or thought, but also various sensory or affective states. A central goal of the various meditative techniques described in the text is to achieve a state of mental stillness in which these *vṛttis* have subsided.

Since our conscious lives are characterized by the continual dynamic arising of these mental states, what could it mean to achieve a state of mental stillness (*nirodha*)? If the various mental modifications are all there is to the conscious mind, then *nirodha* might be a state of blank unconsciousness like deep, dreamless sleep. A state of stillness would be 'lights out'. However, on the Yoga view, there is more to the conscious mind than its various modifications. The state of mental stillness, then, is not a blank unconscious state. Rather it is a form of calm, lucid awareness. Here we might posit two distinct dimensions of the mind. The first is the calmness-agitation dimension, involving the variety, dynamism, or intensity of mental modifications. The second is the lucidity-dullness dimension, involving the qualities of attention and awareness.[5] So, one might experience a variety of intense mental states while being highly alert and aware. Or one might experience a calmer state while being less alert or aware, as when one is drifting off to sleep. In contrast to these, the practice of yoga here aims at a state of low agitation and high awareness.

Patañjali next tells us: "When that is accomplished, the seer abides in its own nature. Otherwise, there is identification with the modifications" (I.3–4). The idea here is that the mind naturally or habitually identifies with the various mental states and contents. For example, one experiences one's thoughts or feelings as one's own, as reflecting one's identity or nature. However, when these mental fluctuations have subsided and one has maintained a lucid awareness, then the true nature of the seer (*draṣṭṛ*) is revealed. That is, the practitioner recognizes her true nature as the seer, which is *puruṣa* or pure consciousness. In the commentary on the main text, we see "[when] the mind that has arrived at 'I am' manifests only 'I am' that is eternally peaceful, like a motionless great ocean" (I.36). Furthermore, Patañjali tells us (I.16) that the highest form of non-attachment occurs when pure consciousness clearly sees itself as distinct from the various qualities of nature (*guṇas*). As in several other Indian schools, this recognition of the true nature of the self is key to spiritual liberation.

In short, Yoga aims at the recognition that the self as pure consciousness is distinct from all the varied mental states and objects of awareness with which we habitually identify. Further, drawing from the ontology of Sāṅkhya, the Yoga school posits a hierarchical tripartite structure of the human person consisting of the body, mind, and conscious self. The body (*rūpa*) comprises the whole complex human organism, including the brain, nervous system, biological functions, and so on. Importantly, the body includes ten faculties or instruments (*indriyās*), divided into two sub-categories. The *jñānendriyās* or sensory-cognitive faculties are the five senses: seeing, tasting, touching, hearing, and smelling. These function to contact and gather information about the world. They are characterized in terms of *input* or movement from the world to the body. The *karmendriyās* or active faculties are speaking, moving, grasping, procreating, and excretion. They are characterized in terms of *output* or movement from the body to the world. The *indriyās* cover both the particular bodily organ or part and its characteristic function, for example, the mouth and its function in tasting and speaking.

The mind (*antaḥkaraṇa*, 'internal organ') is divided into hierarchically ordered functions. The first is *manas*, which functions as a "central processor that continually attends to, filters, analyzes, and assimilates the inputs received from sensory sources" (Rao 2017, 214). In contemporary terms, *manas* is a form of bottom-up processing that selectively integrates lower-level sensory and affective input from the body. Once the sensory input is selected and integrated in or by the *manas*, it is available for other cognitive, conative, and affective functions. For example, the smell of fresh-baked cookies might trigger pleasure, childhood memories, desire to eat, and movement toward the kitchen.

The second basic mental function is *ahaṃkāra*, literally the "I-maker." This is "the ego function that appropriates the processed inputs and engenders the sense of "me" and self-consciousness" (Rao 2017, 214). In the normal course of experience, one has an implicit sense of oneself as the subject of experience and as the owner of one's various thoughts and feelings. On this view, when viewing the sunset, the full description of the experience includes the sense that *I* am viewing the sunset. When thinking about a problem, there is a sense that these are *my* thoughts, and *I* am the thinker. The basic senses of self and mental ownership are a function of the *ahaṃkāra*. On the Yoga model of the mind, then, *manas* and *ahaṃkāra* work together to provide the basic framework of being a distinct subject confronting a world of objects: a someone 'in here' engaging a world 'out there' through cognition and action.

In addition, Patañjali links the *ahaṃkāra* the existential affliction (*kleśa*) of egoity, *asmitā*. He writes:

II.3 The afflictions [*kleśas*] are ignorance, egoity, attachment, aversion, and clinging to life.
II.4 Ignorance is the field [of the other *kleśas*] … whether they are in a dormant, weak, attenuated, or active state.
II.5 Ignorance is the notion which mistakes the eternal, pure, joyful self for the impermanent, impure, painful non-self.
II.6 Egoity (*asmitā*) is to confuse the seer and the power of seeing as one self.

Here we see that *asmitā* arises from ignorance and is an impediment to spiritual development. Ignorance (*avidyā*) is the primordial confusion that conflates self and non-self, *puruṣa* and *prakṛti*. This ignorance might take gross form in the false identification with external forms, such as one's social status, power, or bodily form. However, egoity is thought to be a much subtler form of ignorance at the very root of one's normal sense of self. Indeed, this basic egoity gives rise to the further afflictions of attachment, aversion, and clinging to life.

The third mental function is *buddhi*, intelligence or intelligent awareness. As Rao states, "In virtue of the *buddhi*, we discriminate, remember, and have unified awareness" (Rao 2017, 214). We might think of *buddhi* as the higher-order functioning of the mind. When sensations are brought together into perceptual states by the *manas*, *buddhi* allows the further integration of those perceptual states into a unified conscious experience. This unified experience is then available for top-down conscious attention, verbal report, reasoning, and more. These are functions associated with *buddhi*. Further, in conjunction with the *ahaṃkāra*, *buddhi* constitutes the first-person perspective around which our conscious lives are organized. Finally, according to Yoga, *buddhi* is the function of the mind most like or closely associated with pure consciousness itself. And as we will see below, this is the source of a deep confusion that the discipline of yoga is meant to remedy.

The fourth function is *citta*,[6] here referring to the deeper or more latent aspects of mind. These include latent aspects (*saṃskāras*) such as memories, habits, dispositions, and karmic traces. It also includes conative states such as desires or drives such as hunger. We can compare *citta* here to the contemporary notion of the preconscious or unconscious mind. However, as will be discussed below, in Sāṅkhya and Yoga, strictly speaking all four functions of the mind are unconscious or not inherently conscious.

Returning to the body, Sāṅkhya and Yoga distinguish between the gross body (*sthūlaśarīra*) and the subtle body (*liṅgaśarīra*). The gross body is the body as observable, including its material and biological properties and functions. We might think of the gross body as involving those aspects of the body (or living organism) that are available to third-person investigation, from weighing to brain scans. The subtle body is not observable from a third-person perspective, but includes, for example, the 'energetic' and felt dimensions of embodiment. Furthermore, as both Sāṅkhya and Yoga affirm the reality of rebirth, upon death the subtle body is said to continue to the next birth. Importantly, the gross and subtle bodies, and the process of rebirth are aspects of nature or *prakṛti*.

We now come to one of the most distinctive aspects of Sāṅkhya and Yoga philosophy. On their account, mind or mentality (*antaḥkaraṇa*) *is an aspect of prakṛti*. It is therefore natural and, in their distinctive sense, material. Indeed, the mind in its various functions is deeply interwoven with the subtle dimension of embodiment, which in turn depends on the gross dimension. Now, the distinctive functions of mind like perception, memory, or feeling are not reducible to the functions of the gross body such as metabolism. Rather, mentality emerges from the complex operation of the physical and biological dimensions of the body or organism. In this way, the Sāṅkhya and Yoga systems anticipate contemporary forms of non-reductive naturalism about the mind. On these types of views, mental states and processes arise from and depend on physical and biological states and processes such as those of the brain. However, mental states or processes are not reducible to "lower-level" physical states because they have distinctively *mental* features. Depending on the account, this might be a distinctively mental functional role, representational profile, felt quality, or some combination of these. For example, a particular visual state is about or represents something in the visual environment, it can guide action, it can give rise to memory or thought, and it feels like something to be in it. It depends on the brain, nervous system, and eyes, of course, but its reality as a *mental* state concerns its distinctively mental features. Nonetheless, on this view, mental states and processes are fully natural aspects of the lives and capacities of certain living organisms like us and other animals.

4.3 Self and World

As we have discussed so far, classical Yoga adopts the dualism of *puruṣa* and *prakṛti* already developed within the Sāṅkhya school. That is, the two fundamental realities are *puruṣa* (pure consciousness) and *prakṛti* (nature or material reality). In this section, we will take a closer look at these two basic ontological principles and some of the philosophical issues to which they give rise.

What is *prakṛti*? Broadly considered, *prakṛti* is the whole domain of objective material phenomena, roughly corresponding to what we would now call the natural cosmos. It is the domain of space, time, causality, and the various phenomena that arise within that spatiotemporal and causal framework. Cosmologically, *prakṛti* is beginningless and eternal, though various worlds (*loka-s*) that arise within it go through cycles of creation and destruction. Further, *prakṛti* can be understood in terms of two distinct levels or aspects. The first is *mūlaprakṛti*, which is the root or base (*mūla*) level of materiality. This level of *prakṛti* is described as primordial (*pradhāna*), unmanifest (*avyukta*), and without mark or observable properties (*aliṅga*) (O'Brien-Kop 2023). *Mūlaprakṛti*, then, is the ontological ground and metaphysical substrate of all material phenomena. And as the source of material phenomena, *mūlaprakṛti* is creative (indeed, *prakṛti* is cognate with 'procreate'), giving birth to the causal tapestry of the observable world (Ashton 2020).

The second level or aspect is simply called '*prakṛti*'. It is manifest (*vyukta*) and with marks or observable properties (*liṅga*). Again, following Sāṅkhya, classical Yoga affirms a theory of causation called *satkāryavāda*. This is the view (*vāda*) that the effect (*karya*) in some way pre-exists (*sat*) in the cause. Thus, the primary form of causality is the transformation (*pariṇāma*) or manifestation of *mūlaprakṛti* as *prakṛti*. Root materiality manifests as observable material phenomena and their various connections and transformations. This is possible because of the three fundamental qualities (*guṇas*) of materiality: *sattva*, *rajas*, and *tamas*. As we see in the *Yogasūtra*, (2.17) "*Sattva* has the character of light. *Rajas* has the character of action. *Tamas* has the character of fixity" (O'Brien-Kop 2023, 23). The *guṇas* are not separate substances or individuals, but rather the primordial features or "strands" (another meaning of *guṇa*) of materiality. Karen O'Brien-Kop glosses them as "dynamism (*rajas*), inertia (*tamas*), and balance (*sattva* – a word also used to express the notions of 'truth' and 'purity')" (O'Brien-Kop 2023, 22–23). The differentiated, observable phenomena of the world are combinations of these three strands in different proportions. And these same *guṇas* are present in primordial materiality, in a latent form or static equilibrium. Manifest materiality, then, is seen as a real transformation of primordial materiality, sharing its nature as a mix of these three gunas.

Now, as discussed in the previous section, *prakṛti* is not limited to material phenomena such as stones or storms. Such phenomena are categorized as gross material (*sthūla*) phenomena and the Sāṅkhya and Yoga schools understood them in terms of the basic elements of earth, fire, water, air, and space. Yet, beyond gross material phenomena, biological and psychological phenomena are also forms of *prakṛti* or materiality. The difference between these types of phenomena consists, in part, of different configurations of the three gunas. For example, a living organism, as dynamic and active, is more *rajasic* than a stone, which is more inert or *tamasic.* A human being, as sentient and cognitive, is more *sattvic* than either a simple organism or a stone. Despite these important differences, though, a human being's body and mind are manifestation of *prakṛti*, just like any organism or other material system.

There is, therefore, a sharp metaphysical distinction between the human person as a body-mind complex, and the true self which is pure consciousness. So, what am I? It certainly seems as if I am my body and my mind. I can raise my arm at will (and feel it from the inside when I do), and when I think or perceive I have a deep sense that these states are *mine.* Indeed, it seems that I don't just possess them like I possess a pair of shoes. My thoughts and perceptions seem like states *of me*, no more separable from me than a kick is separable from the kicker. Yet, while this view might be fine for practical purposes, the Yoga school firmly rejects it as a true description of the nature of the self. The mistake arises from a deeply rooted but erroneous perception of "self in non-self – through external instruments, be they animate or inanimate, or in the body, which is the basis of enjoyment, or in the mind, which is an object for consciousness (*puruṣa*) – these are all perception of self in non-self" (YS 2.5). The human mind is subject to a systematic illusion, the illusion that the body and mind are aspects of the self. Further, this illusion gives rise to a false sense of self (*asmitā*) wherein the sense of ownership is attached to mental and bodily phenomena, rather than the pure light of consciousness itself. This false sense of self is the root of the existential bondage of samsara, and the goal of yoga is overcome this illusion.

Is such a systematic illusion possible? Classical Yoga does not offer a formal proof or psychological etiology of the illusion. However, it is worth pointing out that our usual sense of self and ownership is more variable that we might initially expect. Regarding the sense of bodily ownership, disorders such as somatoparaphrenia show that a person can lose the sense that a limb belongs to them (Feinberg and Venneri 2014). For a person with this condition, their right arm, for example, might not feel like their arm. Indeed, it may feel like another person's arm, rudely invading their space. On the other hand, phenomena like the rubber hand illusion show that one's felt sense of bodily ownership can be extended to inanimate objects (Rohde et al. 2011). Regarding the mind, we also find several disorders of typical mental ownership. For example, in the phenomenon of thought insertion, an individual may experience thoughts, perceptions, or other mental contents as alien intruders in his mind. In other cases, a patient may experience certain sensory modalities as unowned. Finally, in some cases of Cotard's syndrome, a person feels that they do not exist (Grover et al. 2014). Of course, there is a rich empirical and philosophical literature on these matters that is beyond the scope of this chapter. The point here is just that our usual sense of ownership or identification regarding body and mind is more variable than one might assume.

The examples just given are instances of neuropsychological pathologies or disorders. One might also point to contemporary research on meditation (Repetti 2022) or psychedelics (Letheby 2021) for evidence of the variability of our usual senses of self or ownership. However, evidence of variability is not necessarily evidence that our usual sense of self is erroneous. Rather it shows that our usual modes of self-identification could be otherwise, and that it makes sense to ask about the philosophical justification of these usual modes. This is a question I will take up in the next section in discussing the yogic goal of *kaivalya*.

For now, I will focus on another puzzle that arises for the Sāṅkhya-Yoga for dualism. If I am not really the body or mind, but rather pure consciousness, then am I a human being? And how should we understand our normal uses of the first-person pronoun *I*? When I say, "I am six feet tall," or "I have a pain in my shoulder," or "I am thinking about classical Yoga," must these claims be *false*? If I am not the body, can *I* be six feet tall? If I am not the mind, can *I* think about Yoga (or anything else)? One approach to this puzzle is simply to bite the bullet and accept an error-theory about our usual uses of 'I'. Our systematic identification with the body-mind is mistaken—we are selves, not human beings constituted by a body-mind—so our typical uses of 'I' are just wrong. We might go along with them for practical purposes, but if the Sāṅkhya-Yoga theory of self is correct, they are still systematically erroneous.

Another approach is to accept a pluralist view of self-identification and self-reference. The idea here is that, as Galen Strawson puts it, "*I* doesn't always refer to the same thing, or kind of thing, even in the thought or speech of a single person" (Strawson 2017, 214). For instance, in many contexts, 'I' refers to the human being as a whole. In other contexts, 'I' refers strictly to the self as the subject of experience and essence of the individual. As Strawson explains:

> I'm a human being, then, and I take it that I'm also a self. I take it, in fact, that I = GS [Galen Strawson] and I = S [self]. I don't, however, think that the self that I am is the human being that I am: I deny GS = S.

How can I do this? I don't reject the logic of the identity relation. That would be silly. I reject the assumption that *I* is univocal in the thought or speech of any given individual. I've assumed that there is such a thing as the self distinct from the human being considered as a whole, and this opens the way to the possibility that the reference of *I* standardly shifts between these two different things in my thought and speech and in the thought and speech of others. Certainly *I* is sometimes used with the intention to refer to a human being considered as a whole, and sometimes with the intention to refer to a self, and these are two things which have quite different identity conditions, one being a part of the other.

(Strawson 2017, 216)

Strawson's metaphysical and phenomenological views of the self are very different from those of Sāṅkhya and Yoga. However, his suggestion that the referent of 'I' may shift depending on context may still prove helpful for proponents of the Sāṅkhya-Yoga view. In the context of everyday life, 'I' can be taken to refer to the whole person—body (*rūpa*), mind (*citta*), and spirit (*puruṣa*). In the context of deep metaphysical reflection or in mediation, 'I' can be taken to refer strictly to the self. The shifty nature of 'I' might also help account for the deep confusion Sāṅkhya-Yoga attributes to the normal person. One systematically conflates distinct contexts of self-identification, yielding the mistaken sense that one is *just* the body-mind complex. But when, through discriminating discernment (*vivekakhyāti*), one correctly identifies the 'I am' (*asmitā*) with *puruṣa*, the mind becomes "eternally peaceful, like a motionless great ocean" (PS 1.36).

Having discussed the ontological principle of *prakṛti*, let's now turn to *puruṣa*. Whereas *prakṛti* is pure materiality, serving as the basis for dynamism, causation, temporality, and evolution, *puruṣa* is pure awareness—changeless, independent, and non-active. *Puruṣa* is the constant or unchanging light of consciousness, in which light the various manifestations of *prakṛti* become phenomenally manifest. Further, *prakṛti* is ultimately *one* reality underlying its many manifestations. In contrast, there are ultimately and irreducibly *many* distinct *puruṣas* (*puruṣa-bahutva*). That is, Sāṅkhya and Yoga are monists about *prakṛti* and pluralists about *puruṣa*. We can say that, according to the Sāṅkhya-Yoga view, a *puruṣa* has the following features:

1) simplicity
2) luminosity
3) individuation
4) transcendence.

The self or *puruṣa* is simple in that it has not separable parts. Rather it is a fundamentally unitary entity. This is not to deny that the *puruṣa* has various properties or powers, but only that it isn't any kind of aggregate, system, or collection of parts. Note, then, the sharp contrast between *puruṣa* and the body and mind. The body is an incredibly complex material system that gains and loses parts over the course of a lifetime. The mind is a complex psychological system of various functions, capacities, and processes. The mind continuously changes its states and contents in causal and functional interaction with the body and the environment. The self remains the pure, changeless witness of these transformations.

The self is luminous because its very nature is conscious awareness. Here consciousness is not an intrinsic property of particular mental states or acts. When a person consciously perceives or thinks, this is a function of inherently unconscious mental states being illuminated by the inherently conscious self. Here consciousness is like the constant light of the sun shining on the ever-changing surface of water.

The self is individuated in that it is a basic metaphysical fact that each *puruṣa* is distinct from every other *puruṣa*, and from *prakṛti*. All *puruṣas* have the same nature as pure consciousness, but they are not the same entity. This is in important contrast to ultimately non-dual views like Advaita Vedānta. On the Advaita view, the nature of the self is pure consciousness, but there is ultimately only *one* consciousness, namely *brahman*. The individuation of selves is therefore merely apparent. However, in Sāṅkhya it is argued that there must be really distinct selves because, otherwise, all changes in the manifest world would affect the self all at once. What we find instead are distinct conscious perspectives within which distinct sets of phenomena come into view. So, the argument goes, these distinct perspectives must be grounded in distinct subjects. Note also that this line of argument does not depend on the distinctness of bodies and minds, but rather the irreducible phenomenological distinctness of the first-person perspective.

Finally, the self or *puruṣa* is transcendent in that it is both phenomenologically and metaphysically distinct from the empirical world, the world of changing phenomena. The self, on this account, is not identical to any of its varied contents. Every object of conscious appears only in the light of consciousness and when it no longer appears, consciousness remains. Consciousness itself is always subject and never an object. Moreover, as metaphysically distinct from *prakṛti*, the self transcends space, time, causality, and change. Of course, this raises the significant problem of how (or whether) the radically distinct principles of *prakṛti* and *puruṣa* could be connected. On the one hand, the answer cannot be in terms of either efficient or material causality, because these are exclusive features of *prakṛti*. On the other hand, the answer cannot be that they are completely separate, because that would fail to explain our experience of a reality in which consciousness illuminates variegated empirical phenomena. As Rao puts it:

> Let us recall, the *puruṣa* is consciousness-as-such or pure consciousness. *Prakṛti* is the materiality-as-such or the principle or substratum of all objects of experience. *Puruṣa* is that which makes awareness possible. *Prakṛti* is what the awareness is about. In their transcendental abstraction, they are pure, independent and self-subsisting principles of reality. But in the existential human context, there is an entanglement of the two in the form of an interface between them. When and how this interface takes place is unknown for the reason that we are cognitively closed to it as we are a product of that interface. For this reason, it may be considered to be without a beginning.
>
> (Rao 2017, 102)

I will take up the possibility of cognitive closure in section 4.5, when we consider the "hard problem of consciousness." It is worth noting here that, in the *Yogasūtra* Patañjali asserts that (manifest) *prakṛti* exists *for the sake of puruṣa*. As a basic ontological principle, *mūlaprakṛti* is not dependent on *puruṣa*. However, at least some of its manifestations (*prakṛti*) depend on *puruṣa*. So, while *mūlaprakṛti* is the efficient and material cause of manifest *prakṛti*, perhaps *puruṣas* are *final* causes of prakṛti. Hence the interface between these ontological principles might be *teleological*.

4.4 *Luminosity*

As discussed throughout this chapter, in classical Yoga, the very nature of the self is luminous consciousness. The self as witness or seer (*draṣṭā*) lights up the world of objects. And one way to understand this illumination of objects is as a form of intentionality. That is, the metaphor of 'lighting up an object' can be explained philosophically as consciousness being *of* or *about* its object. So, when I consciously see an elephant, my seeing is a conscious act or state that is *of* the elephant. 'Luminosity' (*prakāśatā*) is just a way of talking about this basic form of conscious directedness to an object and therefore is closely related to the notion of cognition (*jñāna*). Indeed, as we saw in Chapter 2, this is how the Nyāya proponents of other-luminosity might characterize the matter.

The Sāṅkhya-Yoga tradition sees matters differently. As Patañjali writes in a section of the *Yogasūtra* summarizing the Sāṅkhya system:

The seer is merely the power of seeing; [however] although pure he witnesses the images of the mind.

The essential nature of that which is seen is exclusively for the sake of the seer.

Although the seen ceases to exist for one whose purpose is accomplished [the liberated puruṣa], it has not ceased to exist altogether, since it is common to other [not-liberated] puruṣas.

(II:20-22)[7]

On the Sāṅkhya-Yoga view, pure consciousness is not itself intentional, its luminosity is not understood in terms of a discrete state or act directed at an object. Intentionality as cognitive directedness is in fact a function of the mind (*citta*) and therefore *prakṛti*. When I see the elephant, this perceptual state is the result of a complex set of causal, sensory, and cognitive processes leading to a state of mind that is *of* the elephant. The whole complex chain is entirely within the domain of *prakṛti*. However, what makes the perceptual state *conscious* is that it is illuminated by the unchanging light of *puruṣa*. As Patañjali says in the above passage, the pure seer witnesses the images (or contents) of the mind. Thus, there is a bifurcation between intentionality and consciousness in Sāṅkhya-Yoga. From the perspective of the human perceiver, it may seem as if consciousness itself is in perceptual contact with the object, this is not ultimately the case. Rather, the perception is a complex material cognitive state, witnessed by *puruṣa*.

Given this account, Yoga seems committed to what we can call the *radical transparency* of consciousness. Here consciousness is understood as a kind of pure openness to which various phenomena may appear. Consciousness in itself is not directed at this or that object but rather is that which *allows* any object whatsoever to appear. An implication of this radical transparency is what Mark Rowlands calls the No Content Thesis:[8]

(NCT) Necessarily, any intentional object is outside consciousness.

(Rowlands 2020, 107)

There are two ways or levels at which the NCT applies to the Yoga view. First, on the standard interpretation, Patañjali is an ontological *realist* about external objects of perception. As he states:

The things [of the world] are objectively real, due to the uniformity of [the gunas that underpin] all change.

Because there is a multiplicity of minds [perceiving an object] but yet the object remains consistent, there is a difference in nature between the object and the mind [of the observer].

> An object is not dependent on a single mind [for its existence]; if it
> were, then what happens to it when it is not perceived [by that particular
> mind]?
>
> (IV:14-16)

Here Patañjali appeals to three related considerations. He appeals to the
observed uniformity on external objects due to their underlying material
features (the *guṇas*). He appeals to the public or intersubjective consistency
of perceptual objects. That is, objects are available in a consistent way to
multiple perceivers. And he appeals to the (seeming) continued existence
of objects when not being observed by a particular observer. That is, we
naturally assume that the elephant exists even when I don't see it. Patañjali's
realism here, as his commentator Vijñānabhikṣu (c. sixth century CE) points
out in the *Yogavārttika*, is in sharp contrast to the idealism the Yogācāra
Buddhists. They hold the view that while perceptual objects *appear* to be
material objects external to the mind, in fact they are internal perceptual
images. And they go on to argue (cf. Chapter 5), on metaphysical grounds,
that mind-independent material objects are impossible. In any case, the key
point here is that the intentional objects of cognitive states like perception are
external to the perceiver, and therefore external to consciousness.

The second application of the No Content Thesis is more subtle. One may
readily admit that perceptual objects such as elephants or trees are "outside"
consciousness. But what about feelings, pains, thoughts, or perceptions? That
is, what about mental states? At least when such states are conscious, one
could plausibly argue that these states are not outside consciousness, but
rather they are *what the conscious mind is doing* at that moment. A stabbing
pain or a powerful emotion are not like external material objects. Instead,
they are different states or activities of the conscious subject and when they
are known, it is the conscious subject being aware of itself. However, in
contrast to this view Patañjali asserts:

> The permutations of the mind are always known to its master, the puruṣa
> soul, because of the soul's unchanging nature.
>
> Nor is the mind self-illuminating, because of its nature as the object
> of perception.
>
> (IV.18-19)

Here Patañjali argues that the mind (*citta*) is not inherently self-aware or self-
illuminating (svābhāsam). Rather mind and its various contents (*vṛttaya*), are
illuminated by the *puruṣa*. The mind and its contents are themselves *objects*
(*dṛsyatvat*) of the pure awareness of the self as seer (*draṣṭṛ*). So, on the Yoga

view, even the internal contents of the mind are objects outside consciousness in that they are not themselves *states* or *activities* of consciousness. As an example, take an experience of pain in one's leg. One might analyze this experience as an awareness of a physical object (the leg) which is external to one's mind. But what about the feeling or sensation of pain itself? Is it the pain sensation a property of the leg, like it's mass? It is certainly felt in the leg (though some pains are not so easily located) but we normally think of sensations and feelings as mental states. Thus, one might want to say that the pain sensation is a feature of consciousness, not the leg itself. One might say the leg (the object) is experienced painfully. However, on the Yoga view, neither the leg nor the pain sensations are features of consciousness. As a discrete mental state, the pain sensation is itself an *object* of consciousness, not a state or mode of consciousness. In itself, consciousness is a radically transparent medium in which phenomena appear.

Patañjali highlights two reasons why the mind (*citta*) is not self-illuminating. The first reason appeals to nature of discernment or attention. He writes, "There cannot be discernment of both [the mind and the object it perceives] at the same time" (IV.20). The idea here seems to be that the mind cannot cognize another object and itself at the same time. When I perceive the elephant, the elephant is the object of cognition. To take my *seeing* as the cognitive object, I must shift my focus from the elephant to my own mind. Here, it is attention that selects the intentional object of the cognition. Thus, Patañjali is rejecting the kind of view found in Franz Brentano (1874), that the mind is self-illuminating in that it can (and perhaps always does) have its own states as secondary objects alongside the primary object. Just as in cutting, the knife does not cut itself, so in cognizing, the cognition does not cognize itself. The second reason appeals to the problem of regress. Patañjali writes, "If [the mind] were cognized by another mind, then there would be an infinite regress of one intelligence [being known] by another intelligence. Moreover, there would also be confusion of memory" (IV.21). Now, the terminology here is somewhat confusing, because Patañjali seems to be arguing against a Buddhist opponent and using their technical vocabulary.[9] The problem, though, is relatively straightforward. If a cognition is not conscious in virtue of illuminating itself, then perhaps it is illuminated by another cognition. But the second cognition is either conscious (illuminated) or not. If it *is* illuminated, how is it so? Self-illumination has already been ruled out, so it must be illuminated by another. But now we are off on a regress of cognitions. Further, such a proliferation of cognitions and meta-cognitions would overwhelm the ability of memory to retain one's various conscious mental states. On the other hand, if the second cognition is *not* itself illuminated, then it is unclear how two unilluminated (unconscious) cognitions could yield illumination.

Based on these two lines of reasoning, Patañjali thinks the mind cannot be self-illuminating either through reflexively self-illuminating cognitions or through distinct meta-cognitions of cognitions. Rather, the various states and contents of the mind are illuminated (rendered conscious) through the distinct light of the self. As he concludes "Although it is unchanging, consciousness becomes aware of its own intelligence by means of pervading the forms assumed by the intelligence" (IV. 22).

On the Yoga account, then, the conscious mind is a hybrid phenomenon. In themselves, mental states (*cittavṛttis*) go on "in the dark"—they are not inherently conscious. They become conscious mental states when they come within the scope of *puruṣa* as pure consciousness. Patañjali's commentator Vācaspati Miśra compares this process to light reflecting on water. The various ripples on the surface of water are illuminated by reflecting the rays of light from (in his example) the moon. So illuminated, the conscious mind can yield conscious knowledge of its objects. As Patañjali states, "The mind, colored by the seer as by that which is seen, knows all objects" (9.23). Hence the conscious mind is the interface between objects and the self. It is the mind's predominately *sattvic* nature that allows it to reflect the light of consciousness. Recall that the *sattva guṇa* is considered the most subtle, rarified, and pure or clear *guṇa*. This, like the surface of clear water, it naturally reflects the light of *puruṣa*.

As discussed in sections 4.1 and 4.2, the goal of Yoga is a type of spiritual freedom (*mokṣa*) called *kaivalya*, "isolation" or "aloneness."[10] As we saw in the opening chapter of the *Yoga Sūtras*:

I.2 Yoga is the stilling of the modifications of mind.
I.3 When that is accomplished, the seer abides in its own nature.
I.4 Otherwise, there is identification with the modifications [of mind].

The idea here is that in calming the mind, the misidentification with mental fluctuations (*cittavṛtti*) ceases and the confusion between *prakṛti* and *puruṣa* subsides. Then the self as the seer abides in its own true nature (*svarūpa-pratiṣṭhā*). The *puruṣa* is recognized in its "aloneness"—that is, as the independent reality it has always been. Note, then, that there are both ontological and phenomenological dimensions to *kaivalya* (not to mention the existential and spiritual dimensions). Ontologically, *puruṣa* has always been independent from *prakṛti*, so *kaivalya* does not change this. Phenomenologically however, the normal experience of the individual is one of deep confusion between the body-mind and pure consciousness.

Spiritual liberation entails the removal of this confusion, and this makes an experiential difference.

What does it mean for the seer to abide in its own nature? One way to think of this is as a form of self-recognition, a recognition of pure consciousness as one's true nature. But given the strict difference between pure consciousness and the mind in the Yoga theory, what could this recognition amount to? It can't be a thought or other form of cognition, since that is a function of the mind, not the self. Nor could it involve taking the self or oneself as an *object* of self-knowledge, since, according to the No Content Thesis, anything that could be an intentional object is outside consciousness. In grappling with this puzzle, classical commentators distinguished between self-knowledge (*svabuddhisaṃvedana*) and self-awareness (*svābhāsa*). Here self-knowledge is a type of reflective cognitive grasp (*saṃvedana*) on the contents and activities of one's own mind (*svabuddhi*), for example, 'I am thinking' or 'I am seeing'. In contrast, self-awareness here refers to the non-reflective, non-objectifying self-presence of consciousness.[11] Consciousness is self-luminous not because it turns itself into its own object, but because, to borrow a Sartrean phrase, its being is being-for-itself. Interestingly, in his commentary, Vyāsa shifts from a metaphor of light, to one of space:

> As the other organs and objects like light and sound, being knowable, are not self-illuminating, so is mind. In this case fire is not an appropriate example because fire does not illuminate its own unmanifest self. The illumination caused by fire is the outcome of contact between the illuminer and the illuminated and has no connection with the true nature of the fire. Moreover, if it is said that the mind is self-illuminating, it will mean that the mind is not knowable by anything else; as when we say that ākāśa is self-supporting we mean that ākāśa is not supported by anything else. But the activity of the mind is knowable through a reflection of the cognitive action in one's own mind (svabuddhi) like modifications such as "I am angry," "I am afraid," "I like it." This would not have been possible had there been no "grasping" of what was happening in one's own mind (YBh, 4.19).
>
> (Funes Maderey 2020, 6)

On this account, self-awareness as *svābhāsa* is more fundamental that self-knowledge as *svabuddhisaṃvedana*. It is the inherent presence of consciousness to itself that 'lights up' or 'creates space' for the conscious experiencing of objects in the world and the contents of one's own mind. As Anna Funes Maderey puts it,

The self-as-consciousness (puruṣa) understood from a phenomenological perspective is precisely the consciousness that cannot and need not know itself because it is present to itself in a non-thematized, non-reflective way. This is why, according to the Yoga of Patañjali, self-awareness becomes more evident in moments of stillness (nirodha)—both bodily and mental—when the absence of 'fluctuations' allows it to 'appear' as a spacious presence.

(Funes Maderey 2020, 9)

4.5 Comparative Connections

As we have seen so far, the sister schools of Yoga and Sāṅkhya delve deeply into issues of consciousness, subjectivity, body, mind, and more. And the views they develop have both a powerful internal logic and are quite distinctive in the philosophical contexts of India and more globally. There are, however, some interesting and potentially fruitful connections between Yoga philosophy and current discussion in philosophy. In this section, I will draw three such comparative connections. The first is to the (in)famous "hard problem of consciousness." The second is to the problem of mental causation. And the third is to issues of monism and dualism (or pluralism) in metaphysics.

Various versions of the mind-body problem have occupied thinkers in many traditions, including in India and the West. Indeed, "the" mind-body problem would be better described as several interconnected problems, including issues of causation, agency, intentionality, consciousness, and the self. David Chalmers coined the "hard problem" of consciousness in his book, *The Conscious Mind: In Search of a Fundamental Theory* (Chalmers 1997). As Chalmers puts it, "Consciousness poses the most baffling problems in the science of the mind. There is nothing that we know more intimately than conscious experience, but there is nothing that is harder to explain" (Chalmers 1995, 200). Here 'consciousness' and 'conscious experience' refers to phenomenal consciousness, which is frequently characterized in terms of 'what it's like' for a subject to experience or be aware of something. More specifically,

What makes the hard problem hard and almost unique is that it goes beyond problems about the performance of functions. To see this, note that even when we have explained the performance of all the cognitive and behavioral functions in the vicinity of experience—perceptual discrimination, categorization, internal access, verbal report—there may still remain a further unanswered question: *Why is the performance of these functions accompanied by experience?*

(Chalmers 1995, 202)

The mind sciences have made incredible progress in understanding various cognitive and behavioral functions associated with consciousness, as well as their biological and chemical bases. According to Chalmers, these are the "easy" problems of consciousness, though he is quick to say that they are not scientifically easy! Rather, because they are causal and functional explanations like we find in other scientific fields, they are less philosophically puzzling—hence philosophically "easy"—than the core problem of consciousness. And that core problem is how and why *any* of these functions are associated with phenomenal consciousness at all, rather than simply occurring "in the dark." Indeed, standard causal-functional explanations don't rely on these processes being conscious, and there doesn't seem to be anything logically or conceptually incoherent about them occurring in the absence of any consciousness at all. And yet, we *are* conscious, and our consciousness appears tightly correlated with various functional states of our brain. Similarly, Joseph Levine (Levine 2001) points to the persistent "explanatory gap" between the physical and consciousness. This gap shows up because, according to Levine, even our very fine-grained physical explanations of structures or processes in the brain, or of various cognitive functions, leave open the question of consciousness. Such explanations do not *entail* that consciousness exists, nor do they entail that specific conscious states are correlated with specific physical states. We also lack any explanatory *bridge* between consciousness and the physical. And in the absence of such a bridge, even ever more sophisticated and fine-grained explanations on the physical side by themselves fail to close the gap.[12]

Now, these problems of consciousness have spawned an enormous contemporary literature. And many philosophers and scientists working on consciousness either reject the existence of a distinctively "hard" problem of consciousness or are otherwise optimistic that any current explanatory gap eventually can be closed. For now, though, I want to grant the hard problem and the explanatory gap and explore what classical Yoga might have to say about them. The first thing to note is that a persistent hard problem or explanatory gap is not at all surprising from the perspective of Yoga. Indeed, their model of consciousness and the material world predicts that no account of the causal-functional states of the body or mind alone could explain consciousness. On the Yoga view, there is simply no discernable route from strictly objective or third-person phenomena of the body-mind to the strictly subjective or first-person phenomenon of consciousness.

The Yoga and Sāṅkhya schools give philosophical priority to the first-person perspective of consciousness. As mentioned above, many contemporary thinkers characterize phenomenal consciousness in terms of 'what it's like for a subject to experience something'. The 'something' here is the object or content of experience, which often involves *intentionality*. The 'what it's like' here is the *qualitative* character of experience, for instance, how a pain feels or what red looks like to the subject. And the 'for a subject' here is the *subjectivity* or *first-person perspective* of consciousness. On the Yoga view, consciousness is understood in terms of the subject-perspective—consciousness is the self (subject), the 'seer', the 'witness', the 'unchanging light'. *Puruṣa* is the conscious point of view *to which* various phenomena are manifest and *without which* no phenomena are manifest. This yields an important asymmetry between subjectivity and the qualitative and intentional aspects of conscious experience. On this view, subjectivity or the subject-perspective is what makes it possible for there to be qualitative or intentional modes of experience. If there's no subject-perspective, then there's nothing it is like *for the subject* to experience something. In other words, qualitative feels and experiential contents don't exist independently of a conscious perspective. Moreover, this asymmetry means that subjectivity is an invariant dimension of experience, while the qualitative and intentional aspects are highly variable. Finally, on the Yoga view, subjectivity is self-evident in that cannot be denied and it cannot be revealed by anything other than consciousness itself. In this way, Yoga affirms the *primacy* of consciousness. It is as Adam Frank, Marcelo Gleiser, and Evan Thompson explain the primacy of consciousness:

> There is no way to step outside consciousness and measure it against something else. Everything we investigate, including consciousness and its relation to the brain, resides within the horizon of consciousness … Consciousness is the horizon for the world's disclosure: The world appears and is present to us from within the horizon of consciousness. Consciousness is the horizon of anything we can perceive, think about, and investigate, including when we are doing science. We can observe, imagine, and investigate things only within the horizon of consciousness, and anything that we determine to be real or factual gets this determination from within the horizon of consciousness.

(Frank et al. 2024, 186)

If consciousness has this kind of primacy, then it is not (just) one object of knowledge among others, it is that by which *any* object is knowable. Therefore, on this kind of view, subjective consciousness is *in principle* irreducible to any object or system of objects. That is, *puruṣa* is irreducible to *prakṛti*.

On the Yoga view, there is no solving the hard problem, if that means showing how subjective consciousness could arise from purely objective things. The problem isn't incomplete information about things like the brain, but rather a kind of category mistake. The mistake is in trying to account for first-person consciousness in third-person terms. If, on the other hand, solving the hard problem means showing how consciousness and the physical can be coherently accommodated within the larger scheme of things, then the Yoga ontology of *puruṣa* (subjectivity) and *prakṛti* (the world of objective phenomena) offers one possible solution. As Chalmers argues, if we have principled reasons for the irreducibility of consciousness, then:

> Conscious experience is not 'postulated' to explain other phenomena in turn; rather, it is a phenomenon to be explained in its own right. And if it turns out that it cannot be explained in terms of more basic entities, then it must be taken as irreducible, just as happens with categories such as space and time.
>
> (Chalmers 2010, 33)

Arguably, then, realism about phenomenal consciousness or first-person subjectivity combined with recognition of the hard problem pulls in the direction of non-physicalism.[13] That is, given the undeniable reality of consciousness and the absence of any epistemically transparent account of how it relates to the physical, we have reason to believe that the explanatory gap reflects an ontological gap.

Yet, any viable philosophy of mind must also confront the problem of mental causation, the problem of explaining (or explaining away) how mental events could be part of the causal fabric of the world. And many contemporary philosophers have thought that the problem of mental causation is especially difficult for non-physicalist views. As Owen Flanagan writes:

> Regarding mind, it is true that immaterial mental properties are not completely ruled out by mind science. But the inference to the best explanation (aka "abduction") based on everything we know, taking all the evidence and all reasonable hypothesis into account, is that there are no such things. The reason has to do with mental causation. If mental events—for example, intentions to act—are, as they seem, causally efficacious, then the best explanation is that they are neural events. This is neurophysicalism, the thesis that mental events are brain events or, at least, bodily events, and that the subjective character of experience is

explained by the way nervous systems are connected to the persons that house them.

(Flanagan 2011, 65–66)

Intuitively, desires, pains, beliefs, and perceptions are causally efficacious. And yet, many hold that every physical event has a sufficient physical cause. Thus, when I raise my hand, it appears to be the case that there is a sufficient physiological cause for this event. But if the hand raising can be explained purely physiologically, then what explanatory role is there for my beliefs and desires? It is very hard to see how mental events *qua* mental can play a non-redundant role in explaining the behavior of sentient beings. Unlike the hard problem, then, the problem of mental causation pulls in the direction of physicalism. This is because, as Flanagan argues, it seems that the only way to account for the causal efficacy of mental events is to identify them with physical events. If mental events *just are* neural events, the thinking goes, then there's no mystery about how they can be the cause of other physical events.

So, we have a significant tension between the irreducible reality of phenomenal consciousness and the distinctive causal efficacy of mental events or states. But as Paul Schweizer (Schweizer 2019) has pointed out, the Sāṅkhya-Yoga theory of consciousness-mind dualism—in contrast to the more familiar mind-body dualism—offers a distinctive approach to resolving this tension. On this view, mental states are natural, physical states, so there seems to be no deep *metaphysical* problem of how they can be part of the causal fabric of the physical world. Perhaps mental states (*cittavṛttis*) are all token-identical to brain states, as in Flanagan's neurophysicalism. Here any thought, perception, or feeling *just is* some brain state, but it doesn't follow that any two states that are the same psychological *type* (for example, 'pain' or 'thought') will also be of the same neurophysiological type. On the other hand, perhaps mental states merely *supervene* on brain states, such that there can be no change in a mental state without there being a corresponding change in brain states, even if the two states are not even token-identical. In any case, what makes a state or event *mental* will have to do with its distinctive role in the life of the organism, in virtue of its function, informational profile, representational content, affective valence, or the like. And none of these distinctive features are obviously incompatible with mental states being a kind of natural, physical state.

But notice again that these distinctively mental features still fall within the scope of Chalmers' *easy* problems. Indeed, as Schweizer argues:

A central feature of this model is that there is no intrinsic representational or functional difference between conscious and unconscious mental processes. Instead, there is a material continuum out of which representational structures are composed, where the composition of thought-forms can be more or less transparent, and hence more or less susceptible to illumination, just as ordinary translucent objects can retain local variations in opacity. Conscious illumination takes place only with respect to a small portion of the causally efficacious material mind, and is not an intrinsic property of mental activities.

(Schweizer 1993, 858)

Certain physical states are apt for the extrinsic illumination from consciousness but are not inherently conscious—they are physical states reflecting the non-physical "light" of consciousness. Of course, this means that the Sāṅkhya-Yoga theory has a strictly *acausal* theory of consciousness. That is, consciousness itself is causally inert and strictly independent from the causal functioning of the mind and body.

The Sāṅkhya-Yoga view therefore accommodates both mental causation and the irreducible reality of consciousness, but at the cost of a strict separation between the *light* of consciousness and the inner *life* of the conscious human person. This raises the possibility that the ultimate goal of Yoga, *kaivalya*, is not so much a form of freedom as it is a form of *alienation.* The worry is that the subject is an inert consciousness absurdly coupled to a zombie—namely, essentially unconscious—body-mind. Furthermore, pure consciousness has no agency, no thoughts, no feelings, no desires, no values. The mind and body operate within the causal order of nature, causally and functionally independent of consciousness. That is, the human body-mind is a philosophical zombie in Chalmers' sense.

In response to this worry, it is important to note that the Yogic goal of *kaivalya* is multifaceted, showing a different facet depending on different perspectives. Recall that the human person is a confluence of body, mind, and consciousness. From the perspective of the body-mind, *kaivalya* entails dispelling the root ignorance that leads to suffering and existential bondage. This means the body-mind of the liberated person is free of suffering, confusion, negative passions, maladaptive desires, and so on. The conscious mind is calm, clear, and intelligent. Moreover, the path to liberation requires the cultivation, and eventual perfection, of virtue. In particular, Patañjali mentions the virtues of, for example, non-harming (*ahiṃsā*), truthfulness (*satya*), contentment (*saṃtoṣa*), and self-discipline (*tapas*). He also states:

By cultivating an attitude of friendship toward those who are happy, compassion toward those in distress, joy toward those who are virtuous, and equanimity toward those who are nonvirtuous, lucidity arises in the mind.[14]

(I.33)

From the perspective of consciousness itself, *kaivalya* entails unconditioned awareness and joy, culminating in existential freedom from the conditioned realm of *prakṛti*. So, far from alienation, the Yogic ideal is one of lucid, virtuous personhood free from ignorance and suffering, coupled with a recognition that one's essential nature is unconditioned happiness and awareness (MacKenzie 2018).

4.6 Questions

1. What is Patañjali's definition of yoga?
2. What is the difference between Yoga dualism and standard forms of dualism in the West?
3. Do you think Yoga theory of consciousness offers a plausible response to the hard problem and the problem of mental causation?

Notes

1 While Sāṅkhya is one of the oldest philosophical systems in India, the oldest extant Sāṅkhya text is Īśvarakṛṣṇa's (c. 350–450 CE) *Sāṅkhyakārikā*.

2 Unless otherwise specified, I will use consciousness and awareness interchangeably.

3 The moral restraints concern that which should be avoided, such as *hiṃsa* (harm) to other beings. The observances concern that which should be done or cultivated, such as *santoṣa* (contentment).

4 All translations are my own. See Bryant (2009) for the full Sanskrit text, translation, and commentary.

5 These dimensions correspond somewhat to the modern psychological constructs of activation (arousal) and alertness (vigilance) respectively. In the Sāṅkhya-Yoga theory of the three basic *guṇas* (qualities), an agitated state is highly rajasic, a dull state is tamasic, and a lucid state is sattvic.

6 *Citta* can also refer to the mind as a whole or to conscious awareness. Here it is used to refer to the latent dimensions of mind. Moreover, this dimension is not always treated as a function distinct from *manas*, *ahaṃkāra*, and *buddhi*.

7 Translations in this section are from (Bryant 2015).

8 The Sāṅkhya-Yoga view of radical transparency entails the NCT, but NCT does not entail the Sāṅkhya-Yoga view. For instance, Sartre (about whom

Rowlands is writing in the quoted passage) held both the consciousness is inherently intentional and (indeed, *therefore*) it is contentless.

9 IV.21 *Cittāntradṛśye buddhibuddher atiprasangaḥ smṛtisaṅkaraś.* Another gloss might be, "If a mental state (*citta*) were cognized (*dṛśye*) by another mental state, then there would be a regress (*atiprasangaḥ*) of one cognizing by another cognizing (*buddhibuddheḥ*) causing a confusion of memory (*smṛtisaṅkaraś*)."

10 From *kevala*, "alone, isolated."

11 This tracks Wolfgang Fasching's distinction between two meanings of 'self-consciousness': "(1) the self-identification with certain configurations of what one experiences and (2) the self-presence of experiencing itself" (Fasching 2008, 464).

12 Here it is important to note the distinction between Type-A (a priori) and Type-B (a posteriori) physicalism (Chalmers 2010a). Type-A physicalism denies that there is any ultimate explanatory gap between the physical facts and the mental facts. However, Type-B physicalism admits that there could be an unbridgeable gap between the mental and physical facts. This gap, though, is only epistemic-conceptual and not metaphysical. Type-B physicalism maintains that the mental facts are grounded in (for example, supervenient upon) the physical facts.

13 The following discussion of mental causation draws on (MacKenzie 2019).

14 These virtues—friendliness (*maitri*), compassion (*karuṇā*), sympathetic joy (*muditā*), and equanimity (*upekṣā*)—are known as the four immeasurables (*brahmavihāras*) in Buddhism.

Further Reading

Bryant, Edwin F. 2015. *The Yoga Sūtras of Patañjali: A New Edition, Translation, and Commentary.* Farrar, Straus and Giroux.

Burley, Mikel. 2012. *Classical Sāṁkhya and Yoga.* Routledge.

Kṛṣṇa, Īśvara. 1995. *Sāṁkhya Kārikā of Īśvara Kṛṣṇa.* Translated by Swami Virupakshananda. Advaita Ashrama.

O'Brien-Kop, Karen. 2023. *The Philosophy of the Yogasūtra: An Introduction.* Bloomsbury Publishing.

Schweizer, Paul. 1993. "Mind/Consciousness Dualism in Sāṁkhya-Yoga Philosophy." *Philosophy and Phenomenological Research* 53 (4): 845–59.

5

Yogācāra

5.1 The Yogācāra School

As elaborated in Chapter 3, the Abhidharma schools inaugurate systematic philosophy in the Buddhist tradition. Further, the different sub-schools of Abhidharma—for example, Theravāda, Vaibhāṣika, Sautrāntika—were affiliated with the mainstream, Nikāya or Śrāvakayāna, tradition of Buddhism. These thinkers drew on the early Buddhist discourses (the Nikāyas) and developed the systematic Abhidharma literature. As discussed in Chapter 3, a key aspect of Abhidharma thought is the careful, reflective analysis of sentient experience using the various methods and tools developed in the Buddhist tradition, such as dependent co-arising, momentariness, and no-self. Abhidharma thought laid the foundation for subsequent developments in Indian Buddhist philosophy and remained an important tradition in its own right.

Starting in approximately the first century BCE a newer set of Buddhist traditions, practices, and texts emerged. This new movement came to be called the Mahāyāna or "great vehicle." The Mahāyāna movement developed a very large and rich corpus of sūtras and other texts attributed to the historical Buddha as well as other figures, such as *bodhisattvas* (awakened beings) and even the future Buddha, Maitreya. Important Mahāyāna sūtras include the *Saddharmapuṇḍarīka Sūtra, Prajñāpāramitā Sūtras, Avataṃsaka Sūtra, Laṅkāvatāra Sūtra*, and the *Mahāparinirvāṇa Sūtra*. The distinctive spiritual path of the Mahāyāna is that of the *bodhisattva*, in contrast to the earlier path of the *arhat*. The traditional path of the *arhat* aims at achieving awakening and escape from *saṃsāric* bondage for the individual practitioner through the cultivation of wisdom, ethics, and contemplative self-mastery. In contrast, the Mahāyānists view the bodhisattva path as the higher or more noble. The bodhisattva path entails striving for the full and complete enlightenment of Buddhahood and doing so with the altruistic motivation to facilitate the liberation of all sentient beings.

In addition to this new soteriological emphasis, the Mahāyāna tradition is associated with several distinctive philosophical views. For example, we find an emphasis on a higher mode of insight or knowledge, *prajñāpāramitā* ('perfection of wisdom'). The mode of awareness is often characterized as non-conceptual, non-grasping, penetrating (illusions), and nondual (that is, beyond the reification of subject and object). In the *Heart Sūtra* (*Prajñāpāramitā Hṛdaya Sūtra*), the perfection of wisdom is understood as a direct insight into emptiness (*śūnyatā*) of all phenomena (*dharmas*): "all phenomena are empty, that is, without characteristic, unproduced, unceased, stainless, not stainless, undiminished, unfilled" (12). Roughly, this amounts to a thoroughgoing rejection of the (supposedly deeply entrenched) idea that phenomena have a fixed nature or substantial reality. Other texts emphasize overcoming pernicious dualities, such as the duality between subject and object, or "grasper" (*grāhaka*) and "grasped" (*grāhya*). Furthermore, with development of Mahāyāna we find new and often radical reinterpretations of core Buddhist ideas like dependent origination, no-self, impermanence, and the distinction between conventional and ultimate truth.

There are two principal philosophical schools associated with the emergence of Indian Mahāyāna. The first is Madhyamaka (Middle Way), the name of which likely derives from the broader idea of Buddhism as a middle path (*madhyama pratipad*) between the extremes of eternalism and annihilationism. The most well-known philosopher associated with this school is Nāgārjuna, whose *Mūlamadhyamikakārikā* (Root Verses on the Middle Way) is focused on the idea that all phenomena are empty (*śunya*) of an inherent nature or substantial existence (*svabhāva*). Thus, Madhyamaka is often called *śunyavāda*, the doctrine of emptiness. The second principal school is Yogācāra, which is the subject of this chapter. The term Yogācāra means "yoga practice" (*yoga + acara*) and may also be in reference to one of the early philosophical texts associated with the school, the *Yogācārabhumi*. The central focus of Yogācāra is the nature and functioning of the mind, as indicated by other terms for the school: *vijñānavāda* ("doctrine of consciousness"), *vijñaptimātra* ("cognition-only"), and *cittamātra* ("mind-only"). The two main philosophers associated with the development of Yogācāra are Vasubandhu—already discussed in Chapter 3 concerning his earlier work in the Abhidharma tradition—and his half-brother Asaṅga (300–370 BCE). Additionally, the later Buddhist *pramāṇavāda* (logico-epistemological) tradition of Dignāga, Dharmakīrti, and their successors is also associated with Yogācāra. Indeed, some Tibetan doxographers call this tradition Yogācāra-Sautrāntika. However, the focus of this chapter is the earlier Yogācāra of Vasubandhu and Asaṅga, while the later tradition will be discussed in Chapter 7.

There are several key philosophical themes and innovations in Yogācāra. First, Yogācārins developed a new account of the mind, drawing on but expanding earlier Abhidharma views. Recall from Chapter 3 that Abhidharma philosophers identified six distinct modes or functions of the mind: visual, tactile, auditory, gustatory, olfactory, and mental. These are distinct types of consciousness because they present different types of objects (or contents). For example, visual consciousness presents color and shape. Each type arises based on specific causes and conditions, and while lasting only a moment, plays a distinct causal-functional role in the mind-stream (*citta-santāna*). Yogācāra thinkers add to this model two further types of consciousness. The first is *kliṣṭamanas* (defiled mind or consciousness), which is responsible for the persistent sense of self. The second is *ālayavijñāna* (storehouse, base, or substratum consciousness), which is a continuous subliminal consciousness that serves as the basis (or storehouse) of a variety of latent mental functions. Further, as discussed in section 5.2, on the Yogācāra model, these different levels or types of consciousness interact and structure each other in complex and dynamic ways.

The second key theme or innovation in Yogācāra is the theory of the three natures (*trisvabhāva*) of phenomena. Any given phenomenon can be understood in terms of three natures: the constructed nature (*parikalpita svabhāva*), the dependent nature (*paratantra svabhāva*), and the perfected nature (*pariniṣpanna svabhāva*). As elaborated in section 5.3, the constructed nature is how the phenomenon appears to the unenlightened (hence distorted) consciousness. The dependent nature points to the fact that the imagined nature depends on a set of causes and conditions. And the perfected nature is how the phenomenon really is, which is also how it appears to an enlightened (hence undistorted) consciousness.

The third key theme or innovation concerns the Yogācāra doctrines of emptiness and nonduality. As mentioned above, the Madhyamaka school understood the emptiness of phenomena in terms of lack of substantial or essential nature (*niḥsvabhāvata*). In contrast, the Yogācāra school generally understood the emptiness of phenomena in terms of the absence of any ultimate duality of subject and object. As an ordinary unenlightened being, it certainly *seems* like I am a real self ('in here') experiencing an independent world ('out there') of material objects and other conscious beings. But, as we will discuss in detail in section 5.4, the Yogācāra school rejects this ordinary view of things and aims to offer a rigorous philosophical alternative.

5.2 Eight Dimensions of Consciousness

Overall, Yogācāra can be viewed as a creative synthesis and development of the early Abhidharma style of analysis and the newer Mahāyāna emphasis on emptiness, the two truths, and compassionate activity in the world of *saṃsāra* (Waldron 2023). Abhidharma thinkers analyze the nature and functioning of the mind in terms of complex, plural interactive events and processes rather than fixed enduring substances. These events and processes—such as perceiving, feeling, or conceptualizing—are then further analyzed into basic explanatorily units (*dharmas*), which are ontologically distinct, causally efficacious, and momentary. Moreover, Ābhidharmikas argue that supposedly stable objects and subjects of cognition are in fact constructs of more fundamental events and processes. That is, what appear to be stable objects and subjects are, upon further analysis, constructs of fleeting *dharmas*. The apparently fixed, unified, and enduring is analyzed and reduced to the changing, plural, and momentary.

Abhidharma thinkers understand the mind broadly in terms of perception (*pratyakṣa*), conception (*prapañca*), affect (*vedanā*), and intention (*cetanā*). In the standard formulation, there are six modalities of perception. The first five correspond to the standard sense faculties: visual, auditory, olfactory, gustatory, and tactile. The perceptual process depends on a sensory domain, a functional sense organ, and a sensory faculty (or capacity), giving rise to a moment of sensory consciousness. For example, to have an olfactory sensory experience, there (typically) needs to be a sensory stimulus in the environment, a sensitive nose, and whatever sensory processing is required to translate sensory stimulus into experience. Importantly, each sensory modality operates independently, yielding distinct moments of sensory experience. Yet, in our normal experience we don't have radically separate and disconnected sensory experiences. Rather, our sensory experience is in some way integrated or multi-modal. Further, our integrated sensory experience is available for various cognitive operations such as attention, concept-formation, or thinking. On the Abhidharma view, these functions are accomplished by the sixth type of perception, *manovijñāna* ("mental consciousness") or *manas* ("mind"). Like the other five modes of perception, mental awareness or perception requires a particular domain and an underlying faculty or system. The specific domain for mental awareness is not the external sensory environment, but rather internal environment of other mental states and processes. Importantly, since these more basic mental events are momentary, the domain of mental awareness is in the past. It is the immediately prior mental events that serve as input to mental awareness. The underlying system or faculty is *manas* (mind) here understood as the network of mental capacities such as attention, memory, thinking, and so on. Thus, like some Western notions of an inner sense or mind's eye, the *manovijñāna's* role is to access, integrate, and cognize other mental states or events. In this way, it serves as a bridge between more basic sensory (and affective) states and higher cognitive processes.

This sixfold model of the mind provided a philosophically robust basis for the Abhidharma analysis of sentient experience. Yet, Yogācāra thinkers expanded the standard Abhidharma account into an eightfold model of the mind, adding the ideas of *kliṣṭamanas* and *ālayavijñāna*. Why? According to William Waldron, Yogācāra developed the expanded model to address what he calls the "Abhidharma Problematic." As Waldron comments, the Abhidharma project involves two philosophical goals:

> On the one hand, to overcome illusion on the path to liberation, Abhidharmic analyses of mind deconstruct our sense of self as a singular unchanging entity. On the other hand, these analyses assume the coherence and continuity of what we normally call a *person*. These two necessarily go together.
>
> (Waldron 2003, 84)

And yet, they are in tension with one another, yielding the Abhidharma Problematic: "The indispensable relationship between causal conditioning and temporal continuity—how the past continues to affect the present—becomes nearly inexpressible in an ultimate analysis in which only momentary, presently effective dharmas are truly real" (Waldron 2003, 86). More broadly, Waldron sees the Abhidharma Problematic as a tension between the accounts of the synchronic coherence of the person and the diachronic continuity of the person. For instance, it is not clear that the causal continuity of the mental continuum can be explained entirely in terms of discrete momentary events. Further, it is not clear that the latent aspects of the mind (*saṃskharas, vāsanās*) are well-explained in terms of momentary mental *dharmas*. At the level of philosophy of mind, this tension is between the account of the momentary mind (*citta*) and mental factors (*caitta*), and the continuity of the mind-stream (*citta-santāna*).

The Yogācāra theory of eight dimensions of mind or consciousness can be understood in part as an attempt to address and overcome this tension. Yogācāra divides the eight levels into three distinct categories: *mūlavijñāna* (base consciousness), *kliṣṭamanas* (defiled consciousness), and *pravṛttivijñāna* (manifest or emergent consciousness).[1] The base or root (*mūla*) consciousness is the eighth consciousness, *ālayavijñāna*, the continuous background stream of mentation which forms the basis for all other forms of mentation. The *kliṣṭamanas* is the seventh consciousness, constituting our basic sense of self and self-consciousness. The manifest or emergent (*pravṛtti*) levels include the other six levels. The *pravṛttivijñānas*, as in Abhidharma, are changing and discontinuous. In contrast, the *kliṣṭamanas* and *ālayavijñāna* are more stable and diachronically continuous. Thus, the Yogācāra model helps to address the Abhidharma Problematic by developing a richer account of the diachronic and synchronic dimensions of mind and how their interactions constitute the overall nature of mind and experience.

We might think of the *pravṛttivijñānas* as forming the foreground of our moment-to-moment experience. So, for instance, at a given time the emergent dimension of my experience might involve seeing my desk, smelling coffee, feeling my chair, and thinking about philosophy. It will also involve various mental factors such as being focused, feeling pleasantly relaxed, and intending to meet a writing goal. These distinct perceptual, cognitive, affective, and intentional aspects come together to form much of my overall state of experience. And again, this overall state is dynamic, shifting and changing from moment to moment. In the next moment, I may hear a loud noise outside, shift attention, have a new visual experience, and feel startled or annoyed.

This account of the *pravṛttivijñānas* is quite similar to a standard Abhidharma view. However, an important difference is that Yogācāra accepts the simultaneity of multiple types of consciousness, whereas Abhidharma held that distinct moments of consciousness occur sequentially. Thus, on the Abhidharma view, one cannot in fact see and hear at the same time. Rather, a moment of visual consciousness is succeeded by a moment of auditory consciousness so rapidly that we cannot detect the difference, so they *seem* simultaneous. In contrast, on the Yogācāra view multiple *pravṛttivijñānas* can arise from the base consciousness at the same time, constituting a genuine multi-modal synchronic unity or coherence of consciousness.

The seventh consciousness, *kliṣṭamanas*, is responsible for our basic sense of self and self-consciousness. It is called 'defiled' or 'afflicted' (*kliṣṭa*) because, on the Buddhist account, the sense of self is at the root of the various afflictions (*kleśas*) of unenlightened existence.[2] Be that as it may, the seventh consciousness plays several important roles in the Yogācāra model of the mind. First and foremost, the *kliṣṭamanas* explains the depth and pervasiveness of the sense of self. As in Abhidharma, *manas* (sixth consciousness) is responsible for occurrent thoughts, including self-referential thoughts such as "I am hungry" or "The bus is moving toward me." Yet, we are not always thinking about ourselves. Yet even when we are not entertaining I-thoughts, we still have a sense of *being someone*, of being a subject or self in a world of objects and other subjects. This involves, for example, having a conscious point of view, having a sense of agency, and having a sense of mental and bodily ownership. Even when I am concentrating on a task and not thinking about myself, I still have a conscious perspective on the world, a sense that I am engaging in the task, and a sense that my thoughts, desires, and body are *mine*. This core sense of self is a function of the *kliṣṭamanas*. Second, *kliṣṭamanas* serves as the *basis* of *manas* or *manovijñāna*. On the Abhidharma view, the five types of sensory consciousness have as their basis (*āśraya*) the corresponding sense faculty. Yet, *manas* has only prior mental states as its basis. On the Yogācāra view, the *kliṣṭamanas* serves as the deeper basis for the manifest, intermittent activity of the *manas*. Hence, we might think of the *kliṣṭamanas* as the deeper cognitive architecture that allows for various forms of mental activity. Note also that the *kliṣṭamanas*, in turn, has its basis in the *ālayavijñāna*. Third, the *kliṣṭamanas* explains how the deep sense of self pervades or structures the manifest operations of mind. That is, even when we are not explicitly self-focused, the sense of being a subject interacting with an independent world provides the basic framework of our experience. In perceiving an object, I see it from my point of view and in relation to my body. In experiencing a pain, I feel it as *my* pain. When I think "I'm hungry," I don't first identify someone who is hungry and then ask, "Is this hungry person *me*?" Additionally, the *ātmadṛṣṭi* (view of the self) grounded in the *kliṣṭamanas* involves memory, self-conception, and a sense of personal identity or continuity over time.

While the *kliṣṭamanas* is more basic and constant than the six *pravṛttivijñānas*, on the Yogācāra model, it is still dependent and only relatively constant. It is only relatively constant because it can cease functioning in particularly, admittedly rare, states of consciousness. Vasubandhu mentions that the *kliṣṭamanas* ceases in certain deep meditative states, in very advanced Buddhist practitioners, and upon enlightenment (Triṃś 7). As mentioned above, the *kliṣṭamanas* depends on the *ālayavijñāna*. Like the six *pravṛttivijñānas*, the *kliṣṭamanas* arises from the *ālayavijñāna*, which therefore serves as its causal basis. Further and unlike the *pravṛttivijñānas*, the *kliṣṭamanas* has the *ālayavijñāna* as its object. That is, the *kliṣṭamanas* is ultimately a kind of subliminal awareness of base consciousness. It interprets or represents the continuous base consciousness *as if* it were an enduring unified self. In doing so it produces a synchronic and diachronic sense of self that in turn pervades and structures the *pravṛttivijñānas*. Yet, on the Yogācāra account, the *ālayavijñāna* is *not* an enduring self or subject. The *kliṣṭamanas* is a misrepresentation of the base consciousness. Therefore, the deep sense of self that structures our minds is a *false* construction.

We should distinguish two aspects of the claim that the sense of self is a false construction. First is the idea that the sense of self is a construction. This might simply mean that the sense of self is not simple and fundamental but is rather built up from more basic psychological features (states, capacities, processes, and the like). Second is the idea that the sense of self is false or in error. In a broader philosophical or scientific context, simply pointing out that something is a construction does not entail that it is false, erroneous, or unreal. For example, one might describe the complex series of psychological operations that construct a particular perceptual state, but this does not entail either that the perceptual state is erroneous or that the state itself is unreal. Likewise, it is not uncommon in philosophy or science to argue that the sense of self is a psychological construction, or even that *the self* is constructed in some way. However, Yogācārins, like other Buddhists, argue that construction is the mark of conventionality (*saṃvṛtti*), so the sense of self is *at best* merely conventionally real. However, the constructed sense of self also mistakes the non-self for a self. The problem here is not that the *kliṣṭamanas* is a constructed representation, but that it *misrepresents* its object. Hence, we can say that Yogācārins have an error theory of the sense of self or self-consciousness. In section 5.5 we will discuss a contemporary neurophilosophical version of the error theory of self.

The eighth consciousness, *ālayavijñāna*, is the continuous basis for all other mental operations. We might think of the *ālayavijñāna* in terms of the three interrelated functions of base, background, and storehouse. As the base or root (*mūla*) of mind, the *ālayavijñāna* is the source and cause of the other levels of consciousness. It is the source and cause in two ways. First, it is the core form of mind that flows from lifetime to lifetime within the Buddhist theory of rebirth (*pratisaṃdhi*), thereby allowing for the emergence of the various forms of mentation in the lifetime of a particular individual. Second, it is the more basic level of mind that allows other mental states to arise (in conjunction with the world, the sense faculties, and so forth) at any given time. Regarding its role as background, Yogācārins argued that various *pravṛttivijñānas* could arise and cohere simultaneously because they emerge from a single basis. This helped respond to the argument that, without a real unified self, the synchronic unity of consciousness would be impossible. Moreover, Yogācārins argue that there is two-way interaction between the base and emergent levels of consciousness, which we might think of as constituting the foreground and background functions of the mind. The *pravṛttivijñānas* emerge from and feed back on the base, creating a dynamic in which the foreground and background mutually condition one another. In this way, the *ālayavijñāna* is similar to Evan Thompson's view of base or background consciousness as "the antecedent and 'rolling' experiential context of perception [which] modulates the way the object appears or is experientially lived during the moment of perception, and the content of this transient conscious state reciprocally affects the flow of experience" (Thompson 2007, 355). And because the base operates continuously, the Yogācārins have an account of how even temporally discontinuous states of consciousness can shape the flow of mind. For instance, in deep sleep, anesthesia, or deep states of meditative absorption (*nirodhasamāpatti*) there may be a gap in consciousness. And yet, upon regaining consciousness, there is typically a sense of mental continuity across the gap. This is hard to account for on the Abhidharma view in which there is no enduring self and mental events are momentary and caused by the immediately prior mental event. In positing the deep continuous base consciousness, the Yogācāra model offers a more robust account of the temporal coherence of consciousness.

Regarding its role as storehouse, the *ālayavijñāna* is posited as the locus for the various latent factors of the mind. These latent factors include memories, habits, cognitive schemas, linguistic understanding, the *kleśas*, and karmic potentials. These latent potentials can be triggered in the right circumstances, producing or shaping occurrent, manifest forms of experience. Yet, as Asaṅga argues in the Yogācārabhumi, these latent and persisting mental factors are not explained by the manifest and momentary *pravṛttivijñānas*. The *ālayavijñāna*, then, serves as the continuous locus or storehouse of the various 'seeds' (*bījas*) or latent potentials in the mindstream. Interestingly, the Yogācārins also argue that the base consciousness is karmically neutral. At the level of manifest experience, we find from one moment to the next karmically positive, negative, or indeterminate states, actions, and so on. Each of these arises from the interaction between the individual mindstream and its environment and leaves a karmic trace within the storehouse consciousness. The storehouse is neutral in that it stores all types of traces, and its operation does not itself produce further positive or negative karma.

Finally, on the Yogācāra theory, each level of consciousness is said to have its own domain or type of object. As we've seen, the five types of sense consciousness have their respective sensory objects. The domain of the sixth consciousness, *manovijñāna*, is other occurrent mental states. The object of the *kliṣṭamanas* is the *ālayavijñāna*. But what of the *ālayavijñāna* itself? On the Yogācāra view, the base consciousness has as its objects the body and the surrounding world or environment (*bhājanaloka*). As Asaṅga explains, "Briefly, *ālayavijñāna* arises with two supports: with the perception (*vijñapti*) of the inner appropriation (*upadana*); and with the perception of the external, shared world whose aspects are not clearly delineated" (Waldron 2023, 207).

The base consciousness is said to 'pervade' the body, providing an implicit awareness of the body as a whole. Additionally, the base consciousness is said to have an external function, providing some sort of awareness of the surrounding world (*bhājanaloka*). Yet, since it is not one of the five forms of external sensory consciousness, how could the *ālayavijñāna* provide access to the world? According to Asaṅga, "The 'perception of the external shared world whose aspects are not clearly delineated' means: the continuous, uninterrupted perception (*vijñapti*) of the continuity of the shared world based upon that very *ālayavijñāna* that has inner appropriation as its support" (YcBh (1.b)A.2) (Waldron 2023, 207). "Inner appropriation" here refers to the internal, bodily (interoceptive) aspect of the *ālaya*. So, on Asaṅga's view, the vague sense of the external world is based on the interoceptive aspect and is characterized by an uninterrupted sense of the continuity of the shared world. As we will see in the next two sections, Yogācārins are concerned with how our minds *construct* an experience of a shared world of independent objects and subjects. The various latent dispositions and schemas, habits, concepts, memories stored in the *ālayavijñāna* play a central role in the Yogācāra account of this construction process. As Waldron explains:

> The subtle perception of our shared world is *correlative* with the subtle impressions of the names and concepts of our imagined [constructed] entities, which are constantly shaping our underlying, equally subtle *ālaya* awareness. How does this work? As a species, we humans share not only similar faculties but also similar dispositions, which help us navigate our surrounding world in similarly human ways-as compared to bats, butterflies, or bacteria. The ways we subliminally experience our world are continuously but unconsciously shaped by our embodied but subliminal categories and concepts …
>
> (Waldron 2023, 208)

Finally, it is important to note that, while the *ālayavijñāna* is an important innovation, it is still conceived within the larger Buddhist philosophical framework. In particular, while the *ālaya* is temporally continuous, Yogācārins insist that it is made up of dependently originated moments, just like any other persisting phenomena. Like the broader Buddhist notion of the *cittasantāna* (mind-stream), the *ālaya* is an impermanent or constantly changing process, not an enduring entity of any kind. Moreover, the *ālaya* is not itself a subject or self. Rather, it is the deep, subliminal mental process out of which the mistaken sense of self or subjectivity is constructed.

5.3 Three Natures of Phenomena

As just mentioned, Yogācāra thinkers were interested in the constructive power of the mind and its role in the creation and maintenance of our experience of being (or seeming to be) an enduring subject in a world of independent objects and other subjects. Further, as Buddhist thinkers, they are keenly aware of how the constructive powers of the mind may perpetuate the delusions and afflictions of saṃsāric or unenlightened existence, which must be uncovered and extirpated on the path to enlightenment. Pursuant to this larger project, Yogācāra thinkers developed a framework for analyzing all phenomena in terms of three natures (*svabhāva*) and three forms of naturelessness (*niḥsvabhāvatā*). The three natures are the fabricated or constructed nature (*parikalpita-svabhāva*), the dependent nature (*paratantra-svabhāva*), and the perfected nature (*pariniṣpanna-svabhāva*).[3]

In the opening verses of *Treatise on the Three Natures* (*Trisvabhāvanirdeśa*) Vasubandhu explains:

1. Fabricated, dependent and perfected: So the wise understand, in depth, the three natures.
2. What appears is the dependent [*paratantra*]. How it appears is the fabricated [*parikalpita*]. Because of being dependent on conditions. Because of being only fabrication.
3. The eternal non-existence of the appearance as it appears: That is known to be the perfected nature [*pariniṣpanna-svabhāva*], because of being always the same.
4. What appears there? The unreal fabrication. How does it appear? As a dual self. What is its nonexistence? That by which the nondual reality is there.

'The fabricated' (*parikalpita*) here connotes mental construction and to say that an experiential object has a fabricated or constructed nature in this sense is to point to the way in which the object *qua* experienced depends on the constructive activities of mental processes. It is a core claim of the Yogācāra approach that objects of experience can only appear through the constructive activity of cognition and that this activity makes an essential contribution to *how* the empirical object is given. Thus, to say that an object is mentally constructed is not to say that it is a mere hallucination, since any object of experience is constructed in this way. Yet, the fabricated nature is inherently misleading in that, in normal experience, we do not experience objects *as* mentally constructed. Rather, our default mode is a form of naïve realism that takes the mind to present objects as they really are independently of the contribution of the mind. This leads to the *paratantra-svabhāva*, the dependent nature of phenomena. Despite the fact we tend to experience objects as experience-independent, on the Yogācāra account, they depend on constructive mental activity. The rainbow *qua* experiential object depends on the sensory-cognitive systems of perceivers like us. Since the object as a construct is not pre-given in its conditions, our deep sense that cognition is the simple mirroring or recovery of pre-given objects of experience is mistaken.

The deeper truth, on this analysis, is the *absence* of the constructed nature from the dependent nature. Finally, the *pariniṣpanna-svabhāva*, the perfected nature, is the true or undistorted nature of phenomena. This is understood in terms of how an enlightened being would experience phenomena, namely, as the dependent nature absent the distortions inherent in the constructed nature, most fundamentally the subject-object dichotomy.

Minimally, on the Yogācāra analysis, we start out as naïve realists about the experienced world (including our own subjectivity), but through careful analysis we can come to see clearly the ways in which our experience of the world and ourselves is dependent on our own mental processes. But the Yogācārins go further. As Vasubandhu boldly asserts in the *Viṃśatikā* or *Twenty Verses*, "Everything in the three realms is only appearance (*vijñaptimātra*)" (Viṃś 1). The 'three realms' here refers to the worlds or states of being into which sentient beings are born. Thus, the shared phenomenal worlds of sentient beings are appearance-only. And this means, Vasubandhu makes clear in his auto-commentary, that the three realms are nothing but *citta* and *caitta* (mental processes and their variegated qualities or factors) and there are no mind-independent objects (*artha*). In so far as reality can be positively characterized at all, it is *cittamātra*, consciousness-only or experience-only. Experiential objects, then, are immanent to experience, despite appearing as independent of experience. The fabricated appearance of independent subjects and objects is a distortion of the nondual flow of experience. As he puts in the *Triṃśikā*, "The metaphors of self and external phenomena, functioning in various ways, take place in the transformation of consciousness" (Triṃś 1). And in TSN 5, he writes, "What is this unreal fabrication? Mind. For it does not exist at all in the way it is fabricated or in the way it fabricates a thing" (Gold 2014, 244). Indeed, Vasubandhu famously likens the distortion to a persistent perceptual illusion—the appearance of hairs in the visual field of one with an eye disease (Viṃś 1).

One way to flesh out the Yogācāra view is in the direction of an internalist-representationalist account of mind. This account fits well the historical and conceptual connections between Vasubandhu's Yogācāra and the indirect-realist and representationalist views propounded in the Abhidharma sub-school of Sautrāntika. It also makes good sense of some of Vasubandhu's arguments against naïve and direct realist accounts of the mind. Another way to flesh out the model of the three natures is in the direction of a more radically nondualist account of experience. This account makes good sense of Vasubandhu's emphasis on overcoming subject-object duality and on the flow of experience as fundamental, and will be taken up in the next section.

The internalist-representationalist interpretation is based on a representational theory of experience wherein the contents of experience are logically independent of their cause. So, in the familiar fashion, an experience can be a visual presentation as of a shiny red apple, whether that experience is a dream, a hallucination, or a veridical perceptual experience. Indeed, what we are directly aware of in experience are not external objects, but mental images or representations (*ākāra*), which can be caused in a variety of ways. Dreaming and perception alike involve the phenomenal presentation of experiential objects but differ in their causal constraints. As Vasubandhu argues in the *Viṃśatikā*, those general features of waking experience that the realist attributes to interaction with experience-independent objects can also be found in dreams, which both parties admit do not involve the apprehension of independent objects.

> Restriction as to place, etc. is demonstrated as in a dream. (3a) Now how is this? In a dream, even without an (external) object of sense or understanding, only certain things are to be seen: bees, gardens, women, men, etc. and these only in certain places, and not everywhere. And even there in those places, they are to be seen only sometimes, and not all the time. In this way, even without an (external) object of sense or understanding, there may be restriction as to place and time.
>
> (Viṃś-vṛ 2)

Moreover, the character of a representation derives from the capacities and conditioning of the mind that creates it. Thus, depending on the differences in their karmic conditioning, one being will experience crystal clear water, while another experiences a river of pus. "For all the *pretas* who are in a similar situation due to a similar retribution for action, and not just one of them, see a river filled with pus." This extreme difference in experiential contents is not explained by appeal to independently existing objects.

The stream of consciousness, then, is a causal process whereby virtual worlds of experience are brought forth moment by moment. The *cittasantāna* is in the business of dreaming up worlds of experience, whether we are asleep or awake. Yet, we are by default naïve realists about the virtual worlds our minds create. We do not recognize our mental constructs as mental constructs but take them to be mind-independent external objects. Thus, the fabricated nature here refers to the mentally constructed objects within the virtual world of experience. The dependent nature refers to the fact that, despite appearances, experiential objects are mind-dependent (both causally and constitutively). The dependent nature by extension also refers to those causal processes by which mental objects are constructed. Recognition of the absence of the constructed nature from the other dependent nature amounts to a recognition that the direct objects of experience are merely mental constructs or representations (*vijñāptimātra*) that continuously emerge from causal processes that we are not directly aware of. Seeing through to the true nature of experience, finally, is to experience the perfected nature.

There are two types of case that may help to understand Vasubandhu's position. The first type of case concerns persistent auditory hallucinations. People who suffer from persistent musical hallucinations often report that the music is experienced as if it were like any other music playing in their environment. It can be experienced as loud or quiet, as nearby or far away, as clear or muffled, and so on. While some people quickly realize that they are experiencing hallucinations, others remain for extended periods under the impression that their auditory experience is veridical. According to Paul Coates (Coates 2013), the transition process follows three stages. In the 'deceptive phase', the music is experienced as externally produced, spatially located, and public. Here the auditory experience is constructed as an external sound event. Eventually, in the 'transition phase' the subject realizes that the auditory experience does not correspond to bodily movements in the right way—moving toward or away from the apparent location of the sound does not change its sensory character—or that others can't hear it, and so forth. In the final 'realization phase', the subject has come to fully recognize the hallucination *as* a hallucination. What this involves, according to Coates, is a shift in the way the auditory phenomenon is automatically conceptualized. So, while the subject can still describe the various phenomenal features of the auditory phenomena (volume, pitch, timbre, and the like), she no longer takes it to be an objective sound event. It is important to see that, on Coates' view, this is not a merely intellectual change. Rather, because our experience involves an integration of sensory and cognitive aspects, a change in how a sensory phenomenon is automatically conceptualized is a change in the overall phenomenal character of the experience. What was experienced as an objective event is now experienced as an internal merely subjective event.

The second type of case is lucid dreaming. In cases of lucid dreaming, subjects are dreaming but are aware that they are dreaming and possess memory of both waking life and dream life, as well as the experience of attentional, cognitive, and behavioral agency (Windt and Metzinger 2007). The lucid dreamer recognizes the dream world as a dream world and therefore recognizes the virtual world of experience as virtual. This type of global recognition of the mind-dependent character of the dream world can also carry over into waking life such that waking is also experienced as dream-like. On the internalist-representationalist interpretation of Vasubandhu's Yogācāra—and following an analogy used in the tradition itself—the transformation at the basis (*āśrayaparāvṛtti*) associated with awakening is like the global recognition found in lucid dreaming. To realize the consummate nature is to have not just lucid dreaming, but lucid experiencing as such.

According to Yogācāra, what we are directly aware of in conscious experience are not observer-independent features of the external world, but mental images caused by the interaction between a broader causal nexus and our cognitive system. We are usually unaware of both the constructive activity of the mind in producing these images (*vijñapti*) and we are unaware that they *are* images, rather than external objects. The mind constructs a virtual world-model that is transparent to us. But Vasubandhu's view is more radical than many other internalist-representationalist views of the mind in that he applies the model of the three natures to the *subject* of experience as well. For him, the fundamental structure of the *parikalpita-svabhāva* is the subject-object framework itself. Like the observed objects, the observing self is a virtual construct (*kalpita-ātmanā*) of a cognitive system. Indeed, Vasubandhu will agree with the Nyāya (and Kantian) point that there is a deep interdependence between grasping an objective world and grasping oneself as a persisting subject of experience. It's just that, on his view, this goes to show that *both* are distorted mental fabrications, appearance-only (*vijñaptimātra*). As discussed in the last section, the sense of self arises from the way the cognitive system models itself and draws the self-other distinction. This is the *kliṣṭamanas* (afflictive mentation), which mistakes the selfless flow of the *ālayavijñāna* (base consciousness) for a persisting self. It is also the basis for the general sense of mental ownership and for thinking self-referential thoughts involving 'I', 'me', and 'mine' (and their contrasts). Yet, for Vasubandhu, there is no such *entity* as a self, only the self-model of an impermanent cognitive system. What we take to be the self is like an avatar in the virtual world created by the mind.

5.4 Nonduality

According to the analysis of phenomena in terms of three natures, the everyday world of our experience is constructed by more fundamental mental processes of which we are normally unaware. It *appears* as if there is a fixed and persisting self "in here" interacting with an independent world of objects "out there." However, on the Yogācāra view we've been considering, the world of everyday experience is in fact *vijñaptimātra* (appearance only) or *cittamātra* (mind/consciousness only). This claim has two important elements. First, experiential objects and subjects are mental in nature—subjects and objects are something like constructed mental images (*vijñapti*). Second, these mental images arise from causes and conditions that are themselves mental. Specifically, the mental contents of everyday experience arise from the base consciousness, which includes the traces left by prior moments of manifest experience. Hence Vasubandhu's bold claim that "the triple world [namely, the various worlds of experience] is mind-only."

Another important feature of the Yogācāra analysis is its thoroughgoing critique of the duality of subject and object, or "grasper and grasped" (*grāhaka-grāhya*). On the Yogācāra view, the sense of the reality and independence of subjects (or selves) and objects provides the basic framework for ordinary experience. Yet, on their view, this framework is a false construction. Indeed, in Yogācāra texts we find appeal to the Mahāyāna notion of emptiness (śūnyatā) in this context. The perfection of wisdom (*prajñāpāramitā*) involves insight into the emptiness of subject-object duality. Indeed, Vasubandhu argues in the *Treatise on the Three Natures* that the perfected nature, which is grasped by perfected wisdom, is the *absence* of the constructed nature (subject-object duality) from the dependent nature (the flow of mental events).

Emphasizing the emptiness of the subject-object duality may suggest a somewhat different interpretation of Yogācāra from the internalist-representationalist one presented in previous sections.[4] On this nondualist interpretation, we start, not from the constructed nature of experiential objects, but from the perfected nature of subject-object nonduality. The key to the nondualist interpretation is to see that Yogācāra constitutes a radical critique and revision of the notion of mentality or experience. Given our deeply entrenched realist and objectivist assumptions, it is hard to resist the idea that, in claiming that the phenomenal world is *vijñāptimātra*, the Yogācārins are positing experience as a veil of appearances between subject and world. But this is to confuse the *parikalpita* with the *paratantra*—that is, it conflates the fabricated distortion of experience with the real nature of experience itself. Experience (*vijñāna* or *anubhāva*) as *paratantra* is neither a medium nor a partition between the subjective and objective realms. It is the dynamic causal process out of which subjects and objects emerge. And since there is no subject apart from this more basic causal-experiential process, the process itself cannot serve as a medium or a veil between a subject and its world. On the nondualist interpretation, the problem with the internalist-representationalist approach is that the attempt to overcome the subject-object dichotomy by simply *internalizing* the phenomenal world is insufficiently radical. It tries to overcome the dichotomy by treating the mind as self-contained and therefore it does not transcend the subject-object or inside-outside duality, but rather absolutizes one side of it. Instead of the thoroughgoing interdependence of mind and world, the internalist-representationalist account of the three natures treats the mind as an autonomously intelligible domain.

The nondualist alternative, then, is to treat the distinctions between inside and outside, subject and object, mind and world as distinctions drawn *within* experience rather than *between* experience and something else. Moreover, on the nondualist understanding, Yogācāra constitutes a radical decentering of the subjective, first-person point of view. As the later Yogācārin, Sthiramati (c. sixth century CE), writes in the *Madhyāntvibhāgaṭīkā*, "Subjectivity (*grāhakatvam*) is not possible if no object (*grāhya*) exists." And, "Since there is no object in the absence of a subject, it is not possible for there to be a subject when there is no object" (Shaw 1987, 233). Within the *parikalpita* (or experience as *abhūtaparikalpita*) subjectivity and objectivity are mutually specifying, and so mentality cannot be understood as an autonomous, private domain. Subjectivity and objectivity are interdependent fabrications of the process of experience, and therefore the subject is always a subject-in-a-world. Additionally, the subject's world is a *shared* world, based on similarities in latent karmic tendencies within (relatively) distinct interacting streams of experience (*cittasantāna*).

Vasubandhu makes this point quite vividly in his *Viṃśatikā* (3–4), where he discusses hell realms and the human realm as projections of the similar negative karma of the beings that experience themselves as in those realms. According to the Buddhist cosmology Vasubandhu is drawing on in the *Viṃśatikā*, humans and *pretas* share a world, the human realm, which is a *bhājana-loka* or 'receptacle world'. They share an apparent physical locus and both perceive a river in the same place. However, Vasubandhu says, humans see clear water while *pretas* see puss. In contrast, hell-beings exist in a realm that is spatially distinct from the human realm, where they experience torture at the hands of demons. However, the demons are not independent beings in their own right, but rather collective projections of the negative karma of the poor beings in hell. The key point here, though, is that interacting causal-experiential streams co-create shared intersubjective worlds. And these shared worlds provide the context for on-going karmic activity, which in turn shapes the subjectivity of beings within these worlds. So while a dream experience may be understood as the imaginative play of an individual mind-stream, waking experience is understood as the intersubjective co-creation of shared (or overlapping) phenomenal worlds. On this account, the first-person perspective of the subject is not the privileged basis of experiential construction, but simply one more fabricated aspect of it. And individual subjectivity cannot be understood apart from intersubjectivity and shared phenomenal worlds.

Finally, it is important to appreciate the central role of conceptual-linguistic construction in the Yogācāra view. The construction of shared worlds of experience relies on the operations of various conceptual and linguistic imprints or predispositions: conceptual imprints (*vikalpavāsanā*), linguistic imprints (*abhilāpavāsanā*), and discursive imprints (*prapañcavāsanā*). These *vāsanās* are critical to the construction of shared worlds (*bhājana-loka*) and are themselves intersubjective. As we see in early Yogācāra, the *ālayavijñāna* has both individual (*asādhāraṇa*) and shared or common (*sādhāraṇa*) dimensions, and the conceptual and linguistic predispositions are directly associated with the common dimension. For the Yogācārins, to a large degree we share a common life-world because we share (mostly subpersonal) conceptual and linguistic schemas. This stated clearly in the *Saṃdhinirmocana Sūtra* (V.2):

> The mind with all the seeds (*ālayavijñāna*) matures, congeals, grows, develops, and increases based upon ... the substratum of the material sense-faculties along with their supports and the substratum which consists of the predispositions toward conceptual proliferation in terms of conventional usage of images, names, and conceptualizations.
>
> (Waldron 2003, 95)

The individual aspect of base consciousness is largely grounded in our sensory faculties, while the shared aspect is largely grounded in our conceptual-linguistic schemes. Furthermore, these cognitive predispositions suffuse (or 'perfume') our experience and play a central role in the fabrication of our subjectivity. Thus, it isn't just our shared world that is intersubjectively constructed, human subjectivity, on this account, is also conceptually and linguistically constructed.

Returning to Coates' three phases of recognizing a hallucination, on the nondualist view, the deceptive phase is just naïve realism about lived experience. We experience ourselves as isolated Cartesian subjects confronting other Cartesian subjects within a fully independent objective world. In the transition stage, we come to deeper understanding of the constructing and constructed nature of experience. This leads to the realization stage, a recognition that subjectivity, intersubjectivity, and objectivity are thoroughly interdependent co-constructions of causal-experiential processes that are both *beneath* and *beyond* subject and object. Reality, in so far as it can be positively characterized at all, is seen, to borrow a phrase from Timothy Sprigge, as "a vast system of interacting streams of experience," beyond all duality (Sprigge 2006, 484).

5.5 Comparative Connections

In this section we will discuss some recent work in philosophy and cognitive science that has interesting resonances with Yogācāra. This recent work has been dubbed by Jan Westerhoff "virtual world theory" (Westerhoff 2016) and is well-represented by the philosopher Thomas Metzinger (Metzinger 2009) and the cognitive scientist Donald Hoffman (Hoffman 2016). After discussing virtual world theory, we'll turn briefly to the question of philosophical idealism.

Virtual World Theory (VWT) is a version of what I have been calling an internalist-representationalist approach to the mind. The basic idea is that our conscious experience is a virtual world created by the brain. As Metzinger puts it, "The idea is that the content of consciousness is the content of a simulated world in our brains, and the sense of being there is itself a simulation" (Metzinger 2009, 23). It seems to us that we have direct experiential access to mind-independent objects in the world around, however, according to VWT we do not. Rather, experiential objects are items in a virtual world model, grounded in brain-based mental representations. Of course, in the normal case our mental representations are *transparent*—we do not experience them as representations at all. As Metzinger explains, "a representation is transparent if the system using it cannot recognize it as a representation. A world-model active in the brain is transparent if the brain has no chance of discovering that it is a model" (Metzinger 2009, 41). He goes on to say that our various mental representations are:

> seamlessly integrated into your overall conscious space of experience. Because it has been optimized over millions of years, this mechanism is so fast and so reliable that you never notice its existence. It makes your brain invisible to itself. You are in contact only with its content; you never see the representation as such; therefore, you have the illusion of being directly in contact with the world. And that is how you become a *naïve realist*, a person who thinks she is in touch with an observer-independent reality.
>
> (Metzinger 2009, 43)

The naïve realist believes that their consciousness is like a transparent window that allows them direct (namely, unmediated) access to observer-independent reality. In contrast, on Metzinger's view, the 'conscious space of experience' is like a digital screen displaying images based on a dynamic representation *model* (a "virtual world model") of the environment beyond the brain. The model is only transparent in the sense that we don't realize we're experiencing a model and not the independent world itself. In this sense the everyday level of experience in VWT is like the constructed or fabricated (*parikalpita*) nature of phenomena. The world model is constructed and it elides its construction, creating the "user illusion" of naïve realism. Further, the underlying neurocognitive processes, which Metzinger says are "optimized over millions of years," play a role like the dependent nature (*paratantra svabhāva*) in the Yogācāra theory.

So far, VWT looks like a contemporary form of indirect realism, a view defended in both India (for example, the Sautrāntika school discussed in Chapter 3) and the West. However, Metzinger's version of VWT has a deeper similarity to Yogācāra (and other Buddhist philosophies) in that he is a strong error-theorist about the self. As he bluntly states, "no such things as selves exist in the world: nobody ever had or was a self" (Metzinger 2004, 1). This is a straightforwardly ontological claim: selves do not exist. Whereas Patañjali, for example, thinks that the self exists but we are in error regarding its true nature, Metzinger sides with the Buddhist denial of the self as such. Yet Metzinger readily admits that it very much *seems* like we are selves. On his view, the sense of self or what he calls "phenomenal selfhood" is the product of an underlying process of self-modeling. That is, a particular cognitive system models or represents itself *as if* it were a self—an independent, enduring locus of consciousness, first-person perspective, agency, and so on. But, like the other content of the virtual world model, the self is only a virtual mental image. Metzinger writes:

> The brain is like a *total flight simulator,* a self-modeling airplane that, rather than being flown by a pilot, generates a complex internal image of itself within its own internal flight simulator. The image is transparent and thus cannot be recognized as an image by the system. Operating under the condition of a naive-realistic self-misunderstanding, the system interprets the control element in this image as a nonphysical object: The "pilot" is born into a virtual reality with no opportunity to discover this fact. The pilot is the Ego.
>
> (Metzinger 2009, 108)

The self-modeling aspect of the cognitive system, then, corresponds to the Yogācāra idea of the *kliṣṭamanas,* which *misrepresents* deeper mental processes as belonging to a real self. And, like Vasubandhu, Metzinger thinks that the self-world or subject-object framework is central to our ordinary experience. He argues, "we cannot mentally simulate the conscious experience of a world in which we are not present as selves, but which we nevertheless experience from a first-person perspective," and that "If anything grounds our naive-realistic world-view that reality is composed out of individual substances possessing intrinsic, context-invariant properties and standing in certain relations to each other, it is exactly the phenomenology of selfhood" (Metzinger 2011, 283).

Donald Hoffman and colleagues have developed their own distinct version of virtual world theory, which they call the interface theory of perception. Hoffman compares the contents of perceptual experience to the virtual desktop of a computer. The desktop serves as an interface between the user and the complex underlying functioning of the computer. The icons on the desktop are not (and are not meant to be) accurate pictorial representations of what's going on in the computer. The file icon has a shape, color, and spatial location on the desktop, but the computer file represented does not have any of these properties. As Hoffman and Prakash state, "So to even ask if the properties of the icon are true is to make a category error, and to completely misunderstand the purpose of the interface. One can reasonably ask whether the icon is usefully related to the file, but not whether it truly resembles the file" (Hoffman and Prakash 2014, 3). They continue:

> Turning now to apply the interface metaphor to human perception, the idea is that natural selection has not shaped our perceptions to be insights into the true structure and causal nature of objective reality, but has instead shaped our perceptions to be a species-specific user interface, fashioned to guide the behaviours that we need to survive and reproduce. Space and time are the desktop of our perceptual interface, and three-dimensional objects are icons on that desktop.
>
> (Hoffman and Prakash 2014, 4)

Like Metzinger, Hoffman thinks what we take to be a transparent window on the world is in fact an evolved representation, a "species-specific user interface." Further, Hoffman argues that these representations are geared toward survival and reproduction, not representational accuracy. As he puts it, "natural selection does not favor perceptual systems that see the truth in whole or in part. Instead, it favors perceptions that are fast, cheap, and tailored to guide behaviours needed to survive and reproduce. Perception is not about truth, it's about having kids" (Hoffman 2016, 155). In this respect, Hoffman's view differs from Metzinger's. Both reject naïve realism about perception in favor of an inner-representationalist account. But Hoffman goes further in arguing against representational accuracy. The truth or falsity of perception is beside the point and that kind of accuracy should not be confused with the relative *usefulness* of perception.

Virtual world theories like those of Metzinger and Hoffman immediately raise skeptical worries. If the objects, events, relations, and so on that figure in our everyday conscious experience are really items in a virtual model or species-specific user interface, then what reason do we have to think that we could gain knowledge of the external world or even to believe that the external world exists? Metzinger, at least, affirms that such knowledge is possible: "Of course, an external world does exist, and knowledge and action do causally connect us to it—but the conscious experience of knowing, acting, and being connected is an exclusively internal affair" (Metzinger 2009, 23). His support for this affirmation is that "if an internal representation of the system itself exists, according to the fundamental assumptions of any naturalist theory of mind there also has to exist a physical system which has generated it" (Metzinger 2004, 278). That is, the virtual world model (including the self-model) must be generated by some underlying system, and the scientific naturalist can assume that this is a physical system such as the brain. One might also argue that the best explanation for the regularity and coherence of our representations is the existence of an independent external (presumably) physical world.

In contrast, Hoffman takes a more radical approach to this issue. Based on his evolutionary interface theory, he argues that "space-time and three-dimensional objects have no causal powers and do not exist unperceived. Therefore, we need a fundamentally new foundation from which to construct a theory of objects" (Hoffman and Prakash 2014, 5). The new foundation is that consciousness is fundamental, and that the world consists entirely of interacting conscious agents. So, Metzinger accepts the reality of the physical world, treats consciousness as derivative, and rejects the existence of the self or conscious subject. Hoffman, on the other hand, denies the physical world, treats consciousness as fundamental, and affirms the (sole) reality of conscious subjects.

Let's now return to Yogācāra. Vasubandhu begins his Viṃś with the statement that "Everything in the three realms is only appearance (*vijñaptimātra*)." The three realms are the different worlds into which sentient beings are reborn, depending on their karma. In Vasubandhu's Yogācāra, these are worlds of experience, akin to dreams (or nightmares as the case may be). The experiential objects and subjects in these worlds are *vijñapti*, mental contents or experiential forms, not ontologically independent things. Hence, Vasubandhu might agree with Metzinger and Hoffman that our worlds of experience are merely virtual, despite our ingrained tendency to naïve realism. Crucially, in Yogācāra it is *both* subjects and objects that are virtual constructs. Thus Vasubandhu, like Metzinger, rejects the reality of the self and, like Hoffman, rejects the reality of an independent material world.[5] In this way, Yogācāra is more radical than the contemporary virtual world theories we've examined.

If, according to Yogācāra, the world of experience is not grounded in the brain (or some other physical system) or in a really existing self (or "conscious agent"), what grounds it? One answer would be that the world of experience is grounded in the *ālayavijñāna*. The *ālayavijñāna*, as we've seen, is a selfless flow of mental events from which the other seven layers of consciousness emerge. On this account, Yogācāra can be understood as a form of philosophical idealism in that it holds:

1) objects of experience are formed or constructed by the mind,
2) knowledge of the world depends on the constructive activity of the mind, and
3) reality is fundamentally mental, not physical.

Moreover, this idealism would be pluralistic in that the *ālaya* is analyzed in terms of momentary mental *dharmas* and because these mental *dharmas* form many relatively distinct but interacting streams. This form of idealism, then, is quite different from the strong monistic idealism of Advaita Vedānta (Chapter 6) or the theistic idealism of George Berkeley.

Another answer would not treat the *ālayavijñāna* as the ultimate ground of the experiential world. The reason has to do with Buddhist (especially Mahāyāna) views about the limitations of conceptual thought and language in grasping the true nature of things or suchness (*tathatā*). As Vasubandhu writes in the Vimś:

21. Awareness of other minds is illusory. How? Just like one's awareness of one's own mind. Because one's own mind is unknown to one in the manner in which it is known to the Buddhas.
22. I have established the doctrine of appearance-only according to my capacities; but it is in fact not thinkable in its entirety. It is grasped by the Buddhas.

The ultimate reality or suchness (*tathatā*) here is beyond thought, though grasped in the enlightened awareness of the Buddhas. So even a philosophically basic notion like the *ālaya* is in the end recognized as a limited conceptual construct. Finally, this interpretation might entail that consciousness is itself grounded in an ontologically fundamental but ineffable reality, somewhat like Immanuel Kant's notion of a noumenal reality. However, as Jan Westerhoff has argued (Westerhoff 2020), this interpretation might also lead to the rejection of the very idea of a fundamental ground, thereby affirming the Mahāyāna idea of the groundlessness of all phenomena.

5.6 Questions

1. What are the eight dimensions of mind or consciousness in Yogācāra? Does the addition of the 7th and 8th dimensions improve on the earlier Abhidharma theory?
2. What are the three natures of the phenomena? What role does the three natures view play in the Yogācāra account of experience?
3. What is the status of the external world in Yogācāra?
4. How is the *ālayavijñāna* similar to and different from a self?

Notes

1 Some Yogācāra texts include the *kliṣṭamanas* in the *pravṛttivijñāna* category because it is dependent on the *ālayavijñāna* and is not strictly uninterrupted in its operation.
2 The false view of the self (*atmadṛṣṭi*) is associated with the *kleśas* of greed, hatred, and ignorance, as well as self-love (*ātmasneha*), self-conceit (*ātmamana*), and self-delusion (*ātmamoha*).
3 This section draws from (MacKenzie 2018).
4 I make the case for this alternative interpretation in MacKenzie 2018, from which this section draws, as well as (MacKenzie 2022).
5 In the *Twenty Verses*, Vasubandhu responds to objections to his appearance-only view and offers positive metaphysical arguments against the independent reality of material objects. See (MacKenzie 2018) for further discussion of Vasubandhu's use of mereological arguments.

Further Reading

Anacker, Stefan. 2002. *Seven Works of Vasubandhu: The Buddhist Psychological Doctor*. Motilal Banarsidass.

Gold, Jonathan C. 2014. *Paving the Great Way: Vasubandhu's Unifying Buddhist Philosophy*. Columbia University Press.

Kachru, Sonam. 2021. *Other Lives: Mind and World in Indian Buddhism*. Columbia University Press.

Waldron, William S. 2003. *The Buddhist Unconscious: The Ālaya-Vijñāna in the Context of Indian Buddhist Thought*. 1st edition. Routledge.

Waldron, William S. 2023. *Making Sense of Mind Only: Why Yogācāra Buddhism Matters*. Simon and Schuster.

6

Advaita Vedānta

6.1 The Advaita Vedānta Tradition

Vedānta is one of the six orthodox (*āstika*) schools or textual traditions of classical Indian philosophy. The term *vedānta* means 'end' (*anta*) of the Vedas, referring to the Upaniṣads. Thus, Vedānta names the tradition (or really several related traditions) concerned with the interpretation, elaboration, and defense of the philosophical and spiritual teachings of the Upaniṣads. This tradition is also called Uttara Mīmāṃsā ("higher inquiry or exegesis") because it deals with the *jñānakāṇḍa* (knowledge section) of the Upaniṣads in contrast to its sister school, Pūrva Mīmāṃsā, which deals with the *karmakāṇḍa* (ritual action section) of those texts. The three major sub-schools of Vedānta are Dvaita (dualist), Viśiṣṭadvaita (qualified nondualist), and Advaita (nondualist), the last of which is the subject of this chapter.

While Advaita Vedānta may have its origins in the first or second century CE, the earliest systematic works of Advaita[1] are from the philosophers Gauḍapāda (sixth century CE) and Śaṅkara (eighth century CE). Gauḍapāda is best known for his *Māṇḍūkyakārikā*, a commentary on the *Māṇḍūkya Upaniṣad* which sets out the core tenets of Advaita Vedānta. Śaṅkara was a prolific writer and energetic promoter and defender of Advaita. He wrote commentaries on the triple canon of Advaita, namely the *Brahmasūtras*, *Bhagavadgītā*, and the ten principal Upaniṣads. He also wrote a commentary on Gauḍapāda's work and composed his own treatise, the *Upadeśasāhasrī* (*A Thousand Teachings*). He is purported to have travelled throughout India engaging in philosophical debates and establishing centers for the learning and practice of the Advaita tradition. According to tradition, he died at the age of 32 (Pande 1994).

As the name suggests, the Advaita school defends an ultimately nondualist view of reality. The central Advaita ideas are summed up in the saying from Śaṅkara's *Brahmajñānāvalīmālā* (20), *brahma satyam jagan mithyā jīvo brahmaiva nāparaḥ*.

> "*Brahman* is true, the world is false; the self is not different from *brahman*."

The ultimate reality is *brahman,* the transcendent and immanent divine source. The world (*jagat*), despite appearances, has no reality independent of *brahman.* The individual self (*jīva*) too may appear separate and independent, but in reality, it is not other than *brahman* itself. That is, *ātman* (the true self) is identical to *brahman* (the divine source). Direct knowledge of this identity is liberation (*mokṣa*).

Śaṅkara developed a rich and systematic philosophical articulation of these core Advaita ideas, and we will focus on his views in this chapter. More specifically, there are four main philosophical themes discussed in the remainder of the chapter. First, on Śaṅkara's Advaita view, the self (*ātman*) is pure consciousness. It is the non-relational, non-intentional witness (*sākṣin*) of all inner and outer objects of experience. As such, it is always subject, never an object. Second, this pure witness consciousness is distinct from the mind, and it is the source of identity amidst the changing states and contents of mental life. Third, while the world is ultimately none other than *brahman,* it has a practical reality and exists independent of any finite mind. Fourth, in the final analysis, *brahman* is the only reality, and it is pure nondual consciousness. Thus, there is only one absolute consciousness that appears as everyone and everything.

6.2 Consciousness as Witness

The *Bṛhadāraṇyaka Upaniṣad* describes the self (*ātman*) as:

> [T]he unseen seer, the unheard hearer, the unthought thinker, the unknown knower. There is no seer other than him, no hearer other than him, no thinker other than him, no knower other than him. He is your self, the inner controller, the immortal. Other than him is the sufferer.[2]
>
> (BU 7.23)

In the same text, the sage Yājñavalkya says:

> The self is indeed his [the person's] light; with the self as light, he sits, runs around, does his work and returns.
>
> The self is its own light; it is self-effulgent; it is self-luminous.
>
> (BU 3.7-8)

In these passages the self is the seer, hearer, thinker, knower, and inner controller. That is, the self is the subject and locus of mental life. And yet, the self is unseen, unheard, unknown, and so on. So, the self is both at the center of mental life and elusive, not being graspable in the same way as ordinary objects. As Yājñavalkya puts it, the self is like a light, providing the awareness (illumination) required to engage with the world. And in a familiar by now metaphor, the light of the self illuminates other objects and is at the same time self-luminous. The self is elusive because it cannot be found among the objects it illuminates, but it is undeniable in its self-manifest luminosity.

These Upaniṣadic ideas are given rigorous philosophical development in Advaita Vedānta. Śaṅkara argues that the self is pure consciousness. It is not a substance (*dravya*) that has consciousness as one of its qualities (*guṇa*). Nor is consciousness an act of the self. Rather, the self (*ātman*) *just is* consciousness (*cit, caitanya*). In Śaṅkara's terms, the relation between the self and consciousness is not inherence (*samavāya*), but identity (*tādātmya*). For him, consciousness is the very essence of the self.[3]

The light of the self is the light of consciousness. In ordinary experience the self is bound up with an individual body and mind. The integrated system of body, mind, and self is a *jīva*, an individual person or embodied subject of experience. In this context, Śaṅkara understands the self as the witness (*sākṣin*) of all outer and inner objects or contents of experience. He states, "[*ātman*] is consciousness, self-shining, the seeing, immediate awareness and inactive. [It] is the witness-consciousness directly cognized inside everybody, constant, qualityless, and nondual" (BrSūBh 2.18.26). But what does it mean to say that consciousness is the witness (*sākṣin*) or seer (*dṛṣṭā*)? Śaṅkara states, "A thing is the witness of another thing when the latter is experienced by the former. For an object which is not experienced by anyone, there is no need for positing witnesshood" (VC 215). So, the witness is that which experiences and the witnessed is that is experienced. Or, we might say, there is a distinction between what is *presented* and that *to which* it is present. Advaita thinkers explore this distinction through the practice of *dṛg-dṛśya viveka*, or inquiry into the "seer" and the "seen." Given this distinction, we can now ask what kinds of things might be presented to or within consciousness. In various contexts, Śaṅkara mentions, for instance: objects of perception, the body and its various states and actions, objects of thought, one's own mental states, and the sense of "I." Further, the various objects or contents of experience are quite variable. One can be aware of multiple distinct objects at one time and one can be aware of radically different things over time. And yet, whenever there is the presentation of an experiential object or content, there is (necessarily) that *to which* it is present—the witness.[4] On Śaṅkara's view, the witness is the unchanging subject or conscious perspective of the varied and changing contents. And if the various contents come and go, they are not of the essence of consciousness. As Bina Gupta argues, Śaṅkara seems to hold "the principle that anything that becomes an object of consciousness could not belong to the nature of consciousness" (2003, 103).[5] She continues:

> Things in the world or in nature (*prakṛti* or *saṃsāra*) come and go, arise, and last for some time (not necessarily for an instant), and perish; they are different from each other and they contain internal differences as well. But all these entities are known by consciousness, so consciousness is radically different from them, as light is from darkness.
>
> (Gupta 2003, 103–4)

The notion of consciousness as pure witness distinct from all contents or objects, then, has several important philosophical implications.

First, the distinction between consciousness and objects implies that consciousness cannot be given as an object. On the Advaita view, awareness of an object requires the object, a mental state that takes the form of the object (namely, represents it), and consciousness, which apprehends the mental state and its represented object. Hence, awareness of an object involves transitive intentionality, that is, it involves a mental state that is *of* or *about* a distinct object. The intentional object is given *through* or *by way of* a mental state which grasps the object in virtue of having a particular intentional content or representational form.[6] This form is apprehended by (witness-) consciousness as that *to which* the intentional mental state represents. In other words, we have a connection between the seer, the seeing, and the seen. In the case of visual perception, for instance, there might be a jar (the object), a visual perception of the jar, and the consciousness in which the seeing and the seen are given. Following Itay Shani, we may refer to the *accusative* and the *dative* aspects of experience. He writes,

> I maintain that conscious intentional acts exhibit two complementary sides: a transeunt perceptive aspect, which provides for the grasping of intentional objects; and an immanent receptive aspect, which serves as the subjective ground for the unfolding of contentful streams of experience. Put differently, the distinction pertains to two complementary ways consciousness is, in that consciousness reaches out to grasp its objects while, at the same time, being the addressee to whom things are given and in whom they are presented. I call these two antipodes of experience the accusative mode, and the dative mode, respectively.
>
> (Shani 2024, 183)

Given this distinction, we can see why witness-consciousness eludes objectification. To be given as an object (at least in the standard case) entails being given as distinct from both the mental state that represents it and the subject to which it is given. If a mental state were to represent consciousness itself as an object, that would still require a distinct subject (or dative "addressee"). In other words, with regard to itself consciousness cannot occupy the accusative mode and the dative mode at the same time.[7] Indeed, the Advaitin would go further, insisting that witness-consciousness as the dative mode cannot be captured through the accusative mode at all. Anything that is an object is distinct from that which is the subject or dative of all manifestation (*svapracāra sākṣī*).[8]

Second, consciousness must be self-luminous and self-evident. Since consciousness is not an object, one might think that it is therefore unknown or unknowable. However, Advaitins hold that consciousness or the self is self-evident. Consciousness of objects entails consciousness, even if consciousness itself is not an object. And even to deny consciousness presupposes it. So how is consciousness itself known? It is known by its own intransitive self-luminosity. It manifests itself in manifesting its objects. And it manifests itself *subjectively*—that is, as the subject, witness, or "subjective ground"— while it manifests all other things *objectively*. This self-luminous aspect of consciousness is presupposed by all other cognitive processes that take place within consciousness experience. Hence, none of those other modes could be the source of basic self-knowledge.

Indeed, Śaṅkara argues in the *Brahmasūtrabhāṣya*, it is consciousness itself that is self-luminous rather than the various mental states or processes. As discussed in the next section, on an Advaita view, consciousness is distinct from the various mental states (*vṛttis*) it illuminates. For a mental state to be *conscious*, it must be revealed to or illuminated for the subject. Śaṅkara, then, would accept the Transitivity Principle that a mental state is conscious just in case the subject is in an appropriate way aware of it. Yet, he explicitly rejects the view of the Buddhist reflexivists (see Chapter 7) that conscious mental states are self-illuminating. He does so on the grounds that a reflexive or self-illuminating cognition would have to act on itself. He writes, "Then like assuming that fire burns itself, you [the Buddhist] assume that something can act on itself by itself, which is absolutely opposed to reason" (BrSūBh 2.2.28). In response the Buddhist argues:

> If a cognition has to be known by some entity other than itself, that second one will have to be known by another, and that one again by another. This will lead to an infinite regress. Moreover, since cognition is an illuminator like a lamp, if you should imagine a second cognition (to know it), then since both the cognitions are similar there will be no

revelation of the one by the other, so that this whole assumption will fall
to the ground.

(Ibid.)

That is, if to be conscious, a transitive or object-directed mental state must
be revealed by another transitive mental state, then a vicious regress looms.
On other hand, if transitive mental states are not conscious by nature (or
intrinsically conscious), how does one unconscious state manage to make
the other conscious?

In response, Śaṅkara states:

> Both these arguments are wrong, for once an awareness of the cognition
> occurs, no further desire to apprehend the witness of the cognition
> can arise; and so there is no possibility of infinite regress. And since
> the witness and the cognition are different by nature, there can be a
> relationship of the perceiver and the perceived among them. Besides, the
> self-evident witness cannot be denied. There is another consideration.
> When you assert that cognition shines by itself like a lamp without
> requiring some other cognition, you virtually say that a cognition is
> not apprehended by any other means of knowledge or by anything else,
> which would be like saying that a thousand lamps shine (unknown)
> within a massive boulder.

(BrSūBh 2.2.28)

On Śaṅkara's view, the various transitive mental states ("cognitions") are
directly present (*pratyaktva*) to their subject, witness-consciousness. The
various transitive mental states are apprehended directly by the intransitively
conscious subject. No mediation by second-order mental states is required
and so no regress looms. Moreover, according to Śaṅkara, cognitions can
only be conscious when they are apprehended by their subject. Otherwise,
they are like lamps shining unseen. In other words, the various "accusative"
cognitions are not conscious unless they are apprehended or received by the
"dative" subject.

Third, consciousness is prior to and more fundamental than any of its
contents. As Śaṅkara states, "The Self is changeless and all-pervading on
account of It being the witness of the functions of the mind" (Upad. XV.17).
The various states of the mind (*antaḥkaraṇa*) come and go, and they are only
conscious when revealed by the light of witness-consciousness. Thus, on
Śaṅkara's view, the light of consciousness must be unchanging or constant to
serve as the unified subject of the various mental states at a time and over time.
Like the sun, the self shines continuously. In this way, the self or witness is the

subjective ground of the synchronic (at a time) and diachronic (over time) unity of mental life or experience. Regarding synchronic unity, the various mental states are all given or present to the single conscious perspective of the witness. They are parts of the same field of consciousness because they are illumined by the same source. Regarding diachronic unity, mental states that arise at different times within the same stream of experience are unified in that they have the same persisting subject.

On Śaṅkara's view, then, the temporal continuity of consciousness is not grounded in the various mental states or other "functions of the mind" including memory. Rather, these states and functions presuppose or are grounded in the temporal continuity of consciousness. This is in sharp contrast to the Buddhist approach which denies that mental continuity requires a persisting consciousness or self. Against a Yogācāra Buddhist opponent Śaṅkara argues:

> The mental impressions must have an abode. Without that they cannot exist. But the doctrine of momentariness denies permanency to everything. Even the *ālayavijñāna* is momentary and cannot be that abode. Unless there is a permanent principle connecting the past, present, and future, there cannot be remembrance or recognition of an experience originating at a particular time and place. If the *ālayavijñāna* is said to be something permanent, then that would go counter to the doctrine of momentariness.
>
> (BrSūBh 2.2.5)

A series of momentary mental events, even if causally connected, does not yet constitute an experientially continuous stream of consciousness. And yet, the argument goes, this is what is needed for the exercise (or even possibility) of such mental capacities as recognition or memory. That is, on Śaṅkara's view, one cannot remember or recognize what one has not previously experienced. This presupposes that it was the *same* subject (or witness-consciousness) that experienced and later remembers.

Śaṅkara further argues that the phenomenon of recognition implies the persistence of both the subject and objects. Against the Buddhist idea that all things are momentary he writes:

[Śaṅkara]:   Your statement that every moment a different jar in contact with light is produced, is wrong, for even at a subsequent moment we recognise the same jar.

[Buddhist]:   The recognition may be due to similarity, as in the case of hair, nails, etc. that have been cut and have grown anew.

[Śaṅkara]:   No, for even in that case the momentariness is disproved.... .
In the case of a jar etc. we perceive that they are identical.
Therefore the two cases are not parallel.

When a thing is directly recognised as identical, it is improper to infer that it is something else, for when an inference contradicts perception, the ground of such inference becomes fallacious. Moreover, the perception of similarity is impossible because of the momentariness of knowledge (held by you). The perception of similarity takes place when one and the same person sees two things at different times. But according to you the person who sees a thing does not exist till the next moment to see another thing, for consciousness, being momentary, ceases to be as soon as it has seen some one thing. To explain: The perception of similarity takes the form of "This is like that." "That" refers to the remembrance of something seen: "this" to the perception of something present. If after remembering the past experience denoted by "that," consciousness should linger till the present moment referred to by "this," then the doctrine of momentariness would be gone. If, however, the remembrance terminates with the notion of "that," and a different perception relating to the present (arises and) dies with the notion of "this," then no perception expressed by, "This is like that," will result, as there will be no single consciousness perceiving more than one thing. Moreover, it will be impossible to describe our experiences. Since consciousness ceases to be just after seeing what was to be seen, we cannot use such expressions as, "I see this," or "I saw that," for the person who has seen them will not exist till the moment of making these utterances.

(BUBh IV.3.7)

In this passage, Śaṅkara is making the following points. First, in the case of a (seemingly) persisting object, such as a jar, we perceive that it is identical, not merely similar. When one looks at a jar, looks away, and then looks at it again, the two perceptions of the jar are given as perceptions of one and the same jar. Moreover, when one walks around a jar, each profile is perceived as a profile of the same jar. Second, the Buddhist is faced with a dilemma. Because perception of similarity (or identity) requires comparison between an earlier and a later percept, either there is a single enduring consciousness that has both perceptions and the doctrine of momentariness is false, or there is no enduring consciousness, and each perceptual event is locked in the solipsism of the present moment. In the latter case, no perception of similarity is possible. Third, Śaṅkara argues that if consciousness is momentary, then there can be no diachronic continuity of the first-person perspective. Furthermore, note that Śaṅkara sees a deep phenomenological connection between the experience of persisting objects and the experience of oneself as a persisting subject. Thus, on Śaṅkara's view, one must either accept an enduring self or consciousness or be faced with an experientially disconnected series of mental events.

As we have seen so far, Śaṅkara (and Advaita more generally) holds that consciousness is the basis for temporal continuity and diachronic identity, and that consciousness is the essence of the self. The combination of these views creates an interesting problem. If the very nature or essence of the self is continuous consciousness, what about apparent periods of *unconsciousness* such as dreamless sleep or coma? It certainly *seems* that we have periods of unconsciousness. But if the inner light of consciousness shines continuously, then this rules out strict unconsciousness. According to the Nyāya school, consciousness is a property or capacity of the self, not its essence. As discussed in Chapter 2, they also held a strictly other-directed view of the intentionality of consciousness and a higher-order view of self-consciousness. On this view, in deep sleep the self is not cognitively connected to the external world through the senses, nor is the mind (*manas*) producing images as in a dreaming sleep. In the absence of contact with objects or other forms of mental activity, the self's capacity for consciousness is not activated. So, the self is unconscious. Furthermore, diachronic personal identity is preserved by the enduring existence of the self, regardless of consciousness. It is the same person who goes into dreamless sleep and wakes up because the substantial self-endures through states of consciousness and unconsciousness.

In contrast, the Advaita (and Yoga) view is that consciousness remains across the three distinct states of waking (*jāgrat*), dreaming (*svapna*), and dreamless sleep (*suṣupti*). In the states of waking and dreaming, there are various phenomenal contents and objects presented to consciousness. In dreamless sleep however, witness consciousness is disconnected from the mind and body. Thus, no objects or contents are presented. Like a light that shines in a completely empty room, consciousness continues to shine by its nature even in the absence of mental contents. As Śaṅkara explains:

The individual soul (*jīva*) is called awake as long as being connected with the various external objects by means of the modifications of the mind—which thus constitute limiting adjuncts of the soul—it apprehends those external objects, and identifies itself with the gross body, which is one of those external objects. When, modified by the impressions which the external objects have left, it sees dreams, it is denoted by the term 'mind.' When, on the cessation of the two limiting adjuncts (i.e. the subtle and the gross bodies), and the consequent absence of the modifications due to the adjuncts, it is, in the state of deep sleep, merged in the Self as it were, then it is said to be asleep (resolved into the Self).

(BrSūBh I.1.9)

On this account, we might say that in dreamless sleep consciousness reverts to its ground state, which for Śaṅkara is the true nature of the self.[9]

The Advaita (and Yoga) view is counterintuitive because, upon waking, we seem to recognize a temporal gap in our experience. Upon waking in the morning, I may remember drifting off to sleep and part of a dream I had in the night, but I also recognize that there is a time gap between waking and the last thing I remember. Doesn't that prove I was unconscious during that stretch of time? Perhaps not. According to Śaṅkara:

There is distinct cognition of gross and subtle objects respectively in *jāgrat* [waking] and in *svapna* [dreaming]. But during sleep, when the dream is over, there is no sense-organ activity, and there is a stillness of the mind, *manolaya*. So there is no discriminative awareness of objects. There is no *viseśajñāna* because the sense-organs have subsided into their activating causes. Is the *cit* which is the *ātman* present then? Does it shine? Yes … It does in the same way as the sun and moon do during an eclipse, not brightly however, but hidden by the eclipsing agent. Though sun and moon are invisible during the eclipse, we infer their continued existence abiding before, during and after the eclipse. We say that during the eclipse the sun was the same as it was before and that it shines after it is over. Even so, in the case of the man who sleeps, his *cit* is shrouded by *māyā*. When he wakes from his sleep, he establishes in his consciousness a continuity of his personal identity before, during, and after sleep. This gives expression to when, on waking from his sleep, he says: I slept happily; I did not know anything. The awareness of self-identity is called *pratyabhijñā*. (*Dakṣiṇāmūrtistotra* 6)

(Sharma 2012, 60)

In short, on Śaṅkara's account, if I can say (correctly) "I slept happily; I did not know anything," this implies a continuity of consciousness even in deep sleep. Thus, my sense of having slept happily and dreamlessly is a kind of memory, a memory of the *absence* of objects of consciousness. Moreover, upon waking I have the sense of the continuity of personal identity—I waking up feeling like the same person who went to sleep the night before. In contrast to this line of reasoning, Nyāya philosophers argue that the thought "I slept happily; I did not know anything" is based on inference, not memory. We implicitly infer that we slept soundly based on the *gap* in awareness (and perhaps a current feeling of being refreshed). However, from an Advaita perspective, such an inference would not account for the felt continuity of consciousness across a (supposed) gap, nor would the inference be sufficient to justify the belief in personal identity across the gap.[10]

6.3 Mind, Body, World

Like the Sāṅkhya and Yoga schools, Advaita Vedānta defends an ontological and phenomenological distinction between consciousness (*cit*) and mind (*manas, antaḥkaraṇa*). According to Advaita consciousness has several important features:

1. It is the very nature of the self.
2. It is self-luminous and self-evident.
3. It is the ultimate subject or witness of all objects and contents.
4. It unifies experience at a time (synchronically).
5. It unifies experience over time (diachronically).
6. It is a condition of the possibility conscious mental states, processes, and contents.
7. It is immaterial and fundamental.

In contrast, the mind is neither immaterial nor fundamental. As in the Sāṅkhya and Yoga schools, mind is generated by nature (*prakṛti*) through the interweaving of the three *guṇas*: *sattva*, *rajas*, and *tamas*. The mind is a form of subtle matter (*sattva*) that, like a clear reflective surface, can reflect the light of consciousness. It is also a natural, integrated system of mental processes and states that mediates between the body and world on the one hand, and the self on the other.

Advaita thinkers divide the mind into four main functions (Rao 2017). The first is *buddhi*, the intellect or intelligence. This aspect of the mind includes functions like discrimination, discernment, and knowing or cognition. *Buddhi* is the subtlest and highest function of the mind, and this aspect is the most receptive to consciousness. On the Advaita view, *buddhi* is a reflection (*pratibimba*) of consciousness and therefore takes on the appearance or semblance (*ābhāsa*) of consciousness itself. That is, it seems to us that our intelligence is inherently conscious and may even be the self (i.e., "I am this intelligence"). However, *buddhi* is in fact distinct from the self and merely reflects the inherent light of consciousness. The second aspect of the mind is *manas*. This aspect includes the sensory, affective, and conative states and processes. For example, *manas* integrates the sensory inputs from the different external senses, making them available for other mental processes such as recognition or belief formation. It is sometimes called the lower aspect of the mind because it deals with sensation, perception, feeling, and conative states such as desire. In contrast, *buddhi* deals with higher-order functions like judgment or decision-making. The third aspect is *ahaṃkāra* ("I-maker"), which is responsible for the basic sense of an individual self and mental ownership. When I think "I am six feet tall" or "these thoughts are mine," the thoughts are a function of the *ahaṃkāra*. The fourth aspect of the mind is *citta*, which here means the recollective function of mind, especially memory.

According to Advaita, then, the human psyche is constituted by these four integrated functions, centered on and illuminated by the self as pure consciousness. Yet, if the self is both independent of the mind and self-evident, why should there be a distinct *mental* function like the *ahaṃkāra*? Shouldn't the sense of self or the "I" be an inherent aspect of the witness-conscious itself? In response to these questions, it is important to note that for the Advaitin there are distinct layers or levels of self-consciousness or of the sense of self. When I think "I am hungry," "these are my hands," or "I have blue eyes," I am identifying with my body. Yet, according to Advaita, I am not my body. When I think "I feel sad," "I see a cat," or "I have a great idea," I am identifying with my mind and its contents. Yet, I am not my mind. In these cases, the sense of "I" results from a kind of blending or fusion of the self and the not-self that is ultimately a form of ignorance (*avidyā*). The *ahaṃkāra* helps to specify how this fusion takes place. The function of the *ahaṃkāra* is to allow the mind to organize itself around a central self-representation, a representation of the mind as (in Śaṅkara's terms) the 'knower, doer, and enjoyer'. And this self-representational cognitive structure also reflects the inherent light of consciousness (the true self) creating the false impression that the self-representing *mind* is the locus of the conscious self. Moreover, it is also important to recall that Advaita is an ultimately nondualist view. Thus, in its ultimate nature pure consciousness (*śuddha caitanya*) is not localized and individuated. Therefore, the localized and individuated sense of self arises from a process of limitation (*avaccheda*) that depends in part on the association between consciousness as such and the body-mind.

Regarding the body, the Advaita school distinguishes three modes or layers of embodiment, each layer of which is called a body (*śarīra*).[11] The first layer is the gross body (*sthūla śarīra*). This is the flesh and blood physical body with its external sense organs and the 'organs of action' such as the hands, feet, and vocal apparatus. The gross body is associated with the 'food sheath' (*annamaya kośa*), since it is sustained by and made from material elements. It is subject to biological processes such as birth, growth, disease, and death. It is also associated with the waking state. The second layer is the subtle body (*sūksma śarīra*). This covers the less tangible or observable functions, capacities, and states of the embodied person. The subtle body is subdivided into three sheaths (*kośa*). The vital sheath (*prānamaya kośa*) includes processes such as digestion, respiration, and circulation which constitute the various life functions. The mental sheath (*manomaya kośa*) includes the processes of the *manas*, such as sensation, feeling, and conation. The intellectual sheath (*vijñānamaya kośa*) is associated with *buddhi* and its higher cognitive functions. The subtle body is also associated with the state of dreaming. On this account, then, the mind is a subtle aspect of embodiment continuous with the biological processes of life. The third layer of embodiment is the causal body (*kārana śarīra*). This is the subtlest layer, covering the latent or unmanifest aspects of embodiment. These include various tendencies (*vāsanās*), memories, and positive and negative karmic traces.[12] It is also the locus of the deep ignorance (*avidyā*) or cognitive distortion that gives rise to the appearance of duality, individuated identity, and so on. The causal body is associated with deep sleep when only these subtlest mental functions continue. Further, the causal body includes the bliss sheath (*ānandamaya kośa*), which is connected to feelings of peace and bliss as in deep sleep or certain quiescent meditative states.

Beyond the mind and body, Advaitins affirm the empirical reality of the world independent of the mind. That is, everyday objects like trees, pots, or houses exist and they exist independently of their being perceived or otherwise cognized by any finite mind. Thus, Śaṅkara argues against the Yogācāra/Vijñānavāda view that objects of perception are in fact internal mental images rather than everyday objects. Recall from Chapter 5 that, for a Yogācārin like Vasubandhu, what we take to be mind-independent perceptual objects are really *vijñaptis*—mental constructs that emerge from the complex confluence of sensation, mental construction, and latent tendencies carried by the *ālayavijñāna* (storehouse consciousness). Further, Yogācārins argue that mind-independent external objects would be imperceptible and that, being neither identical to nor different from their parts, we should reject their existence in any case. As Vasubandhu argues, perceptual objects are like objects in a dream: they appear to be mind-independent and external but are in fact internal object-images created by deeper mental processes.

In response, Śaṅkara argues that this view misconstrues the nature of perception. He claims that in normal perceptual experience we are presented with external objects, and we can distinguish between, say, the seeing and the thing seen. He writes, "something other than the perception has to be admitted perforce, just because it is perceived. Not that anybody cognizes a perception to be a pillar, a wall, and the like, rather all people cognize a pillar, a wall, and the like as objects of perception" (BrSūBh 2.2.28). The distinction between the perception and the object perceived is fundamental to the phenomenological structure of perception. Indeed, Śaṅkara goes on to say that the Buddhist smuggles this phenomenology into his view when he claims that objects "appear external." On Śaṅkara's view, the basic distinction between perception and its distinct objects has perceptual warrant.[13] Furthermore, objects are perceived through multiple senses, across time, and by more than one person. We are therefore warranted in believing they are real and independent of our mental states.

Additionally, Śaṅkara argues that the Buddhist dream analogy is inapt. He states, "It has been said by those who deny the existence of external things that perceptions of things like a pillar and the like. in the waking state occur even in the absence of external things, just as they do in a dream; for as perceptions, they are similar. That has to be refuted." On his view dream states and waking states are different in nature. Śaṅkara writes:

> In what does that difference consist? We say that it consists in being subject to sublation or not. To a man, arisen from sleep, the object perceived in a dream becomes sublated, for he says, "Falsely did I imagine myself in contact with great men. In fact I never came in contact with great men; only my mind became overpowered by sleep; and thus this delusion arose." So also in the case of magic etc., adequate quate sublation takes place. But a thing seen in the waking state, a pillar for instance, is not thus sublated under any condition.
>
> (BrSūBh 2.2.29)

According to this line of reasoning, the waking state provides an epistemic perspective that assimilates and corrects (sublates, *bādha*) the dreaming state. When I wake up, I realize that the dream object was not real, while the objects I encounter in waking experience are not overturned by future empirical experience. Of course, Śaṅkara is not denying that we can be mistaken in waking experience. A later experience can correct a *misperception*. But it does not correct a *perception*. Śaṅkara continues:

> Moreover, dream vision is a kind of memory, whereas the visions of the waking state are forms of perceptions (through valid means of knowledge). And the difference between perception and memory, consisting in the presence and absence of objects, can be understood by

oneself, as for instance when one says, "I remember my beloved son, but I do not see him, though I want to see." That being so, it cannot be asserted by a man, who feels the difference of the two, that the perception of the waking state is false, merely on the ground that it is a perception like the perception in a dream. And it is not logical for those who consider themselves intelligent to deny their own experience.

(Ibid.)

Dreaming is like memory in that objects can be brought to mind without actually being present. I may dream of or remember a dearly departed loved one without that loved one being present or even still existing. I may dream of or remember a fictional character who has never existed. However, according to Śaṅkara (genuine) perception requires the actual presence of the perceived object. And this difference, he maintains, is available to the subject herself. Indeed, on Śaṅkara's view, it is part of the *nature* of perception that it reveals a real object, whereas it is not part of the nature of either memory or dreaming that it can reveal an actually present (or existent) object. So, pointing out that dreaming can occur in the absence of external objects is beside the point when it comes to perception. Moreover, as mentioned above, Śaṅkara thinks that the mere appearance of externality (as in dreaming) is parasitic on a more fundamental grasp of externality in waking perceptual experience. As Chakravarthi Ram-Prasad explains Śaṅkara's view, "Waking experience is required for the concept of externality, before externality can coherently be denied of dreams. It is thus incoherent to deny the externality of that (waking) experience from which the very concept of externality was first derived" (Ram-Prasad 2013, 59).

6.4 Nonduality

As discussed in the previous section, Advaita Vedānta thinkers maintain a distinction between consciousness as such (*cit*) and the empirical world (*jagat*), including the body and mind. Śaṅkara criticizes the Vijñānavāda or Yogācāra Buddhists for denying the reality of external objects and the enduring self. In these respects, Advaita is in line with realist perspectives found in Nyāya, Sāṅkhya, and Yoga. However, recall that the short summary of the Advaita view is:

brahma satyam jagan mithyā jīvo brahmaiva nāparaḥ.
    "*Brahman* is true, the world is false; the self is not different from *brahman*."

How can Advaita defend the existence of the world and the individual self (*jīvātman*) and yet proclaim that the world is "false" (*mithyā*) and the self is identical to the ultimate ground of reality (*brahman*)? In other words, how can Advaita reconcile the empirical world with nondual *brahman*?

The Advaita tradition proposes that the empirical world and *brahman* can be reconciled through distinguishing levels or layers of reality (and knowledge). *Brahman* is ultimate reality (*paramārthikasattā*), the fundamental existence ontologically prior to space, time, causality, and change. The empirical world is at the level of *vyāvahārikasattā* (practical reality). This is the level of intersubjective experience, practical engagement, individuated objects and subjects, and causation. Importantly, individual persons exist at this level and are parts of the larger causal order of the world they inhabit. Thus, the empirical world transcends the minds of empirical individuals, who must deploy the various reliable means of knowledge (*pramāṇas*) to gain knowledge of the world. This contrasts with the level of *pratibhāsika* (illusion), consisting of mere appearances such as mirages, dream objects, illusions, and so on. Ontologically, the *pratibhāsika* is not a level of reality or existence, but of subjective appearance. Epistemologically, the level is sublated (*bādha*) by the *vyāvahārika* epistemic standpoint. For example, in poor lighting a coiled rope in the corner may appear to be a snake. But on closer inspection, one sees that it is in fact a rope (MK 2.17–18). The second experience corrects the first, giving an adequate empirical perspective on the object in the corner of the room. The rope appeared to be a snake, but the snake-appearance was not anything real.

The empirical world, then, exists as an intermediate domain between mere illusion (*pratibhāsika*) and ultimate reality (*paramārthikasattā*). It is neither entirely real nor entirely unreal. It is not entirely (or ultimately) real because it is dependent and transient. It is not entirely unreal because it appears and functions independently of the minds of finite knowers. Śaṅkara draws on an analogy from the Upaniṣads to illustrate the ontological status of the empirical domain. The relationship between the empirical world and *brahman* is like that between a pot and the clay from which it is made. In particular, the pot depends for its existence on the clay, but the clay does not depend for its existence on the pot. That is, the pot is asymmetrically dependent on the clay. Also, the pot is a transient form (*rūpa*) of the clay. The clay can exist before and after its formation into a pot. (Or we might think of a lump of gold shaped into a statue and then melted down into a lump of gold again.) We call a particular configuration of clay a 'pot' because that form is useful for us. However, it is merely a particular name (*nāma*) attached to a particular form (*rūpa*) of a more basic substance (*dravya*). On Śaṅkara's view, the empirical world is likewise merely *nāmarūpa*, name and form. There are various relatively stable patterns and configurations that we pick out with our concepts and words. But all these forms are transient and depend on a more fundamental reality, *brahman.*

Of course, upon further analysis, clay is also a form. We can analyze the clay into its molecular, then atomic, then sub-atomic components. These components themselves appear to be dependent transient patterns, and so on. Perhaps reality is nothing but dependent transient forms all the way down. However, according to Śaṅkara and other Advaitins, the many dependent and transient forms must be grounded in a fundamental (and unitary) reality. This is linked to their *satkāryavāda* theory of causation, according to which the effect in some way exists in the cause. That is, the primary paradigm of causation is the modulation or transformation of an underlying substance, such as a wave forming in the medium of water or the culturing of milk into yogurt. On this picture, the whole empirical world of plurality is an interconnected network of forms emerging from what Jessica Frazier (2024) calls the "object-constituting medium" of *brahman.*

Given this picture, what is the ontological status of the empirical world? The world of forms is transient and dependent on a deeper reality, so it cannot be ultimately real. It has (at best) a secondary ontological status. So, is the empirical world *real*?[14] Śaṅkara argues that the world has an indeterminable (*anirvacanīya*) status. It is neither ultimate (it is not 'really real') nor mere illusion. It is deceptive in that it appears to exist separately from *brahman*, but it does not. However, the world can be accorded a practical (*vyāvahārika*) and epistemic reality consistent with its ontologically derivative status. Later Advaita thinkers often appeal to the principles of *māyā* (illusion, appearance) and *avidyā* (ignorance) in this context.[15] Here *māyā* is both the creative power of appearing and the collective name for the names and forms which appear. *Avidyā* here is the fundamental ignorance that construes the empirical world as separate or ontologically different from *brahman*.[16] Chakravarthi Ram-Prasad characterizes Advaita broadly as a form of "non-realism." He explains:

Non-realism, in conclusion, grants that there can be no account of experience of the world that explicitly denies externality, determinacy and independent existence. In this way, it saves the appearance of the world, that world in which the sacred texts are found, in which knowledge for the sake of liberation can be sought, and action to remove impediments to liberation can be performed. On the other hand, non-realism argues that externality, determinacy and independent existence cannot coherently be defended, and, therefore, that it cannot be established that the world is irreducibly real (elementary to reality). Since all that is required for liberating knowledge and action is an assumption (i.e., the refusal to deny) externality, determinacy and independent existence, the ultimate impossibility of establishing them is not a worry for soteriology. Indeed, this opens the way for undergoing transformation in consciousness that transcends this world and our experience of it.

(Ram-Prasad 2013, 14–15)

Returning to the issue of consciousness, Advaita philosophers maintain that pure nondual consciousness is the very nature of *brahman*. Following the Upaniṣadic formulation, *brahman* (in so far as it can be positively characterized) is *sat* (being), *cit* (consciousness), *ānanda* (bliss). As we have discussed throughout this chapter, at the empirical level, consciousness is understood to be the witness (*sākṣin*) of the varying contents of outer and inner experience. Object-directed cognition is a function of the mind, but that cognition is illuminated by witness consciousness. Further, witness consciousness constitutes the unified subjectivity to which all contents are given and around which mental life is organized. At the ultimate level, consciousness is beyond individuation. Ultimately there is only one absolute consciousness beyond any distinction between subject and object or between separate subjects. And since there is only one consciousness, there is only one self (*ātman*) which is strictly identical to *brahman*.

If there is ultimately only one self which is absolute consciousness, what accounts for the appearance of distinct individual selves (*jīvātman*)? Here Advaita philosophers adopt and adapt the theory of reflection (*pratibimba*). Śaṅkara writes:

And that individual soul is to be considered a mere appearance of the highest Self, like the reflection of the sun in the water; it is neither directly that (i.e. the highest Self), nor a different thing. Hence just as, when one reflected image of the sun trembles, another reflected image does not on that account tremble also; so, when one soul is connected with actions and results of actions, another soul is not on that account connected likewise. There is therefore no confusion of actions and results. And as that "appearance" is the effect of Nescience, it follows that the *saṃsāra* which is based on it (the appearance) is also the effect of Nescience, so that from the removal of the latter there results the cognition of the soul being in reality nothing but Brahman.

(BrSūBh 2.3.50)

The single light of absolute consciousness is reflected in a variety of reflective media without ever losing its true unity. But what could serve as the reflective medium for the light of consciousness? As in the Yoga and Sāṅkhya traditions, the mind (*antaḥkaraṇa*), in virtue of its *sattvic* nature, has the unique capacity to reflect or mirror the light of consciousness. Specifically, it is *buddhi* (the intellect) that reflects consciousness, making possible the illumination and regulation of other aspects of the mind by conscious intelligence. Of course, in Yoga and Sāṅkhya there are many irreducibly distinct centers of consciousness (*puruṣa*) existing alongside the single reality of *prakṛti*. In contrast, for the Advaitin, consciousness is never truly plural. Rather, the single light is reflected in many distinct minds and the mind subsequently represents itself as being or belonging to a separate self. This is a key function of the *ahaṃkāra*.

On this account, the individual self is an appearance (*ābhāsa*) arising from a process of limitation (*avaccheda*) of the one nondual consciousness. Śaṅkara writes that when the supreme self is "delimited by the conditioning factors—body, mind, sense, intellect, and so forth.—[it] is spoken of in a roundabout way as the embodied soul by the ignorant" (BrSūBh 1.2.6) Yet, he says, the "case is similar to the appearance of space, undivided though it is, as if divided owing to such conditioning factors as a pot, a jar, etc" (Ibid.). That is, we may think of the space inside a pot as distinct from the rest of space, but this is not a deep fact about space itself. Rather space is a single, undivided field that, under certain circumstances, may appear divided. Likewise, the self as nondual consciousness is undivided, but appears divided when (apparently) associated with the conditioning factors of distinct bodies and minds. Furthermore, Śaṅkara goes on to assert that the individual self or embodied soul (*jīvātman*) is to be understood as consciousness identified with or associated with intellect (*buddhi*). In contrast the true or supreme self (*paramātman*) is the undivided nondual consciousness. Thus, we might say that the empirical self is an individuated locus of conscious intelligence, whereas the ultimate self is unified field of consciousness beyond space, time, causality, and so on.

6.5 Comparative Connections

In this section we will take up two comparative connections between Advaita Vedānta and contemporary philosophy, both concerning the fundamental nature of consciousness. The first connection concerns the relationship between consciousness and intentionality. The second concerns the ontological status and scope of consciousness.

In many contemporary discussions, phenomenal consciousness is characterized in terms of the "what it is like" locution (Nagel 1974). When

I am in a phenomenally conscious state (e.g., consciously seeing a red bird) there is "something it is like" for me to be in that state or having that experience. We can further specify what it is like to be in that state (in part) in terms of various qualitative features such as experiencing red, seeing a bird-like form, seeing motion, and so on. These features form part of the *phenomenal character* of the experience. The phenomenal character of a state, then, is what it is like for the subject to be in that state. Following the work of Uriah Kriegel (Kriegel 2009), we may further divide phenomenal character into *qualitative* character and *subjective* character. The qualitative character of the experience picks out its specific qualitative aspects: how the lemon tastes, the specific feel of a pain, how the red bird in flight looks, and so on. The experiential difference between tasting chocolate and tasting a lemon, or between tasting a lemon and puzzling through a hard math problem is (at least in part) a difference in the qualitative character of the different experiences. The subjective character of the experience picks out that it is like something *for me*. That is, the experience is had or undergone subjectively or first-personally. Moreover, on Kriegel's view, while qualitative character tracks differences between experiences, subjective character points to something all my experiences have in common; they are *for me* or subjective.

Returning to our example of seeing a red bird, in addition to the qualitative and subjective aspects, we can also identify an *intentional* aspect of the experience. My experience is *of*, *about*, or *directed at* a red bird. As Gallagher and Zahavi explain:

> 'intentionality' is a generic term for the pointing-beyond-itself proper to consciousness (from the Latin *intendere*, which means to aim in a particular direction, similar to drawing and aiming a bow at a target). Intentionality has to do with the directedness or of-ness or aboutness of consciousness, i.e. with the fact that when one perceives or judges or feels or thinks, one's mental state is about or of something.
>
> (Gallagher and Zahavi 2020, 96)

So, we may now further expand our "what it's like" locution. At least in many instances, a phenomenally conscious state will involve what it is like (qualitative) for a subject (subjective) to be aware of something (intentional). A complete philosophy of consciousness would need to have a fully developed account of these aspects. Here I want to focus on the relationship between consciousness and intentionality, and whether intentionality is intrinsic to consciousness. That is, is consciousness by nature intentional?

On this question we can identify two broad camps (Siewert 2025). *Intentionalists* hold that phenomenal consciousness necessarily involves intentionality (in classical Indian terms, consciousness is necessarily *saviṣayaka*, 'with an object'). *Separatists* hold that consciousness does not necessarily involve intentionality (it is *nirviṣayaka*, 'without an object'). Again, these are not themselves theories of consciousness, but rather broad tendencies. Two proponents of intentionalism (or of separatism) might hold the view based on otherwise radically different views of consciousness.

Nearly all thinkers in the Phenomenological tradition, for example, hold that consciousness is inherently intentional. Consciousness is always (or is best understood as) consciousness-of-something. For instance, on a Husserlian view:

> Regardless of whether we are talking of a perception, thought, judgement, fantasy, doubt, expectation, or recollection, all of these diverse forms of consciousness are characterized by intending objects, and cannot be analyzed properly without a look at their objective correlate, i.e. the perceived, doubted, expected object. The converse is also true: the intentional object cannot be analyzed properly without a look at its subjective correlate, the intentional act. Neither the intentional object nor the mental act that intends it can be understood apart from the other. Acts of consciousness and intentional objects, even if the latter do not exist, are essentially interdependent: the relation between them is an internal rather than an external one.
>
> (Gallagher and Zahavi 2020, 99)

On this type of view, intentionality is a central feature of the life of consciousness. This also implies that genuine or original intentionality is tied up with the qualitative and subjective aspects of consciousness such that intentionality cannot be treated as a separable and merely contingent aspect of consciousness. As Galen Strawson writes:

> [M]eaning is always a matter of something meaning something to something. In this sense, nothing means anything in an experienceless world. There is no possible meaning, hence no possible intention, hence no possible intentionality, on an experienceless planet ... There is no entity that means anything in this universe. There is no entity that is about anything. There is no semantic evaluability, no truth, no falsity. None of these properties are possessed by anything until experience begins. There is a clear and fundamental sense in which meaning, and hence intentionality, exists only in the conscious moment ...
>
> (Strawson 2009, 208–9)

One might also endorse a form of intentionalism for quite different reasons. For example, representationalist theories of consciousness may try to explain consciousness in terms of representation, thereby reducing consciousness to a type or mode of intentionality. And if one can then provide a fully naturalistic theory of intentionality in terms of representation—for example, in teleofunctional (Millikan 1987) or perhaps informational terms (Dretske 1986)—then one has provided a naturalistic reduction of consciousness (Tye 1999).

As with intentionalism, there are many routes to separatism. For instance, one might argue that the primary feature of phenomenal consciousness is its qualitative aspect and that this qualitative aspect can be understood in terms of non-intentional features such as qualia, sensations, or raw feels. One will then want to give a separate analysis of representation or intentionality on the one hand, and qualia on the other. Another route derives from internalist/externalist debates regarding the nature of cognitive representation (Rowlands 2020a). One might give an externalist account of representation such that what a cognition represents in part depends on features of the external environment. However, one might also hold that phenomenal consciousness is an internal matter. That is, what one's experience is like depends only on what is going on, as it were, inside the skin or skull.

The Advaita tradition offers a distinctive and potentially fruitful approach to these complex issues. The Advaita philosopher Citsukha (thirteenth century CE) argues at length in his *Tattvapradīpikā* that, in its basic nature, consciousness is reflexive or self-luminous (*svaprakāśatā*) and objectless (*nirviṣayatā*). He defines self-luminosity as "fitness for being immediately known without being an object of any cognition" (TP 2.1.16). That is, consciousness is immediately self-present (*aparokṣa*) and indubitable (*abādhita*). What is crucial here for Citsukha is that this inherent reflexivity or self-presence is not a form of intentionality. On his view, construing self-presence as a form of intentionality would turn consciousness into just another object *for* consciousness, thereby collapsing subjectivity into a mere object. Moreover, because this self-presence is the very nature of consciousness it is prior to any form of intentionality or representational cognition. As Chakravarthi Ram-Prasad explains:

> This Advaitic conception of consciousness as essentially reflexive in fact is tantamount to saying that it is purely reflexive. Indeed, this is the idea behind the conception of such consciousness as 'witness' (*sākṣin*, drawing on the word for sight that suggests the literal translation 'onlooker'). Just as onlookers do not engage in the events they are witnessing, so

witness-consciousness does not engage with objects. It is present, but is transparent to content, not itself intentionally directed towards (i.e. 'engaged' with) objects.

(Ram-Prasad 2016, 80)

But if consciousness is just pure self-luminosity, how to account for the intentional dimension of experience? Here Advaita thinkers offer a broadly naturalistic, cognitivist account. Recall that the production of a representation or intentional cognition is a function of the mind which is an inner organ or functional system of the natural organism. A key function of the mind is to take non-cognitive or pre-cognitive mental events (*vṛttis*) and shape (*pariṇāma*) them into fully intentional cognitions (*vṛttijñāna*). This is done through several layers of mental processing. For instance, in the case of perception, the reception of sensory data up to the fully cognitive representation of an external object. And importantly, all this mental processing goes on 'in the dark', not intrinsically connected to phenomenal consciousness.

In this respect, the Advaita account is similar to recent naturalistic views of intentionality or cognition (van Hateren 2021). However, they maintain a stringently non-naturalist view of consciousness, the essence of which is the irreducible reality of conscious subjectivity. Here the intentional aspect of conscious experience arises from the natural functioning of the mind, while the qualitative aspect arises from the interface between mental processes (such as sensation or feeling) and witness consciousness. Thus, we might say that on the Advaita view, the hard problem of consciousness is fundamentally the hard problem of *subjectivity*. And since subjectivity is in principle irreducible to any object or objective process, there is no naturalistic solution to the hard problem. Like the Sāṅkhya and Yoga views discussed in Chapter 4, Advaita thinkers developed a *horizonal*, in contrast to a strictly *phenomenal*, view of consciousness.

This contrast derives from the work of J. J. Valberg. According to Valberg, on the common *phenomenal* (or empirical) view, conscious experience:

is a phenomenon: a process or activity or series of states or events. My experience is a phenomenon which occurs on my part—just like the activity (the states, processes, etc.) in my brain. (Perhaps it *is* the activity in my brain.) So, of course, just like the activity in my brain, my experience is a part of the world. Just like the activity in my brain, my experience has a character of its own.

(Valberg 1992, 128)

In contrast, on the horizonal view, conscious experience is, "a horizon within which the world is present, and which is 'mine'. The world is present within the horizon, but since the horizon is nothing in itself, we cannot include it (*it?*) in the world" (Valberg 1992, 124). Because consciousness (or 'experience' as Valberg is using the term) is the horizon within which anything can be present, it cannot be one more phenomenon within the world. On Valberg's account:

> experience (on the horizonal conception) cannot be viewed as something which occurs in the brain or soul. Anything which occurs in the brain or soul would be part of the world; it would have a character of its own. Experience, on the horizonal conception, is not something which 'occurs' at all. It is neither an external object nor an external *phenomenon* (activity, process, series of states).
>
> (Valberg 1992, 125)

Nor, for that matter, is it an *internal* phenomenon. Valberg argues, "If my experience were an internal object (phenomenon), it would, like an after-image, exist only in so far as it is present in my experience-which is absurd. On the horizonal conception, the external-internal contrast does not apply to experience" (Valberg 1992, 125).

The Advaita view of consciousness as pure, luminous witness is aligned with the horizonal conception. The self is the field of consciousness within which phenomena, 'inner' or 'outer', may come to presence. Therefore, witness consciousness (*sākṣin*) must be sharply distinguished from mind (*manas*) and the changing series of mental states (*vṛttis*). For the Advaitin, the mind is necessarily phenomenal, whereas consciousness (*cit*) is necessarily horizonal. Indeed, the phenomenal conception of the conscious mind as a series of cognitive states that have the property of being conscious is a mistaken superimposition (*adhyāsa*) of essentially subcognitive states onto pure non-intentional consciousness. This view occupies a distinctive position in the philosophy of consciousness, allowing for a broadly naturalistic approach to understanding the mind, while recognizing the irreducible nature of consciousness understood as the open horizon within which anything could come to presence.

The Advaita approach to the distinction between intentionality and (horizonal) consciousness as such may help to make sense of two types of experience discussed in both contemplative traditions and recent work in consciousness studies: Nondual Awareness (NDA) and Pure Consciousness Events (PCE). The idea of nondual awareness is linked both to certain philosophical perspectives (such as Advaita, Yogācāra, and Pratyabijñā) and to certain contemplative or meditative traditions such as Mahāmudrā in Buddhism (Dunne 2011) or recent Neo-Vedānta (Dalal 2020).

A central commitment of these traditions, Zoran Josipovich writes, "is that at some fundamental level, human experience is not fragmented into opposing dualities, but that such fragmentation, though a universal condition of human life, is adventitious to a more unified reality underlying our daily experiences" (2014, 2) . In the context of meditation, that underlying reality is said to be Nondual Awareness (NDA):

> a nonconceptual nondual awareness that abides, ordinarily unrecognized, in the background of all conscious experiencing. This background awareness appears in meditation to be unitary and unchanging—a cognizance that is in itself empty of content, yet clearly aware and blissful—whereas various sensory, affective, and cognitive contents, and the various states of arousal appear to it as dynamic processes or, as a well-known metaphor states, like images in a mirror.
>
> (Josipovic 2021, 3)

The aim, then, is to experientially recognize this NDA and to defuse attachment or identification with the shifting contents presented within the horizon of NDA. In Advaitic terms, one comes to rest as the witness consciousness which is the luminous space (or horizon) within which all inner and outer phenomena come into presence (Fasching 2008). In Valberg's terms, one shifts from a *phenomenal* to a *horizonal* mode of consciousness.

Another related type of NDA is pure consciousness. As Jonathon Shear characterizes it, "when the mind has become completely settled (while nevertheless remaining alert) one steps outside all activity of perception, and, silent and fully awake inside, experiences pure, unmanifest, absolutely objectless, consciousness" (Shear and Jevning 1999, 194–95). As one Transcendental Meditation (TM) practitioner reports, "Sometimes in meditation my thoughts drift away entirely, and I gain a state I would describe as simply being awake. I'm not thinking about anything. I'm not particularly aware of any sensations, I'm not aware of being absorbed in anything in particular, and yet I am quite certain (after the fact) that I have not been asleep. During it I am simply awake or simply present" (Forman 1999, 20). Furthermore, some TM practitioners report an elimination of a sense of effort in concentration as well as a loss of the senses of time, space, and body sense (Travis et al. 2004).

Because the Pure Consciousness Event (PCE) purportedly is a form of objectless consciousness, it can be characterized as nondual. The subject–object duality is absent because there is no object, and even the usual duality between the subject's own states and their awareness of them is attenuated or absent. However, there is an important difference between the PCE and the type of NDA already discussed. In the PCE a nondual state is achieved by the absence of explicit phenomenal contents, while in the NDA discussed above, the nondual state is achieved in the presence of phenomenal contents. So, while both states are understood to be a recognition of consciousness itself as distinct from its contents, the phenomenological structure differs. One way to understand the difference here is in terms of the phenomenal unit of identification. The NDA experience involves the maximal unit of phenomenal identification, that is the space or expanse of consciousness as the context of phenomenal contents. In contrast, the PCE involves the minimal unit of phenomenal identification, the simple state of phenomenal consciousness devoid of contents. In both cases, though, there is a shift of self-identification from the typical sense of being a separate subject in relation to an object to a sense of being consciousness itself, whether in its pure form or in its spacious form.

Furthermore, note that in both types of experience there is sharp distinction between intentionality and consciousness itself. In the PCE case, we (apparently) have a form of consciousness in the absence of intentionality, in that it is characterized as objectless or contentless. Of course, the PCE does seem to have qualitative features, but it is important not to conflate qualitative character with intentional content. An experience may feel a certain way without necessarily being *about* or intentionally *directed* at that feeling. In the NDA case, we (apparently) have a form of consciousness that is inclusive of but distinct from intentionality. Here intentionality is a phenomenal or empirical mode of experience occurring within the more basic space of nondual awareness. That is, in this 'spacious' form of NDA, one comes to experience both intentional objects and intentional states as dynamic appearances within the more basic space or condition of NDA. Objects and various mental states and processes (seeing, thinking, remembering) appear, change, and disappear like clouds forming and dissipating in the open sky.

In sum, the Advaita model of witness conscious as the nondual horizon within which mental and physical phenomena appear more readily accommodates PCE and NDA types of experience. As contemporary philosophers and scientists investigate these and other modes of experience, we would do well to take seriously the models of mind and consciousness developed by Advaita and other nondual traditions.

6.6 Questions

1. How is the Advaita Vedānta account of the self different from the Nyāya view?

2. Why does Śaṅkara argue that consciousness can never be an object? Does this argument work?
3. What is difference between the Advaita and the Yogācāra views of perception?
4. What is the relationship between *brahman* and the empirical world (*jagat*)? According to Advaita, is the empirical world *real*?

Notes

1 The term *advaita* can be applied more generally to mean "nondual" or "nondualist." I will use the capitalized *Advaita* as shorthand for the specific tradition of Advaita Vedānta.

2 Translated by Roebuck (2004).

3 As Bina Gupta (2003) points out, there are three main approaches to the relation between self and consciousness in the orthodox schools of philosophy. Consciousness might be (1) a quality or property of the self, (2) an act of the self, or (3) the essence of the self. Advaita argues for (3).

4 As discussed later in this chapter, Śaṅkara argues that we must posit the *same* witness across time, as against the Buddhist view that each moment of cognition is distinct and there is no enduring subject.

5 This is similar to Rowlands' (2020b) *no content thesis* (that any object of consciousness is outside consciousness) mentioned in Chapter 2. Here the thought is that anything variably presented within consciousness is therefore not part of the essence of consciousness.

6 Hence the distinction between the object itself (*vastu*) and the intentional form or content (*viṣaya*).

7 Classical Indian thinkers debated the relationship between what we are here calling the dative and accusative mode. For instance, the Viśiṣṭādvaita (qualified nondualist) philosopher Rāmānuja (c. 1077–1157) argued that subjectivity (dative) and intentionality (accusative) necessarily go together. And as will be discussed in Chapter 7, Buddhist thinkers such as Dignāga and Dharmakīrti hold that each moment of consciousness has a subject aspect and an object aspect. See (Mohanty 1971) and (MacKenzie 2025) for further discussion.

8 The *Dṛg Dṛśya Viveka*, usually attributed to Śaṅkara, states, "The eye is seer and the form (and color) the seen. The (eye) is the seen and the mind is the seer. The witness alone is the seer of thoughts and never the seen" (1).

9 Elsewhere he says that in dreamless sleep the individual self reverts to *brahman* (Sharma 2012).

10 See (Gupta 1998), (Sharma 2012), and (Thompson 2014) for further discussion.

11 The division of the body into three layers and five sheaths goes back to the Upaniṣads (for example, *Taittirīya Upaniṣad*).

12 Hence, the causal body in Advaita plays a similar role to the *ālayavijñāna* in Yogācāra Buddhism.

13 Śaṅkara points out that if Buddhists have warrant to distinguish between successive cognition, then they should also allow a warranted distinction between a perceptual state and its object. He asks, "if one admits a distinction between [cognition] and [cognition], why should not one admit external objects such as a pillar, a wall, and so on?" (BrSūBh 2.2.28).

14 One way to think about the problem here is whether 'real' can come in degrees. Can one thing be *more* real than another thing? If so, one might say empirical things are real, but *less real* than *brahman*. On the other hand, one might want to say that 'real' is not a matter of degree—things are either real or not. Then, one would say that *brahman* alone is real and the empirical world falls short of the status of *real*. The nineteenth century British philosopher, F. H. Bradley (1893), used the term 'appearance' to designate this intermediate ontological status.

15 Śaṅkara himself does not use the term *māyā* very much and, as Anantanand Rambachan (Rambachan 2006, 72) has argued, Śaṅkara generally holds that *brahman* (not the intermediary principle of *māyā*) is the cause of the empirical world.

16 After Śaṅkara there was significant debate regarding the locus of *avidyā*. The Bhāmatī school, associated with Vacaspati Miśra (ninth century) held the *jīva* to be the locus of *avidyā*. The Vivaraṇa school, associated with Prakāśātman (tenth century), held that *brahman* is the locus of *avidyā*.

Further Reading

Gauḍapāda Ācārya. 1998. *Discourses on Māṇḍūkya Upanishads with Gaudapāda's Kārikā*. [Rev. ed.]. Translated by Chinmayananda. Central Chinmaya Mission Trust.

Gupta, Bina. 1998. *The Disinterested Witness: A Fragment of Advaita Vedānta Phenomenology*. 1st edition. Northwestern University Press.

Ram-Prasad, Chakravarthi. 2013. *Advaita Epistemology and Metaphysics: An Outline of Indian Non-Realism*. Routledge.

Śaṅkarācārya. 1965. *Brahma Sūtra Bhāṣya Of Śaṅkarācārya*. Translated by Gambhirananda. Vedanta Press & Bookshop.

Śaṅkarācārya. 1992. *A Thousand Teachings: The Upadeśasāhasrī of Śaṅkara*. Edited by Sengaku Mayeda. State University of New York Press.

Timalsina, Sthaneshwar. 2014. *Consciousness in Indian Philosophy*. Routledge.

Buddhist Pramāṇavāda

7.1 Buddhist Pramāṇavāda

"Buddhist *pramāṇavāda*" is a label used to designate a new approach to Buddhist philosophy inaugurated by Dignāga (c. 540–c. 580 CE) and further developed by Dharmakīrti (550–610 CE). Drawing on earlier Yogācāra and Sautrāntika Abhidharma, this (sub-) school was not separately named in Sanskrit, but later Tibetan philosophers and doxographers referred to it as "those who follow reasoning" (*rigs pa rjes su 'brang ba*), whereas modern scholars refer to it as the Buddhist "epistemological school" (*pramāṇavāda*) (Tillemans 2021).

Dignāga is a pivotal figure in the history of Indian philosophy. He was affiliated with the great Buddhist monastic university of Nalandā, where he lived and taught alongside scholars of the whole Buddhist tradition as well as non-Buddhist scholars such as the famous philosopher-grammarian, Bhartṛhari. On the one hand, Dignāga's work is a continuation and development of the Yogācāra tradition of Buddhist thought associated especially with Vasubandhu (and discussed in Chapter 5). On the other hand, his work was profoundly innovative, synthesizing distinct strands of philosophy and developing rigorous new methods of analysis and argumentation. Indeed, as Jonardon Ganeri remarks, "[a]n emerging scholarly consensus agrees in identifying Dignāga as marking the beginning of a new era in Indian philosophical thought, some scholars emphasizing his theoretical innovations and others his transformation of discursive practice" (Ganeri 2017, 6). Ganeri labels this new epoch in Indian philosophy "the age of dialogue," as it was characterized by vigorous philosophical dialogue and debate deploying rigorous and widely shared new philosophical methods in logic, philosophy of language, epistemology, and other areas.

So, while Dignāga continued and developed the Yogācāra tradition, he is reasonably credited with the inauguration of the new school or sub-school of Buddhist *pramāṇavāda*. The term '*pramāṇavāda*' refers to a broader philosophical inquiry into the nature and reliable means of knowledge undertaken by philosophers from many Indian traditions. The label here is apt because, for Dignāga and his important successor, Dharmakīrti, issues of the reliable or valid means of knowledge (*pramāṇa*) were philosophically central. Dignāga's masterwork, *Pramāṇasamuccaya* (*Compendium of Valid Cognition*) deals extensively with issues in logic, epistemology, and philosophy of mind (all of which fall under the purview of *pramāṇa*). The text was not only influential on subsequent Buddhist thought, but it also prompted detailed and sophisticated responses from non-Buddhist philosophers such as Uddyotakara (Nyāya) and Kumārila (Mīmāṃsā).

Dharmakīrti, like Dignāga, lived and taught at Nālandā. According to Tibetan biographers, he was born in South India and was initially a proponent of the non-Buddhist Mīmāṃsa tradition (Tillemans 2021). Dharmakīrti's largest and most important work, the *Pramāṇavārttika* (*Commentary on Valid Cognition*), is an extensive commentary on Dignāga's *Pramāṇasamuccaya*. Dharmakīrti both defends and modifies Dignāga's views, developing a coherent and sophisticated approach to Buddhist philosophy that proved to be highly influential in subsequent Indian and Tibetan philosophy. So influential in fact that during the 'age of dialogue' the Dignāga-Dharmakīrti school was sometimes treated by critics as the definitive Buddhist philosophical perspective.

In metaphysics, the Buddhist epistemologists were, in Western terms, broadly empiricist, reductionist, and nominalist. Their ontology consists in two basic categories: *svalakṣanas* (particulars) and *sāmānyalakṣaṇas* (universals). *Svalakṣanas* are momentary causally efficacious concrete particulars that might be best understood, in contemporary ontological terms, as *tropes* (Goodman 2004). That is, they are *particular* qualities or features (Williams 2018). On this view, there are both physical and mental tropes. *Sāmānyalakṣaṇas* are not particular, but general and come in two basic varieties. Horizontal particulars (*tiryaglakṣaṇa*) are what we normally think of as universals, such as properties and kinds. So, the particular red of this apple is a *svalakṣana*, while *redness* is a *sāmānyalakṣaṇa*. Vertical universals (*ūrdhvatālakṣaṇa*) are persisting entities.[1] They are universals not particulars because they are, ultimately, constructions of particulars. The apple is a *sāmānyalakṣaṇa* because, in the final analysis, it is synchronically reducible to a bundle of momentary *svalakṣanas* and diachronically reducible to a series of momentary trope bundles. Further, as strict nominalists, Buddhist epistemologists hold that only *svalakṣanas* are finally real because only they are causally efficacious. To be real is to make a difference to how the world goes. Of course, they recognize that universals play an important, indeed indispensable, role in our cognitive and practical engagement with the world. But in so far as they are reducible constructs and have no autonomous causal powers, they have a merely conventional or pragmatic reality, while momentary tropes constitute the causal fabric of the world.

In epistemology, the Buddhist *pramāṇavādins*/epistemologists held that particulars (*svalakṣaṇas*) and universals (*sāmānyalakṣaṇas*) are the two basic types of objects of knowledge (*prameya*). Particulars are known through perception (*pratyakṣa*) while universals are known through inference (*anumāna*). These two are the only basic means of knowledge (*pramāṇas*) in the system.[2] Perception—or more broadly, direct awareness—is non-conceptual and non-linguistic and takes only unique particulars as its object. Inference is conceptual and linguistic[3] and only takes universals—or more broadly, anything general—as its object. As we will discuss more fully below, perception is privileged in that it is has a direct causal connection to real particulars. Inference, though indispensable, is secondary and always distorted (*bhrānta*) because it traffics in constructed universals.

The main subject of this chapter is the distinctive philosophy of mind and consciousness developed by these Buddhist epistemologists. In the remainder of the chapter, we will take up four key interconnected ideas from the Buddhist epistemologists. First is the rejection of the transparency of experience, in favor of a representationalist (viz. *sākāravāda*) view of perception. Second is a dual-aspect (*dvairūpya*) account of the structure and content of experience. Third is the idea that reflexive awareness (*svasaṃvedana*) is a necessary feature of all experience. Finally, fourth is the reconciliation of this (as I have elsewhere termed it MacKenzie (2021) and (2022a)) "dual-aspect reflexivist" philosophy of mind with the Buddhist rejection of the self. What emerges is a rigorous account of the conscious mind as a stream of impermanent, selfless, but self-luminous cognitive events.

7.2 Dual Aspects

The Buddhist epistemologists hold that the mind is by nature (*prakṛti*) luminous (*prakāśa*). It is the nature of awareness to present. From here we may ask both *what* is presented and *how* it is presented. Paradigmatically, perception (*pratyakṣa*) presents an object (*viṣaya*). More generally, Dharmakīrti understands cognition (*jñāna*) in terms of its presenting or taking an object (*viṣayagrahaṇam*) (PV 2.206). I may have a visual perception of a red jar and in that case we would say that the red jar is the object of my perception. However, as the Buddhist epistemologists would be quick to point out, this commonsense account hides much philosophical complexity.

The Buddhist epistemologists hold a representationalist view of perception, according to which the epistemic object (*prameya*) is cognized ('grasped', *grāhya*) by way of a phenomenal form or image (*ākāra*) internal to the perceptual state. Through perception I can gain knowledge of the red jar on my desk, but I do so by way of certain mental images derived from my senses. My perceptual awareness takes on a phenomenal form (*ākāra*) or appearance (*ābhāsa*) that re-presents the jar in my external environment. Therefore, on this view, I am not perceiving the external jar directly, but only indirectly by way of the perceptual image created in my mind. However, (in part) because the jar caused me to have the <red jar> perceptual image, we can say that the perceptual image represents the jar. This representationalist[4] view is called *sākāravāda* ('with-aspect-ism'), the view that a cognition of a certain type grasps its epistemic object by way of a mediating form or image (*ākāra*) which is an intrinsic aspect of the cognition. As mentioned in Chapter 1, the opposing view is called *nirākāravāda*, the view that a certain type of cognition grasps its object without the mediation of a mental image or form.[5] The *nirākāravādin* holds that perception is transparent and direct, whereas the *sākāravādin* holds that it is indirect and representational.[6]

For the Buddhist epistemologists, one role of the form or object aspect of cognition is to mediate and facilitate cognitive access to the world. The object-aspect (*viṣayākāra, viṣayābhāsa*) provides the cognitive link or mode of presentation of the external object within the medium of consciousness.[7] In this way, the object-aspect is an answer to what Michelle Montague terms *the access problem*: "How does one achieve access to the things with which one stands in perceptual intentional relations? When one perceives some particular thing, what makes it the case that one has that very thing in mind? What mechanism determines which object a perception is of?" (2016, 142). In other words, it is the problem of how exactly a cognitive event or system achieves (epistemic or experiential) access to its intentional object. Further, Montague distinguishes between two common but opposed approaches to the access problem, which she terms 'internalist' and 'externalist'. According to the externalist, "the phenomenon of having an object in mind," is explained, "*solely* in terms of external relations (causal or historical) that hold between a thinker's relevant mental state and the relevant object in the world" (2016, 143). As Fred Dretske characterizes the externalist view, "When I am experiencing an object, nothing in my experience of it determines which object I'm experiencing any more than there is something about a gauge's representation of a tire's pressure that determines which tire it is registering the pressure of" (1997, 33).[8] In contrast, according to the internalist, the explanation of having an object in mind must include an internal condition on access. As Montague puts it, "The fundamental idea behind the internal approach to the access problem is that thinking of a particular object essentially involves conceiving of it in some particular manner, or characterizing it in some fashion, and that reference to the particular manner involved is essential for determining which object is being thought of" (2016, 142). It is important to note that the internalist condition, beyond thinking and conceiving, can apply to other modes of intentionality including perception. The key claim is that, in addition to whatever external conditions may be required, there is something about the particular way of cognizing the object that (at least in part) explains having that object in mind.

We can understand Dignāga and Dharmakīrti to hold an internalist view wherein the object-aspect of the cognition plays the role of the internal 'particular-way' condition. For instance, as Dignāga affirms in his *Ālambanaparīkṣā* (*Analysis of the Objects of Cognition*), Buddhist thinkers generally held that there are two conditions on a genuine perceptual cognition (Duckworth and Eckel 2016). First, the object perceived must be the cause of the perceptual cognition. This is an external condition on the perception. Second, the object must *appear* in the perception. When I see a tree, the tree appears to me visually and the tree has caused me to be in that perceptual state. But what is it for that tree to appear in the perception? For *sākāravādins*, it is for the visual consciousness to take on the phenomenal form of the tree, like a clear mirror reflects the form of an object in front of it. The aspect or phenomenal form here is the internal 'particular way' condition that in part determines that the perception is of the tree. In contrast, *nirākāravādins* such as the Naiyāyikas reject the need for an internal aspect to mediate cognitive access to the intentional object. For them, perception is like a transparent window through which things are seen, rather than a reflective surface in which things can appear.

For the Buddhist epistemologists, however, a cognition is not exhausted by its presentation of an intentional object. Consciousness has a two-fold form or content (*dvairūpya*). As Dignāga puts it, "Every cognition is produced with a twofold appearance, namely that of itself (*svābhāsa*) and that of the object (*viṣayābhāsa*)" (PSV 1.9a). As just discussed, the object-appearance or object-aspect is the presentation of the intentional object in cognition. It is what the experience is *as of*.[9] Whatever the further status of the intentional object, insofar as it is given in experience, there is an object-appearance. Consciousness also presents a subject-aspect (*svābhāsa*), which for Dignāga and Dharmakīrti means the way the cognition presents *itself*. When one has an experience as of a tree the experience presents both the tree (the object-aspect) and the experiencing of the tree (the subject-aspect). As Dignāga asserts: "That cognition has two aspects is [known] from the difference between the cognition of the object and the cognition of that [cognition]" (PS 1.11ab). This view of cognition is like that of Colin McGinn. On McGinn's view, experiences are 'Janus-faced'. He writes, "Thus … experiences are Janus-faced: they point outward to the external world but they also present a subjective face to their subject; they are of something other than the subject and they are like something for the subject" (McGinn 1993, 29). On the dual-aspect view of consciousness, the phenomenal character of experience involves both how the object is presented and how the experience itself is presented. This entails a phenomenological distinction between what the object is like and what it is like to cognize or experience the object. For instance, what it is like to see a bright yellow lemon may be different from what it is like to *imagine* the lemon or to *remember* it, even if the lemon itself is presented in the same way (as bright yellow, and so forth.) in each cognition (Zahavi 2020, 23) . Indeed, Jonardon Ganeri characterizes the subject-aspect simply as, "whatever it is in virtue of which attending to one's experience does not collapse into attending to the world as presented in experience" (Ganeri 2012, 170).

For Dignāga, the available features of the cognition itself include subordinate mental factors. He writes: "The mental [perception] which, taking a thing of color, etc., for its object, occurs in the form of immediate experience (*anubhava*) is also free from conceptual construction. The self-awareness (*svasaṃvedana*) of desire, anger, ignorance, pleasure, pain, etc., is [also recognized as] mental perception because it is not dependent on any sense-organ" (PSV 1.6ab). That is, for Dignāga we have direct self-awareness of certain features of our own mental states. Specifically, Dignāga here is appealing to the more general Buddhist *citta/caitta* model of cognition. Here *citta* refers to the moment of cognition as such, whereas the *caittas* or mental factors are analytically discernable aspects of the cognition. According to Asaṅga's *Abhidharmasamuccaya*, there are five omnipresent mental factors: sensory contact (*sparśa*), affect (*vedanā*), cognition (*saṃjñā*), conition (*cetanā*), and attention (*manaskāra*). The basic nature of the cognition is shaped by sensory, affective, cognitive, conative, and attentional factors. Further, for the dual-aspect view, these mental factors contribute to the *svābhāsa*, the way the cognition presents itself in addition to the way it presents its object. There is a discernable phenomenological difference between a vivid, pleasant, attentive, and desirous cognition of a bright yellow lemon and an unfocused, non-desirous, unpleasant cognition of that same bright yellow lemon.

It was suggested above that the object-aspect is meant to solve the problem of cognitive access to objects. What about the subject-aspect? Here there is a different kind of access problem for the cognition itself. There is an *intra-mental* access problem, namely, how can one become directly aware of one's own cognitive states or their (intrinsic) features? Indeed, Dignāga's two main arguments involving the subject-aspect—the introspection argument and the memory argument—concern the possibility of intra-mental access.

Dignāga's introspection or meta-cognition argument for the dual-aspect view (*dvyābhāsatā*) is that if cognitions are transparent, there would be no distinction between a cognition and the cognition of that cognition (PSV 1.11d–12) (Kellner 2010, 210). That is, if a cognition of a tree (C1) has no form other than its object and a meta-cognition of C1 (C2) is also transparent, then, while C2 has as its object C1, C1 has no form other than the form of the tree. Therefore, C2 will collapse into just another cognition of the tree. However, if C1 has two faces, then we can make sense of what C2 grasps when it cognizes C1, namely, the subject-aspect of C1. C2 will also grasp C1's object in grasping C1, but it will not collapse into it. Whatever one makes of the soundness of this argument, the point here is that the subject-aspect facilitates intra-mental access, just as the object-aspect facilitates extra-mental access.

In the memory argument, Dignāga states (PSV 1.11c) that one cannot remember what one has not experienced before. But we can remember our own previous experiences—that is, we can remember not just the *object* of a previous experience, but also the previous experience itself. Thus, the experience must itself have been experienced, in the sense that it was part of the overall content the experience itself. If the prior cognition is cognized by a distinct cognition, as in the higher-order view, then there would occur an infinite regress. This is because, according to Dignāga, the higher-order experience too can be remembered and so must itself have been experienced, and so on. To avoid the regress, he argues, we must hold that experiences are reflexive—that is, that the awareness of the experience is not separate from the experience itself. To be sure, this is a controversial argument[10], but the point here is that Dignāga is appealing to the subject-aspect to mediate intra-mental access. Of course, the intra-*mental* access problem is different from the object-access problem. There is no ontological gap between consciousness and external objects to overcome.[11] Rather, the role of the subject-aspect is to account for the direct availability of cognitions in a way that avoids collapsing the distinction between cognitions and meta-cognitions (memory, introspection) or setting off a vicious regress of cognitions.[12]

So, on this interpretation of the dual-aspect theory of consciousness, the object- and subject- aspects of experiences are *phenomenal modes of presentation*. The object-aspect presents the object (for example, as being yellow and oblong), while the subject-aspect presents the experience itself (for example, as being a pleasant, focused, visual experience, as well as being a cognition of a yellow lemon). They are *phenomenal* modes of presentation in that the object and the experience are presented qualitatively. In modern parlance, we can say that there is something it is like to be aware of a yellow lemon and there is also something it is like to live through an involuntary, attentive, pleasant, visual experience of a yellow lemon.

Yet, while the aspects are both phenomenal modes of presentation, there is an important distinction between them. On the dual-aspect view, both aspects belong to a single cognition. However, as distinct modes of presentation, they must present differently. The object-aspect purports to present an object distinct from the cognition itself, that is, by way of transitive intentionality. In perceiving a pot, the pot is presented as being distinct from the perception and external to the perceiver. This may ultimately be an error or illusion if the object is really itself an immanent mental image. However, the error or illusion itself is based on the gap between how the object is given (*as* independent and external) and how it is understood to be on further analysis. In contrast, the cognition itself, presented through the subject-aspect, is presented *as* within, as immanent rather than transcendent.

7.3 Reflexive Awareness

For Dignāga and his successors, the dual aspects of experience are *appearances* (*ābhāsa*) and, arguably, it is a feature of the conceptual grammar of "appearance" that it is always "appearance-to." Indeed, insofar as our discussion of luminosity has taken it to be a form of phenomenal presentation, the very idea of consciousness as presentation seems to presuppose presentation-to. This fits well with views that accept the self (*ātman*) as the enduring subject of experience or the idea of consciousness as witness (*sākṣin*) but seems to present a problem for Buddhist philosophers for whom *anātmavāda* (the doctrine of no-self) is foundational. In short, if both the objective and subjective aspects are presentations, to whom or to what are they presenting?

For Buddhist reflexivists like Dignāga, the answer is *svasaṃvedana* (self-awareness). Here "self-awareness" or "reflexive awareness" can denote the primitive, direct acquaintance one has with one's own experience. However, given the commitment to the doctrine of no-self, it is more appropriate to understand reflexive awareness in terms of Michelle Montague's *awareness of awareness thesis*: "Conscious awareness always involves—constitutively involves—some sort of awareness of that very awareness" (Montague 2016, 41).[13] To be presented an object in experience is to be aware of the object as it is given in and through that experience, whether or not it is thematized *as* the object experienced. To experience an object is also to live through the experiencing directly. In both cases, we may say there is something it is like to have the experience and that is a function of how the experience presents the object and how it presents itself. Reflexive awareness, then, is the direct awareness of that which is presented (objectively or subjectively) in experience. It is, in other words, the basic awareness of the objective and subjective faces of each cognitive episode.

The Buddhist reflexivists, like other proponents of self-luminosity, are committed to the *Transitivity Principle*, according to which a subject is in a conscious state M only if the subject is, in some suitable way, aware of M (or of being in M). The subject need not be *reflectively* or *attentively* aware of M, but must only be aware of it "in some suitable way." The *Transitivity Principle* does not entail reflexivity, because one might hold the Higher-Order Representationalist (HOR) view that M is represented by a distinct, second-order state. It does, however, entail a rejection of the *independence condition* maintained by Nyāya (see Chapter 2). What is distinctive about the reflexivist view is that self-awareness is *not* a distinct higher-order state, but a feature of the same state of consciousness. It is a same-order view of pre-reflective self-awareness. Moreover, dual-aspect reflexivists such as Dharmakīrti and Śāntarakṣita (725–788 CE) hold that this reflexivity or self-luminosity is the very nature of consciousness (MacKenzie 2017). As Dharmakīrti asserts, "Just as an illuminating light is considered to be the illuminator of itself, because of its nature, just so, awareness is aware of itself" (PV 3.329).

The Buddhist reflexivists, then, are committed to three key ideas. First, they hold that all conscious awareness by its nature involves awareness of itself (awareness of awareness). Second, that any conscious mental state presents itself. Third, that the presentational content of the state and the reflexive awareness of the state are features of the same state or episode of consciousness. In short, the object-aspect, subject-aspect, and reflexive awareness are features of a single episode of consciousness. As Dignāga characterizes the view, "That whose appearance [cognition possesses] is the object that is validly cognized. The form as apprehending and [reflexive] awareness, again, are the means of valid cognition and the result. Therefore, these three [aspects of cognition] are not separate [from one another]" (PS 10). In this way, dual-aspect reflexivism is what David Woodruff Smith (2016) calls a modal model of consciousness, whereby one can analytically distinguish various aspects or factors in the phenomenological structure of a typical act or event of consciousness, while denying that these factors are ontologically distinct or separable (proper) *parts*.

As mentioned above, Dignāga's main argument for *svasaṃvedana* is the memory argument. However, Dharmakīrti deploys a different line of argument that links reflexive awareness to the two access problems already mentioned. In his *sahopalambhaniyama* argument Dharmakīrti states:

> Blue and its cognition are not different because they are necessarily
> perceived together.
>
> For someone who does not perceive perception, the perception of the
> object is not established either.
>
> (PVin 1.54)

Here, 'blue' is the object-aspect of the cognition, while 'its cognition' is the
cognitive state itself in which blue is presented. The claim is that, because
they must be given together, they are aspects of a single state. And, as we
see in the next line, his reason for this is that, without an awareness of the
perception, the perceptual object is not established. He elaborates in the
auto-commentary:

> To explain: (1) a perception of an object is not due to the existence
> of the object, but due to the existence of its perception. (2) And if the
> existence of the object's perception is not established by a means of valid
> cognition (*aprāmāṇika*), then it does not attach itself (*anuruṇaddhi*)
> to forms of behavior that presuppose existence (*sattānibandhanān
> vyavahārān*). (3) If the perception is then unestablished, then the object
> is also unestablished, so that everything would go asunder, for (4) even if
> something exists, it cannot be treated as existent unless it is established.
> Therefore, someone who does not perceive the awareness of something
> is not aware of anything at all.
>
> (PVin 1.54)

The idea here seems to be that perceptual access to an object requires that
the perceiver be in a particular perceptual state. But for that perceptual state
to do its cognitive work, the cognizer must somehow *register* that it is in
that cognitive state. Otherwise, Dharmakīrti argues, the percept would not
be available for downstream operations like behavior.

Here we see a clear contrast between dual-aspect reflexivism and first-
order other-illuminationist (or first-order representationalist) views of
cognition. Recall Dretske's view that a conscious perceptual state is one
that makes the subject aware of objects, but that one should not conclude
that the subject must therefore be aware of the perceptual state itself. The
perceptual state is something the subject is *conscious-with* not something she
is *conscious-of*. Moreover, in a contemporary context, the issue is complicated
by the important distinction between conscious and unconscious cognition
because an unconscious cognition may be available for certain downstream
functions even when the subject is not conscious of the cognition or its
object. Take, for instance, the phenomenon of blindsight (Ajina and Bridge

2017). A lesion in the primary visual cortex (V1) causes a blind spot in the visual field. The subject reports not consciously seeing anything in the blind spot. However, the subject does have access to visual information about what is in the blind spot. In particular, the typical person with blindsight is capable of accurately guessing the presence or absence of the stimulus, movement detection, as well as reaching, pointing, and avoidance behavior.

So, in the blindsight case, there is some degree of cognitive and behavioral access to an object in the absence of any reported conscious awareness of the object or the cognition. This weakens Dharmakīrti's argument but might not defeat it. There are important differences between blindsight and normal sight. First, the degree of access is significantly diminished in the blindsight case. Subjects possess some visual information about the blind spot, but it is impoverished and unavailable to many typical mental functions, such as verbal report, voluntary attention, or fine-grained sensorimotor tasks. Second, based on the first-person reports of blindsight subjects, the visual information is not phenomenally conscious. There is nothing it is like for the subject to perceive an object in the blind spot, in marked contrast to other objects in the conscious visual field. Plausibly, an object in the blind spot is only partially established in terms of access and entirely unestablished in terms of phenomenal presentation. Indeed, blindsight provides a plausible demonstration of the distinction between conscious and unconscious cognition. So, while Dharmakīrti's argument is not successful as it stands, his point about the connection between reflexive awareness and *conscious* cognition may yet stand. Indeed, one could argue that the blindsight phenomenon bolters the transitivity principle. A cognition of which the subject is unaware is, like as in blindsight, an *unconscious* cognition lacking in phenomenal character and to which the cognizer has limited, if any, voluntary direct access.

Again, in contrast to the first-order other-illuminationist view, Dharmakīrti posits a deep link between conscious *content* and reflexive awareness. Consider what Montague terms the Conscious Content Principle:

> If a mental state S is conscious, the (representational) content of that mental state must be consciously entertained (we may say that in this sense the content of a mental state must be conscious). And conversely, if some (representational) content is consciously entertained, the mental state S of which it is the content must be conscious.
>
> (Montague 2016, 55)

The idea here is that consciously occurrent content implies a conscious state, and vice versa. In the blindsight case, it seems we have neither conscious content nor conscious state. On my reading though, Dharmakīrti is concerned with the epistemic status of conscious content and, according to the Conscious Content Principle, this implies a conscious cognition. In virtue of what is the cognition conscious? Dharmakīrti argues that the cognizer must 'perceive the perception'—that is, she must be directly, non-inferentially aware of it.

Mark Siderits (2025, 95–96) reconstructs Dharmakīrti's argument as follows:

1. S [subject-aspect] just is the cognizing of O [object-aspect]
2. Hence the cognizing of O is not distinct from the cognizing of S (by the identity of S and O)
3. Hence one cognizes O only if one cognizes S
4. One only seeks to obtain an object A if one is aware of A[15]
5. In order to be aware of A one must be aware of the cognizing of A (by (3))
6. Suppose cognition of cognition of A occurs only after cognition of A
7. But one does not cognize A unless one cognizes S
8. Then an infinite regress results from the supposition.
9. C: Therefore if cognition did not cognize itself there would be no acting to obtain one's goals.

Now proponents of a first-order view of consciousness, in keeping with the independence condition, can respond that the perception is conscious just insofar as it makes the cognizer conscious of its object. Nothing more. But how is a mental state of which the subject has absolutely no awareness different from the blindsight case? On the first-order view, in the blindsight case the state fails in phenomenally presenting the object whereas in the normal case it succeeds. In neither case does the subject need to be aware of her *perceiving*. What, then, differentiates an unconscious mental state from a conscious mental state for the first-order view? Here a proponent of the first-order view could appeal to a functional notion of access or availability. A mental state is conscious (makes its subject conscious of its object) just in case it is, say, widely available for things like action guidance, belief formation, and verbal report. As we have seen, this is a concern for Dharmakīrti as well. However, while there does seem to be an important link between consciousness and wide access, this purely functional account is not yet sufficient to explain state consciousness.

The view that emerges from these considerations is one in which each discrete moment or episode of consciousness has a dual-aspect form, presenting both an object appearance and a subject appearance, within an inherently reflexive structure. In this respect, Buddhist dual-aspect reflexivism resembles certain accounts of consciousness developed in the post-Husserlian phenomenological tradition. For instance, Aron Gurwitsch writes:

> Consciousness ... is consciousness of an object on the one hand and an inner awareness of itself on the other hand. Being confronted with an object, I am at once conscious of this object and aware of my being conscious of it. This awareness in no way means reflection: to know that I am dealing with the object which, for instance, I am just perceiving, I need not experience a second act bearing upon the perception and making it its object. In simply dealing with the object I am aware of this very dealing.
>
> (Gurwitsch 1940, 330)

Recall that Dharmakīrti states, "Just as an illuminating light is considered to be the illuminator of itself, because of its nature, just so, awareness is aware of itself." For the dual-aspect reflexivist, it is the very nature of consciousness to be reflexive and this reflexivity is the condition of any other phenomenal presentation. It also serves as the dative of manifestation or the receptivity of consciousness—it is that to which the object- and subject-appearances appear. That is, reflexive awareness accounts for the minimal (state) subjectivity of consciousness. Reflexive awareness constitutes the minimal phenomenal point of view within which various phenomenal contents are present. Both objective and subjective appearances appear within the condition of reflexive awareness. And, according to Dharmakīrti, without consciousness' fundamental self-presence, no other phenomenal contents could be present. Furthermore, as the basic condition within which anything can be present, reflexive awareness also constitutes the synchronic unity of consciousness.

Furthermore, according to Dharmakīrti and his commentator Śākyabuddhi, reflexive awareness is more basic than the subject-object structure and intentionality of consciousness.[14] Transitive (object-directed) intentionality presupposes subject-object duality, but on this view the subject-object duality is a cognitive distortion, not a real feature of consciousness. Reflexive awareness, however, is the very nature of consciousness and is therefore nondual and non-intentional. As Śākyabuddhi puts it:

> Since an agent and its patient are constructed in dependence upon each other, these two [i.e. subject and object] are posited in dependence on each other. The expression "subject" does not express mere reflexive awareness, which is the essential nature of cognition itself. The

essential nature of cognition is not construed in mutual dependence on something else because it arises as such from its own causes. The essential nature of cognition is established in mere reflexive awareness (*svasaṃvedanamātra*). Since it is devoid of the above-described subject and object, it is said to be non-dual.

(PVT 203b-204a)

Here we see the philosophical continuity between the Buddhist reflexivist epistemologists and earlier Yogācāra (Dunne 2004, 407). Rigorous analysis of the nature of cognition finally leads beyond all dualistic constructions of subject and object to *cittamātra* (consciousness-only or mere consciousness) which is, by nature, *svasaṃvedanamātra* (reflexive awareness-only or mere reflexive awareness).

7.4 Selflessness

Buddhist *pramāṇavāda* shares several features with earlier Buddhist views of mind and consciousness. As in the broader Abhidharma tradition, they adopt part-whole reductionism and a nominalist rejection of universals (*sāmānya, jāti*). As in Sautrāntika, they develop a representationalist theory of perception, affirm *sākāravāda*, and accept the radical momentariness theory (*kṣaṇikavāda*) of phenomena. As in earlier Yogācāra, they analyze the mind as a complex and dynamic stream of conscious events (*cittasantāna*), the basic nature and functions of which can be explained in largely intramental terms. Yet, despite these similarities, Buddhist *pramāṇavāda* also represents a genuinely new and distinctive approach to mind and consciousness. The dual-aspect structure accounts for both the intentional and subjective features of consciousness in a tightly integrated way. This feature of the view also helps address the two types of access problems mentioned above. Moreover, the idea that consciousness is inherently reflexive addresses three related issues. First, it accounts for what Itay Shani calls a "sentient terminus" in consciousness—that *to which* contents are presented. Second, it accounts for the synchronic unity of consciousness in that reflexive awareness is the direct awareness of all other aspects of a moment of consciousness. Third, it captures at least part of the intuition behind the transitivity principle—that is, a cognition of which one is completely unaware is not a conscious cognition. And it accounts for these in an economical way. The theory of reflexive awareness does not rely on separate higher-order representations, multiple arrows of intentionality, or separately existing subjects of experience.

However, classical Indian critics of Buddhist reflexivism challenged the view, particularly regarding its compatibility with the Buddhist doctrines of no-self and momentariness. Regarding no-self, we will examine two lines of argument. The first, developed by the Nyāya philosopher Uddyotakara, concerns self-knowledge and self-reference. The second, developed by the Advaita Vedāntin Śaṅkara, concerns diachronic self-consciousness.

Uddyotakara writes:

> The consciousness of "I," which conforms to the distinctions of the nature of the object, and which does not depend upon memory of marks, the possessor of the marks, and their relationship, is direct acquaintance just as is the cognition of physical form. Concerning what you yourself, with perfect confidence, establish to be direct acquaintance, in virtue of what is it that it is [said to be] direct acquaintance? You must establish it as being consciousness alone, which does not depend upon the relationships among marks, etc., and which is self-presenting. So then you think there is an I-cognition, but that its object is not the self? Well, then show us its object! (NV 704)

> (Kapstein 2001, 98)

Reflexive awareness can be understood as a form of direct awareness or direct acquaintance with the dual contents of experience. Indeed, Dignāga sometimes calls reflexive awareness a form of *pratyakṣa* (perception), meaning in this instance any form of direct, non-conceptual awareness. Crucially for the Buddhist reflexivists, this is awareness of awareness or consciousness of *itself*, not consciousness of a *self*. What Uddyotakara is interested in here, though, is *ahampratyaya* (I-cognition or self-reference). The idea here is that, when I am perceiving an object, I am aware that *I* am perceiving the object, that it is *me* having this perceptual experience. When having the perceptual experience, is there something further I must do (or think) for me to be aware that I am the one having that experience?

Perhaps I am not directly aware of myself as the subject, the one having the experience. Rather, it might be that I must *infer* that I am the subject. But what is the basis of this inference? How does one go from mental states such as <seeing a tree> or <feeling pain in the foot> to <I see a tree> or <I feel a pain in my foot>? One possibility is that I infer that I am the subject of the perceptual or pain state based on some feature of the state itself. In this case there would need to be some mark (*liṅga*) or inferential sign attached to the mental states that warrants the inference that they are mine and (thus) I am their subject. What kind of mark or sign would that be? It is not clear that mental states come with such a mark. Moreover, the deeper difficulty is that any inference of this kind would seem to presuppose the I-consciousness (self-awareness) it is meant to establish. For the mark to indicate that a mental state is mine (that I am having it), I must already be aware of myself as the subject to whom the mental state might belong. That is, if I detect a mental state, for example, <seeing a tree>, and want to establish that the mental state belongs to me based on a special mark (perhaps it comes stamped *MM*), I must already know that anything so marked is *mine*. It does no good to know merely that any mental state with a certain feature belongs to MM. I must further be aware that *I* am MM. Further, perhaps I could be mistaken about whether a particular mental state belongs to me, but it is hard to see how I could be mistaken about whether *I* am the one inquiring. And that awareness of myself cannot be based on some special mark without setting off a vicious regress.

An alternative, as Uddyotakara points out in the passage, is that first-person self-reference is anchored in a non-criterial, non-inferential mode of self-acquaintance (Shoemaker 1994). But if there is no self, then what are I-cognitions directly acquainted with? What is the subject of experience? Here we come to a fundamental divide between two views of the basic structure of consciousness. Borrowing from contemporary phenomenology, we can call them the *egological* and the *non-egological* views of consciousness. As Dan Zahavi explains,

> an *egological* theory would claim that when I watch a movie by Bergman, I am not only intentionally directed at the *movie*, nor merely aware of the movie being *watched*, I am also aware that it is being watched by *me*, that is, that *I* am *watching* the *movie* … Thus, an egological theory would typically claim that it is a conceptual and experiential truth that any episode of experiencing necessarily includes a subject of experience.
>
> (Zahavi 2008, 99)

On the egological view, a state of consciousness has a triadic structure. The global character of the experience includes an intentional object (the movie), aspects of the experiencing itself (watching, and the like), and a sense of being the subject of the experience. Zahavi calls the third aspect *for-me-ness* and argues that this sense of for-me-ness is closely linked to the first-person perspective that structures consciousness. Importantly, this *me-ness* or I-consciousness is non-inferential and pre-reflective—it is built into the nature of consciousness and does not require introspection or reflective thought. Moreover, it is (part of) what makes possible explicit I-thoughts.

In contrast, non-egological views deny that it is a "conceptual and experiential truth that any episode of experiencing necessarily includes a subject of experience." For example, on a strong *no-ownership* view, experiences are not for a subject at all but are non-subjective. As Jonardon Ganeri characterizes the no-ownership view of Buddhist reductionism (as found, he thinks, in Vasubandhu), "There is nothing that owns mental tropes [states] and they don't aggregate to form subjects (it is the fundamental wrong move to think that any of the mental items, or the collective stream, is a subject)" (2012, 42). We may have a *sense* of being a subject or having a robust first-person perspective, but this is a kind of illusion or distortion of fundamentally selfless and non-subjective phenomena. However, in contrast to this no-ownership view, the Buddhist reflexivists offer a different version of the non-egological theory. Like the non-egological views in phenomenology (Sartre 1991) and (Gurwitsch 1940), Buddhist reflexivists hold that consciousness is always conscious of itself. As we've seen in this chapter, reflexive awareness serves as 1) a phenomenal perspective, 2) a mode of access to phenomenal content (*ākāra, ābhāsa*), 3) a sentient terminus or dative of manifestation, and 4) a basis for the synchronic unity of consciousness. As I have argued elsewhere, these features warrant understanding reflexive awareness as a minimal form of subjectivity (MacKenzie 2024). However, this weak notion of subjectivity differs from the egological view in at least two important respects. First, it is compatible with an anonymous conscious perspective. That is, it is a kind of experiential hosting or what Miri Albahari (Albahari 2006) calls perspective ownership, rather than the more robust form of personal ownership associated with a sense of "I-me-mine" (*asmimana*). Second, reflexive awareness is limited to each distinct moment of consciousness—it is synchronic not diachronic.[15]

So, in response to Uddyotakara's challenge, a Buddhist reflexivist can affirm direct acquaintance with consciousness, but deny that this involves acquaintance with a *self*. On this view, my pre-reflective sense of being a subject (the for-me-ness) is not a distinct or inherent feature of experience. Rather, it is part of the content of the *svābhāsa*, the internal face or profile of the moment of consciousness. The deep sense of being a separate self or subject "in here" looking at a world "out there" is a mental construction (*kalpanā*). And a false or distorted one at that. The bare conscious perspective provided by reflexive awareness (*svasaṃvedanamātra*) is reified into a more robust sense of self.[16] Just as the object-aspect of the cognition is (mis-) taken to be the real external object rather than a mental image, so the subject-aspect is (mis-) taken to be a real self rather than a mental image. On this view, the implicit I-consciousness is a misconstrual of the reflexivity of consciousness. One might say that the moment of consciousness is its own subject (in contrast to the strong no-ownership view), but this is not a self. Further, when one explicitly thinks I-thoughts or has I-cognitions (*ahampratyaya*) one is in fact appropriating or identifying with prior cognitions. But, for the Buddhist reflexivist, in neither case is one acquainted with a persisting subject of experience.

This is what might be called an *illusionist* response to Uddyotakara's objection.[17] In the case of visual illusions such as the Müller-Lyer illusion or the bent stick illusion, one perceives an object, but in a distorted or mistaken way. In the Müller-Lyer illusion one sees two lines, but they falsely appear to be different lengths, whereas in the bent stick illusion one sees the stick, but it is distorted by refraction from being in the water. Likewise, in the case of strong first-person consciousness (I-consciousness or for-me-ness) or I-cognitions, one is aware of a real conscious state—a moment of dual-aspect reflexive awareness—which falsely appears to present a real self.

The second line of argument against Buddhist reflexivism concerns the diachronic aspects of consciousness. As already discussed in Chapter 6, against a Yogācāra Buddhist opponent Śaṅkara argues:

> The mental impressions must have an abode. Without that they cannot exist. But the doctrine of momentariness denies permanency to everything. Even the *ālayavijñāna* is momentary and cannot be that abode. Unless there is a permanent principle connecting the past, present, and future, there cannot be remembrance or recognition of an experience originating at a particular time and place. If the *ālayavijñāna* is said to be something permanent, then that would go counter to the doctrine of momentariness.
>
> (BrSūBh 2.2.5)

The objection here is that basic mental functions such as memory or recognition (of objects or oneself) require the experiential continuity of a genuine stream of consciousness. And this requires, according to Śaṅkara, a persisting subject of experience to ground the diachronic unity of experience. However, if there is really nothing more than a series of momentary mental events (even if causally connected), then there can be no diachronic unity.

The Buddhist reflexivist response to this kind of objection is to appeal to both the causal and cognitive relations between mental events in a stream. The connection between a current mental event and its immediate condition (*samanantarapratyaya*)—that is, the immediately prior mental event—is causal but also synthetic. It is these synthetic cognitive relations rather than the positing on an enduring self that explain the synthetic cohesion (*pratisandhāna*) of the stream. It is the intra-stream relations between events that ground synthetic cohesion, and according to the Buddhist reflexivist, to infer an enduring ontological ground behind the stream imputes a false substantial unity on a series of momentary events.

This response to Śaṅkara tries to show that the diachronic unity of consciousness is unnecessary for memory and recognition. Rather, only the weaker notion of diachronic continuity is required, and that is provided by casual and cognitive connections between momentary mental events. However, it is important to recall that the Buddhist epistemologist's final ontology is very austere. As we saw in section 7.1, their ontology consists in two categories: *svalakṣaṇas* (particulars) and *sāmānyalakṣaṇas* (universals). In terms of our present topic, the momentary mental events are *svalakṣaṇas*, whereas the intra-mental connections that support diachronic continuity are *sāmānyalakṣaṇas*. Indeed, Dharmakīrti argues in his *Sambandha Parīkṣā* (*Examination of Relations*), all relations, including causal relations, are *sāmānyalakṣaṇas* (SP 2.7–24). However, the critical point here is that for the Buddhist epistemologists, in the final analysis, *sāmānyalakṣaṇas* are not real. As strict nominalists, only particulars are real. This means that *any* form of relationality or continuity is ultimately a mental construct or fabrication (*kalpanā*) (SP 1.5). Thus, the Buddhist *pramāṇavādins* in the end must resort to an illusionist account of the diachronic continuity of consciousness as well.

The picture that emerges is that there is a series of momentary mental events or tropes but no persisting self and no real continuous stream (*santāna*) existing over and above the mere series. However, a momentary cognition may still *represent* itself as being part of a temporally integrated stream or as belonging to a self. This would be part of *svākāra* or subject-aspect of the cognition. And as Monima Chadha (2015) has recently pointed out, it is possible to have a temporally thick form of *content* carried by a momentary mental *vehicle* (Dennett and Kinsbourne 1992). That is, just as a two-dimensional image may represent a three-dimensional scene, or a temporally present chart may represent an expanse of time, so a mental moment could represent persisting objects, subjects, and streams of consciousness. Thus, as she reconstructs the Buddhist reflexivist view:

> The principles that constitute conscious sensations and perceptions do not need to glue together temporally contiguous impressions into a diachronically unified stream of experience that accounts for unity of objects and subjects. Rather, conscious sensations and perceptions are constituted by luminous phenomenal forms that supervene on the local distribution of co-temporal *dharmas* made available by the sense faculties, basic consciousness, and other mental factors in the vertical present. But note that there is no veridical awareness of succession: there is only a succession of awarenesses. Diachronic unity of successive

awareness is only an illusion, a conceptual fabrication of the ego-consciousness. This shows too that the doctrine of reflexive awareness is compatible with a no-self view, insofar as the notion of self requires diachronic unity of experience.

(Chadha 2017, 285)

7.5 Comparative Connections

The dual-aspect reflexivism developed by the Buddhist *pramāṇavādins* offers a philosophically rich and flexible account of the nature and structure of consciousness. Further, it is a good example of what phenomenological philosopher David Woodruff Smith calls a "modal model" of consciousness. As he explains:

> [a] *modal model* of (self-) consciousness factors out several different "modal" characters (as I call them) in the phenomenological structure of a typical conscious experience. These characters … define not the way the *object* of consciousness is presented in an act of consciousness, but rather the way the *act itself* is experienced or carried out: that is, *consciously*, with a certain form of *awareness*.

(Smith 2016, 292)

As I explained earlier, according to Woodruff Smith, the 'modal characters' are analytically distinguishable factors that contribute to the overall phenomenological structure of a typical experience or act of consciousness. Additionally, he includes the intentionality of an experience as an additional factor distinct from the various modes of experience mentioned above. The explanatory aim of the modal model is to give a rigorous account of the phenomenological structure of a typical conscious experience as well as a systematic account of the variant and invariant aspects of that structure.

Woodruff Smith lists several factors he takes to be typically present in an act of consciousness:

> These "modal" characters in an act of consciousness include: phenomenality, or how the experience "appears" in consciousness; egocentricity, or how the "I" appears as subject of experience; inner awareness *per se*, or how the experience is reflexively experienced as "this very experience"; a spatiotemporal sense of embodiment, of the "here and now" as experienced (say) in seeing something "here and now before me"; the species of conscious activity (e.g. seeing, thinking,

willing, etc.). These modal characters modify the presentation of the *object* of consciousness: that is, whereby the object is presented as such-and-such.

(Smith 2016, 292)

How might a proponent of the dual-aspect reflexivist model articulate the structure of a moment of experience? First, we may identify the intentional or cognitive (*jñānatā*) aspect of experience, which Dharmakīrti understands as *viṣayagrahaṇam* (grasping or apprehending an object). Grasp of the cognitive object, in this model, is mediated by a phenomenal form (*viṣayākāra*) which would count as one of the discernable modes or factors internal to the experience.[18] Second is the subjective aspect which, as we have seen, includes the various modes or factors. For example, Dignāga includes the mental factors (*caitta*) of "desire, anger, ignorance, pleasure, pain, etc." and we may more generally list the "omnipresent mental factors" of sensory contact (*sparśa*), affect (*vedanā*), cognition (*saṃjñā*)[19], conation (*cetanā*), and attention (*manaskāra*). Arguably, the subjective aspect would also include the sense of self or egocentricity as well as the basic sense of temporality. Indeed, these two factors are linked because they are both based on a (for Buddhists ultimately illusory) sense of persistence within consciousness. Third, we have reflexive awareness itself, which is awareness of awareness or the inner awareness of consciousness itself. The complex interplay of these modes or factors arguably provides a phenomenologically robust account of the basic structure of consciousness.

Several contemporary philosophers have been influenced by and drawn on Buddhist *pramāṇavāda* ideas. For instance, Evan Thompson (Thompson 2014) has drawn on Buddhist reflexivist (and earlier Yogācāra, Yoga, and Advaita Vedānta) ideas to develop a rich phenomenology of dreaming, the hypnogogic state, deep sleep, meditation, and even (so-called) out-of-body and near-death experiences. Specifically, Thompson understands consciousness in terms of the twin capacities for (phenomenal) manifestation (luminosity, *prakāśatā*) and apprehension (cognizance, *samvit*). He then analyzes three distinct aspects of the operation of consciousness: "awareness, the contents of awareness (what we're aware of from moment to moment), and ways of experiencing certain contents of awareness as being or belonging to the self (our sense of self or 'I-Me-Mine')" (Thompson 2014, 16). Finally, Thompson argues that consciousness is self-luminous or reflexive. Thus, he writes, "Consciousness is that which is luminous, knowing, and reflexive. Consciousness is that which makes manifest appearances, is able to apprehend them in one way or another, and in so doing is self-appearing and prereflectively self-aware" (Thompson 2014, 18). While his own views differ from the Buddhist reflexivists in important ways (Thompson 2022), Thompson draws on their ideas of reflexive awareness, objective and subjective aspects, a dynamic stream of experiences, and the fluid and (partially) constructed nature of the sense of self.

Monima Chadha (2023) has drawn on both Abhidharma (especially Vasubandha) and Buddhist epistemological thinkers in her recent work in philosophy of mind and metaphysics. For example, she has argued that *svasaṃvedana* is essential to consciousness and the reflexive nature of consciousness is consistent with the radical no-self and momentariness views characteristic of mainstream Indian Buddhism. She has also applied these Buddhist ideas to issues ranging from the synchronic unity of consciousness to perception, emotions, meditation, depersonalization disorders, and ethical vows. Likewise, in my own work (MacKenzie 2022a) (MacKenzie 2022b), I have drawn on the dual-aspect reflexivist model to understand the nature of consciousness, the distinction between consciousness and the sense of self, the nature of meditation, as well as subjectivity and temporality.

The basic structure of dual-aspect reflexivism as a model may be able to account for several key features (modes or factors) of a typical state of consciousness. But, as Woodruff Smith makes clear, a feature or mode may be *typical* but neither invariant nor essential to all possible states of consciousness. It is an open question whether any particular feature might be invariant or even essential to consciousness *per se*. Furthermore, more recently philosophers such as Jennifer Windt and Thomas Metzinger (2007) have introduced the idea of *Minimal Phenomenal Experience* (MPE), which is hypothesized as the simplest state of consciousness. The MPE hypothesis is then linked to a *minimal model* of consciousness. That is, a model that attempts to isolate the minimal conditions, core invariant features, or causal factors of the MPE. Metzinger hypothesizes that that minimal phenomenal experience, "lacks (i) MPS [minimal phenomenal self] and all other forms of egoic self-consciousness, (ii) time representation, and (iii) a spatial frame of reference" (Metzinger 2020, 2). He further hypothesizes that it would involve the minimal phenomenality of tonic alertness or wakefulness and low complexity of contents (9).

Interestingly, the Buddhist reflexivist Śākyabuddhi appears to offer his own minimal model of consciousness. As we saw in section 7.3, he writes:

> Since an agent and its patient are constructed in dependence upon each other, these two [i.e. subject and object] are posited in dependence on each other. The expression "subject" does not express mere reflexive awareness, which is the essential nature of cognition itself. The

essential nature of cognition is not construed in mutual dependence on something else because it arises as such from its own causes. The essential nature of cognition is established in mere reflexive awareness (*svasaṃvedanamātra*). Since it is devoid of the above-described subject and object, it is said to be non-dual.

(SVT 203b-204a)

Here *svasaṃvedanamātra* or mere reflexive awareness is posited as the essence of consciousness. As sheer self-luminosity, it combines (or is the shared nature of) the two factors of phenomenality and reflexive or inner awareness. If there could be an instance of pure or mere reflexive awareness, based on this passage, it would lack i) a sense of agency, ii) a sense of being a subject or self, and iii) the presentation of a distinct object. Arguably, it would also lack iv) spatial and v) temporal representation. Thus, following Woodruff Smith's account, a typical moment of consciousness might have the following structure:

<phenomenally in this very experience I now here see this red pot>.

However, a moment of mere reflexive awareness might only have this structure (Smith 2016, 298):

<phenomenally there appears this present field of consciousness>.

Here we would simply have an inner awareness of the phenomenal quality of consciousness's own wakefulness, prior to it taking on or reflecting any further phenomenal form of subject or object. Perhaps, then, theoretically austere Buddhist reflexivism—wherein self, object, conceptuality, temporality, and continuity are ultimately eliminated—could provide a minimal model of consciousness.[20]

7.6 Questions

1. What are the two basic ontological categories in Buddhist *Pramāṇavāda*?
2. What are the two aspects of a moment of consciousness and how are they related to reflexive awareness?
3. What is Dignāga's memory argument? Is it persuasive?
4. How do Buddhist *pramāṇavādins* reconcile reflexive awareness with no-self? Is their reconciliation convincing?

Notes

1 Both what we take to be enduring objects (substances) as well as events and processes, then, are ultimately reducible to sequences of trope bundles. Individuation of these constructions is ultimately a matter of our conventions and interests in successful practice (Dunne 2004).

2 Other philosophical traditions accepted as *pramāṇas*, in addition to perception and inference, such means as testimony (*śabda*), analogy (*upamāna*), postulation (*arthapātti*), or absence/non-perception (*anupalabdhi*). The skeptical Cārvāka tradition accepted only perception (Phillips and Vaidya 2024).

3 There was significant debate concerning the relationship between conceptuality and language. At a minimum, conceptual cognition is fit to be articulated in language even if not itself properly linguistic.

4 In terms of contemporary philosophy of perception, "representationalism" sometimes names a direct realist view according to which perceptual states are representational states bearing a certain representational content. However, these views deny the role of mediating mental images. This view is also called (perhaps more appropriately) "intentionalism" (Crane and French 2021). In this chapter I will use "representationalism" in the older sense of indirect perception by way of mental images.

5 Note that this issue is not whether knowledge is mediated by cognitive states, but whether the cognitive state itself has an internal image or form.

6 In the case of the Buddhist epistemologists, however, things are more complicated because they ultimately endorse an idealist metaphysics that does away with mind-independent external objects. See (Arnold 2008) and (Ratié 2014) for further discussion.

7 For purposes of this discussion, the ultimate status of external objects or the external world for these thinkers will be left aside. I will be treating the *pramāṇavādins* external realists who deploy an indirect realist account of perception.

8 Quoted in (Montague 2016, 143).

9 Both *ākāra* ('phenomenal form') and *ābhāsa* ('appearance') are used to refer to these 'aspects'.

10 Cf. (Garfield 2006) and (Thompson 2011).

11 Ultimately, Dignāga will deny any such ontological gap even in the case of the perceptual object, consistent with his Yogācāra idealism. However, Buddhist *pramāṇavādins* typically argued in a way that was consistent with both Sautrāntika indirect realism and Yogācāra idealism (cf. PS 1.9cd). For Dharmakīrti see (Dunne 2004), (Dreyfus 1997), and (Kellner 2011).

12 On my interpretation, the introspection or meta-cognition argument is meant to establish the subject-aspect, while the memory argument is meant to establish reflexive awareness and in doing so relies on the accessibility of the subject-aspect of prior states.

13 The difference is that the awareness of awareness thesis does not mention a self or subject. It is only committed to the idea that conscious awareness is reflexive.

14 There is significant debate among Buddhist reflexivists about the relationship between the aspects and the nature of awareness. Some argue that there is no awareness without the aspects, while others argue that the aspects themselves are in some sense an illusion. See Dreyfus (1997) for an extensive discussion.

15 As discussed in Chapter 8, phenomenological thinkers, whether egological or non-egological, see pre-reflective self-awareness as tightly connected to time-consciousness, and thus as diachronic (Zahavi 2003).

16 Note that this move is like the one found in earlier Yogācāra where the *kliṣṭamanas* misrepresents the *ālayavijñāna* as if it were a persisting self.

17 See (Frankish 2016) and (Kammerer 2021) on illusionism about phenomenal consciousness. See (Cermeño-Aínsa 2025) and (Chaturvedi 2024) on proposed connections between Yogācāra and illusionism.

18 Note that this more indirect or representationalist account of intentionality is quite different from the one developed by Woodruff Smith, which draws from the Husserlian tradition of phenomenology. However, his full model of the ideal phenomenological structure of an act of consciousness includes the "object-presenting sense" as one of the factors. This sense (*Sinn*) (or *noema* in Husserlian terms) plays a role similar to the object-aspect (Smith and McIntyre 1984).

19 The cognitive factor relevant to the subject aspect might include what Woodruff Smith calls the species of conscious activity. Thus, whether the experience is an instance of visual perception or thought would count as part of the subject aspect.

20 For Buddhist thinkers, the austerity of the model would be motivated (at least in part) by their austere metaphysics of momentary particulars (*dharmas, svalakṣanas*). However, a minimal *model* of consciousness need not be coupled with an austere or minimalist metaphysics. The role of the minimal model of consciousness is to isolate its core features, not infer from those core features what really exists. Thus, even if the self does not appear in MPE, it does not rule out the existence of the self. Likewise, one's own brain does not typically appear in experience, but one may hold the metaphysical view that brains exist, and consciousness depends on the brain in some critical way.

Further Reading

Duckworth, Douglas, and Malcolm David Eckel. 2016. *Dignaga's Investigation of the Percept: A Philosophical Legacy in India and Tibet*. Translated by Jay

L. Garfield, John Powers, Yeshes Thabkhas, and Sonam Thakchoe. Oxford University Press.

Dunne, John D. 2004. *Foundations of Dharmakīrti's Philosophy*. Wisdom Publications.

Hattori, Masaaki. 1968. *Dignāga, on Perception: Being the Pratyakṣapariccheda of Dignāga's Pramāṇasamuccaya from the Sanskrit Fragments and the Tibetan Versions*. Harvard University Press.

Pandeya, Ram Chandra, ed. 2024. *The Pramāṇavārttikam of Ācārya Dharmakīrti*. Motilal Banarsidass Publishing House.

Stoltz, Jonathan. 2021. *Illuminating the Mind: An Introduction to Buddhist Epistemology*. Oxford University Press.

8

Pratyabhijñā

8.1 The Pratyabhijñā School

The Pratyabhijñā or "Recognition" school of thought emerged within the rich, cosmopolitan intellectual environment of ninth-century Kashmir. During this period, Kashmir was a crossroads of both trade and culture. Intellectually, "in the complex and varied cultural panorama of ninth-century Kashmir we find all the major components of the religious-philosophical tendencies in India at the time" (Torella 2021, x). These include Buddhist Abhidharma, Yogācāra, and Pramāṇavāda thinkers, as well as Brahmanical Nyāya, Vedānta, and Mīmāṃsā thinkers. The Grammarian school (*Vyākaraṇa*) of Bartṛhari also flourished in Kashmir, as did various traditions of aesthetics and literary criticism (Torella 2021).

The Pratyabhijñā school itself emerged within the broader religious movement of Tantric Śaivism. This movement centers on devotion to Śiva as the supreme divinity, draws on the Vedas and the (Śaiva) Āgamas and Tantras as scriptures, and is associated with distinctive tantric ritual and yogic practices. Further, one can divide the Tantric Śaiva traditions into generally dualistic and nondualistic or monistic varieties. The Śaiva Siddhānta school, for instance, is theistic and dualistic in that Śiva is understood as an ontologically distinct supreme being (theism) and individual selves (*ātman*) are distinct, persisting, ontologically independent substances. This tradition is developed and defended by philosophers such as Bhaṭṭa Rāmakaṇṭha (c. 950–1000 CE), who wrote on a wide range of philosophical topics including a systematic and novel defense of the *ātman* against Buddhist critics (Watson 2006). In contrast, Vasugupta (c. 800–850 CE) develops the nondualistic or monistic strands of Tantric Śaivism in his *Śivasūtras*.

Vasugupta's disciple, Somānanda (c. 875–925 CE), is the founder of the Recognition school. In his philosophical treatise, the *Śivadṛṣṭi*, he engages in the lengthy critiques of Buddhist Yogācāra and Bartṛhari's Grammarian philosophy. He also develops many of the central tenets of his own Pratyabhijñā view. Somānanda's most important disciple was Utpaladeva (c.925–975CE). His major work, the *Īśvarapratyabhijñā* (*[Treatise on] Recognition of the Lord*)— along with his auto-commentary (*Īśvarapratyabhijñākārikā*) and extensive sub-commentary (*Pratyabhijñāvimarśinī*)—is a systematic elaboration and defense of the Recognition school. After Utpaladeva, the great polymath Abhinavagupta (c.975–1025 CE) further enriched and systematized the view in his commentaries on Utpaladeva, the *Īśvarapratyabhijñāvimarśinī* (*Commentary to the Verses on the Recognition of the Lord*) and *Īśvarapratyab hijñāvivṛtivimarśinī* (*Commentary on the explanation of Īśvarapratyabhijñā*), as well as other works. As we will elaborate in this chapter, Pratyabhijñā thinkers see Śiva as the monistic absolute—the unified source and substance of all. This supreme reality is absolute consciousness (*paramśiva*) and creative power (*śakti*). It is identical to the consciousness of each individual self, and its activity or dynamic manifestation is the world. The path to liberation (*mokṣa*) is the full *recognition* that all is ultimately Śiva.

Regarding the philosophy of mind and consciousness, this chapter will explore four related themes developed by Utpaladeva and Abhinavagupta. The first is the inherent dynamism of consciousness (section 8.2). In Pratyabhijñā thought, consciousness has an intrinsically active dimension, related to notions of agency, creativity, and freedom. The second is the view that the self, as the active conscious subject, is revealed directly in experience (section 8.3). Defense of this view requires both an answer to Buddhist critiques of the existence of the self, as well as a distinctive account of nature of self-awareness. As we will see below, the Pratyabhijñā view of the self as dynamic, self-luminous consciousness both borrows from and sharply criticizes Buddhist Pramāṇavāda. Finally, the third theme is a defense of the reality of the phenomenal world and individual selves within a nondual or monistic ontology. As we will discuss on section 8.5, Pratyabhijñā thinkers argue that world is the real expression of the creative dynamism of Śiva-Śakti, rather than an ultimately false (*mithyā*) appearance or illusory manifestation (*vivarta*) as in (some interpretations of) Advaita Vedānta. In this way, the relationship between absolute consciousness (*paramśiva*) and the phenomenal world is parallel to the relationship between the individual subject and her flow of experiences and actions.

8.2 Consciousness and Action

In *Īśvarapratyabhijñākārikā* (ĪPK), Utpaladeva writes:

> I.1.2 What intelligent being could ever deny or establish the cognizer and agent, the Self, Maheśvara, established from the beginning?
> — The Self of all beings, the substratum of the establishment of all objects, who embraces of himself—since otherwise it would be impossible to establish all the various objects—self-luminous, whose

nature is uniquely that of cognizer, formerly established, ancient, possesses knowledge and action. Sovereignty (*aiśvaryaṃ*) is established through inner awareness. Therefore only the foolish strive to establish or deny the Lord.[1]

Several important aspects of the Pratyabhijñā view are introduced in this passage. First, the self is self-evident—it makes no sense (it is "foolish") to attempt to independently establish[2] or deny it. Second, while the self is self-evident (or self-establishing), it is the basis for the establishment of any *object* of consciousness. Objects can only be cognitively grasped or known by a subject, through the means of consciousness. Third, the two essential qualities of the self are knowing and action. The self, according to Utpaladeva, is essentially a "cognizer and agent." And fourth, the self is "sovereign" (*aiśvarya*[3]) or autonomous.

The connection between consciousness and action is one of the most important and distinctive aspects of Pratyabhijñā thought. As we have seen in earlier chapters, proponents of the self (*ātmavādins*) agree that the self must be the principle of synchronic and diachronic unity and identity. Yet they disagree on the relationship between the self and consciousness and between the self and agency (*kartṛtva*). Nyāya thinkers defend the view that self is both knower and agent. However, the capacities for cognition and agency are active only when the self is embodied and in touch with the world. In Nyāya thought, the liberated self is neither conscious nor active. On the other hand, in the Sāṅkhya, Yoga, and Advaita Vedānta schools, the self is identical to consciousness but is not an agent. The self is the light of consciousness, the seer (*draṣṭṛ*), or the witness (*sākṣin*), but the locus of agency is the ontologically distinct mind (*manas*). Consciousness here is essentially passive. In sharp contrast, in Pratyabhijñā the self is consciousness and it is essentially active.

The conscious self, according to Utpaladeva, has two intertwined powers: the power of knowing or cognition (*jñāna-śakti*) and the power of action (*kriyā-śakti*). Abhinavagupta posits a triadic (*trika*) set of powers: cognition, action, and will (*icchā-śakti*). For him, the desire of the will is the background condition of both cognitions and actions. Take a mundane example: Devadatta desires to eat rice. He then searches for the materials necessary to cook some rice. This searching is both cognitive and active, and it is motivated by his underlying desire to eat. Devadatta gathers the materials—firewood, a pot, water, rice—and goes about cooking the rice. For the Śaiva thinkers, following the influence of Bartṛhari, the action 'Devadatta cooks rice' is analyzed in terms of Sanskrit grammatical categories (*kāraka*). Utpaladeva writes:

ĪPK II.2.6 The connection existing between the factors of the action (*kārakāṇām*) is based on the awareness of the action (*kriyā*); the notions of space etc. rest on the connection between limit and limited.

—The notion of action is based on unity-multiplicity, insofar as the various factors that contribute to carrying out the action—wood, saucepan, Devadatta, rice—are internally linked to each other by the verb 'he cooks' and externally differentiated. Also spatial and temporal succession—given the mutual involvement of the objects which act as the limiting and limited element—is merely a particular case of relation characterized in the same way by unity and multiplicity. The notions of universal, individual substance, action, number etc. all rest on inherence (*samavāya*), which is a particular type of relation.

So, the action is here understood as a complex unity made up of several related factors. The different factors (*kāraka*) include the agent (*kartṛ*), instrument (*karaṇa*), the object (*karman*), location (*adhikaraṇa*), where it comes from spatially, causally, and so forth. (*upādāna*), and for whom or what it is performed (*sampradāna*) (Lawrence 1999, 139). In our example, Devadatta (the agent) cooks (action) the rice (object) in a pot (location) using fire (instrument) so that he may eat it (goal, recipient). An action (and the action situation) has an identifiable structure, which for these thinkers is in fact a *syntax*. The syntax of action unifies the diverse elements into an intelligible whole, a unity in multiplicity. Furthermore, this intelligible structure is graspable by the agent or an observer, allowing a discrete series of spatial and temporal events to be identified as an *action*, rather than a mere series of things that happen.

Utpaladeva goes on to state:

II.4.5 Thus, action ... characterized by succession and manifesting itself both internally and externally (*antarbahihsthitiḥ*), being related to an entity that is unitary (*ekasya*) and capable of showing both aspects, is proved to be one.

— This action, though taking place in succession, being both internal and external, is connected with a unitary reality, the agent, established as such through inner awareness, and with an object that is also unitary, since it is recognized as being one by reflective awareness (*aikyena pratyavamṛśyasya*), despite the manifold changeable forms of the manifestation. And it is precisely on the basis of this fact—i.e. that its substratum is unitary—that is unity is proved.

We will discuss the complex issue of recognition through reflective awareness in the next section. Here the important points are that an action is an extended process and that this process has both internal and external aspects. The internal aspect includes the agent's desires, awareness, cognitions, intentions and so on. The external aspects include the external materials and objects, as well as the bodily movements of the agent. For Utpaladeva, the structured unity of an action requires the unity of the agent and the object over time. Two key aspects of this unity are the agent's continuous inner awareness of acting coupled with her continuous external awareness of the object and situation of action. Because the extended process of action straddles the inner and outer, and because it has an intelligible syntax, an action can be interpreted or understood as the outer expression of inner consciousness.[4]

In this way, action expresses the active power (*kriyā-śakti*) of the self and, more deeply, the intrinsic dynamism of consciousness. This active power is manifest not only in overt action, but also in will, desire, perception, imagination, and creativity. The life of the self is continuously expressed through its free agency. Indeed, Isabella Ratié explains:

> Refusing to define it as a static substance capable of bearing transitory qualities, [Utpaladeva] rather presents it as a pure dynamism: according to the Śaiva, the self is nothing but the absolute freedom (*svātantrya*) that constitutes the essence of consciousness. The term *svātantrya* primarily designates the property of that which is autonomous, or exists and acts by itself, without requiring any external prompting or determination (contrary to what is heteronomous, *paratantra*). But translations such as "autonomy" or "independence" fail to grasp the entire range of meaning of the Sanskrit word, because *svātantrya* designates, more than a mere absence of external influence, a positive power that nothing can hinder (the Śaivas often use it as an equivalent of terms such as *aiśvarya*, "sovereignty"), and also because—at least in Śaiva nondualistic literature—it has strong aesthetic connotations: *svātantrya* is the playfulness and aesthetic delight experienced in any artistic process, but also in any act of imagination.
>
> (Ratié 2017, 440)

On this view, the self is essentially a free agent. Thus, whereas some accounts of *ātman* see it as essentially static and receptive (as the pure principle of awareness, seeing, or witnessing), the Pratyabhijñā school sees the self as dynamic and active. However, unlike the Buddhists who analytically dissolve the (supposed) self into a causal series of moments, Pratyabhijñā sees the self as an enduring substratum. The self, according to Pratyabhijñā, is an active substance.

Moreover, this active substance, ultimately, is the *only* substance. As monistic idealists, Pratyabhijñā thinkers hold that absolute consciousness (*saṃvit*) is the ground and underlying substance of all things. Philosophically, absolute consciousness is the highest principle (*tattva*). Religiously, it is the Lord Śiva. Thus, all individual agency is ultimately the agency of Śiva or the divine syzygy, Śiva-Śakti. As Abhinavagupta elaborates:

> Here [according to this system], action is really nothing but the Supreme Lord's [agential] intention [icchā]. [This agential intention] consists of uninterrupted self-recognition [svātmāparamarśa] which has the nature of unobstructed [agential] freedom [svātantya], and is not dependent on another ... For [limited individuals such as] Caitra or Maitra, etc., the inner intention [icchā] [expressed] "I cook" is the action. Thus, even though there is the movements such as putting something on the fire, etc., the [intention] "I cook" is uninterrupted. It is nothing but the intention [icchā] "I cook" which appears as such movements. However there is really no sequence in this [intention]. Thus is that reognitive judgement [vimarśa] of the Lord, which has the nature of intention [icchā, which may be expressed] "I Lord," "I appear," "I manifest in cosmogonic vibration [sphurāmi] ... The essential nature [of such recognitive judgement] is nothing but "I," and it has no sequence.
>
> (ĪPV 2.1.8, 2:24-25)[5]

Thus, in the final analysis, all action is reducible to the unified intention of Śiva to manifest as all phenomena and all individuated selves.

8.3 Memory and Recognition

Utpaladeva opens the ĪPK with brief statement of his view of the self, which he then defends by entertaining a series of objections from a philosophical opponent (*pūrvapakṣin*), in this case a Buddhist. As we saw in the last section, he states (I.1.2) that the self is self-evident or "established from the beginning" so that it does not make sense to try to independently establish or deny it. Yet, while he thinks the *existence* of the self is undeniable, he also holds that the true nature of the self is not discerned because of delusion (I.1.3). Hence the need for a reflective *recognition* (*pratyabhijñā*) of the nature of the self.

Given this situation, one can come to grasp the true nature of the self (in part) through a grasp of its essential powers, namely knowledge and action. To this end, Utpaladeva points out the (provisional) distinction between sentient and insentient aspects of reality and an important epistemic asymmetry between them. He states:

ĪPK I.1.4 Indeed, the foundation of insentient realities rests on the living [sentient] being; knowledge and action are considered the life of the living being.

— There are two kinds of reality: sentient and insentient. The establishment of the insentient rests on the living being; the being such of the living, i.e. life, is represented by knowledge and action.

On this view, insentient things are only experienced or known ("established") by sentient knowers. However, he goes on to argue, (I.1.5) "Knowledge is self-established (*svataḥ siddham*); action, when it manifests itself through a body, becomes cognizable also by others. Thanks to it, knowledge in other can be guessed." Knowledge and action, as two essential powers of consciousness, are self-established. In other words, the conscious mental life of a sentient being is available to that being through self-perception or inner awareness. And when that inner life is outwardly expressed through action, other sentient beings can surmise that the agent is also a sentient being and not a mere thing. Recall from the previous section, Utpaladeva argues that a proper analysis of action established that the self as agent must persist over time and have a persistent awareness of their own action. In short, the self is evident to itself as persisting knower and agent in and through its own internal conscious life.

Now a (hypothetical) Buddhist opponent can object that:

I.2.1-2 There is one type of cognition in which the particular reality (*svalakṣaṇa*) appears and another type of cognition, called mental elaboration (*vikalpa*), inseparably connected with discourse (*sābhilāpam*), which appears in manifold forms. For neither of the two is there any necessity to posit any stable perceiving subject, since he does not appear in them. Also the notion of 'I' (*ahaṃpratītiḥ*) has in reality as referent the body, etc.

The Buddhist opponent here is a Pramāṇavādin (see Chapter 7), who holds that perceptual cognition grasps momentary particulars (*svalakṣaṇa*) while conceptual cognition grasps (mentally constructed) universals or general categories (*sāmānyalakṣaṇas*). The argument here is that a persisting self is not found among the objects of perceptual or conceptual cognition, and therefore the self is not epistemically established. Furthermore, while the Buddhist will admit that we have the notion 'I', this essential indexical does not refer to a real self. Rather, it merely picks out one of the *skandhas* (the body, feeling, sensory consciousness, and so forth) on any given occasion of use. In short, the persistent self is not established by either perception (*pratyakṣa*) or inference (*anumāna*), the only two valid means of knowledge recognized by the Buddhists.

In response to this objection, Utpala deploys a well-known line of argument from memory and recognition developed by earlier Nyāya, Mīmāṃsā, and Advaita Vedānta thinkers. He writes:

> I.1.3 How could we explain memory, which conforms to direct perception when the latter is no longer present, if there were not a permanent self, who is the subject of perception?
>
> — Since the former direct perception has disappeared at the moment of the memory, the memory, whose essential quality is precisely its dependence on that former perception of the object, could not arise, unless one admits the persistence of the awareness of this perception also at the moment of the memory. And this lasting awareness at different times is precisely the self, the perceiving subject.

Utpaladeva's argument here relies on the idea of a temporal continuity of awareness. When I smell fresh brewed coffee in the morning, it is an olfactory experience. But when I remember the smell in the afternoon, I am recalling the earlier delicious coffee smell. At that later time, the earlier smell experience no longer exists, yet I can recall it (or its contents). What seems to be required here is a mechanism by which earlier contents later can be recalled as well as an (at least implicit) awareness that I am now recalling what I earlier experienced. But if, as the Buddhist thinks, there is only a selfless causal series of momentary mental events, how can this work?

The Buddhist response here (I.1.4–5) is that, like any perception, smelling the coffee leaves a mental imprint (*vāsanā*) or trace (*saṃskāra*) on the subsequent mental event. This trace or latent impression is carried—more accurately, replicated each successive moment—within the mental stream until it is later triggered. When it is triggered the latent content manifests as a reconstruction of the earlier sensory impression, which we call a memory. Further, the memory is grasped, not by a persisting self or awareness, but by the inherent reflexive awareness (*svasaṃvedana*) of the momentary mental event itself. The impression that it is the same subject or same awareness that earlier smelled the coffee and later remembered it is an illusion created by the complex interaction of momentary mental events in causal succession.

Interestingly, Utpaladeva in part agrees with the Buddhist interlocutor regarding the importance of both latent impressions (*saṃskāras*) and reflexive awareness (*svasaṃvedana*) in an adequate account of memory. However, he turns these concepts against the Buddhist view. Recall from Chapter 7 that the Buddhist Pramāṇavādins held a dual-aspect reflexivist account of a moment of consciousness. Each moment of consciousness has two faces, or two forms of phenomenal content (*ākāra*)—the object-aspect and the subject-aspect. The object-aspect presents a phenomenal form *as object*, whereas the subject-aspect presents a phenomenal form *as subject*. Thus, in perceiving a clay pot, the object-aspect presents the phenomenal form of the pot, while the subject-aspect presents certain features of the perceptual state itself (for example, hedonic tone, attention, and the like). Crucially, these two aspects are grasped by (and so are present to) reflexive awareness, which is itself an intrinsic feature of that (and every) conscious state. Thus, the two-fold content of a cognition is directly and immediate grasped in the same cognition not by another, distinct cognition (*parasaṃvedana*). With this account the Buddhist Pramāṇavādins aim to secure the immediacy of consciousness and to avoid the possibility of a vicious regress of cognitions of cognitions.

Utpaladeva targets his critique on this picture of consciousness. He states:

I.3.1 However, that form of cognition which is memory, though from the latent impression deposited by the former direct perception, is restricted to itself (*ātmaniṣṭham*) and does not know the original perception.
I.3.2 A cognition is self-revealing (*svābhāsaiva*) and cannot be the object of another cognition, just as the cognition of taste is not known by that of shape. The fact that [memory] arises from latent impressions implies its similarity to the former perception, but not its cognition of that (*tadgatiḥ*).

Now, at first glance, the claim that a cognition cannot be the object of another cognition seems puzzling. For example, I can think about my own mental states, thereby making them an object of a distinct cognition. But here Utpaladeva is referring to the direct awareness we have of our own mental states. According to the Buddhists, this is an intrinsic feature of a momentary conscious state, along with its (two-fold) content. Hence, the state is indeed self-enclosed or "restricted to itself" (*ātmaniṣṭham*). The problem, then, is that there can be no first-person access to earlier mental states even within the same mental continuum. One could only be aware of the earlier state *from the outside*, as if it were a mere object. I might have the thought that I earlier smelled coffee, but I would not be able to *first-personally* remember my earlier smelling of coffee. In memory we seem to be able to recall an earlier experience *from the inside* (namely, subjectively or first-personally), but if each moment of consciousness is self-enclosed, it is not clear how this is possible.

Of course, the Buddhist can appeal to an illusionist or error-theoretic (*bhrānta*) account of memory according to which a memory is a mere fabrication and no earlier mental state is recalled. However, as Utpaladeva goes on to argue, a mere series of self-enclosed cognitions would thereby lack the necessary cognitive synthesis (*anusandhāna*) that underpins coherent mental life, agency, and knowledge of the world. He writes:

> I.3.6 — Cognitions are restricted to themselves only (*svātmamātrapariniṣṭhitāni*) and cannot be the object of other cognitions (*aparasaṃvedyāni*) being by nature [exclusively] conscious of themselves. But then how would the dimension of human activity and behaviours (*lokavyavahāraḥ*) ... be possible, since this consists precisely in the interconnection between the objects of knowledge?

In short, Utpaladeva thinks that without real diachronic synthesis of consciousness, knowledge and agency are not possible. In his commentary on Utpaladeva, Abhinava cogently summarizes the issue:

> And because the [past] experience [that we remember now] does not consist in an object of knowledge, since it consists in a cognition, [we] cannot be aware of it through another cognition [taking it as its object]; rather, it is self-manifest. But if [this past experience] no longer exists when [its] memory occurs, then how could it be manifest [within that memory]? Even if [we] had rather admit that [somehow the past experience still] exists [when we remember it], these two [cognitions] must remain separated from each other, as the manifestation of the memory [on the one hand] and the manifestation of the experience [on the other hand, since one cognition cannot take the other as its object;] so that memory[, which must be somehow connected with the experience that it recalls,] can never occur. So this [memory process] is [only] possible in the [following] way: the self-awareness belonging to the [present] memory is none other than the self-awareness belonging to the [past] experience. And nothing else that would be distinct from this self-awareness—[i.e., a means of knowledge] such as a perception or an inference—can be applied to this [past experience so as to make it known]. And therefore this single self-awareness that stretches uninterrupted[ly] in the period of time [between the past experience and the present memory] is precisely the true nature of the knowing subject—this is [now] established.
>
> (ĪPVV vol. 1, 288-289)[6]

On this view, at the very root of mental life is a single persisting subjective self-awareness, which just is the dynamic self.

8.4 Light and Reflexivity

In the previous sections we have seen that Pratyabhijñā philosophers posit the powers of cognition and action as essential to consciousness. From their critique of the Buddhist Pramāṇavādins, we can also see that they are committed to the self-luminosity (*svaprakāśatā*) of consciousness. Like the Grammarian philosopher Bhartṛhari and the Buddhist philosopher Śāntarakṣita, Pratyabhijñā thinkers hold that reflexivity or self-luminosity is the essential nature of consciousness (Ferrante 2021). Utpaladeva characterizes conscious cognitive states as self-revealing (*svābhāsaiva*) (ĪPK I.3.2). As Abhinava explains:

> [In the verse] the word *dṛś* means "knowledge." This knowledge differs from what is inert, insofar as its nature consists only of illuminating itself. For what is inert must be regarded as different from light. Hence, the expression "a cognition is self-illuminating" (*dṛk svābhāsa*) means that: 1) the unfailing nature of a cognition is the capacity to illuminate (*prakāśamānatā*); or that 2) the proper nature of a cognition consists of illuminating itself.
>
> (ĪPV on ĪPK 1.3.2)[7]

Like Śāntarakṣita, Abhinava contrasts conscious or sentient beings from merely inert or insentient (*jaḍa*) things (MacKenzie 2021). The difference between you and stone is that you have an inner light or consciousness which means—to put it in contemporary terms—there is something it is like for you to be you. This inner light is the capacity to illuminate (*prakāśamānatā*) or make experientially present, and what is most fundamentally present is consciousness *itself*. In short, the very nature of consciousness is self-luminous, and it is in virtue of that capacity that it can also illuminate that which is other.

On the Pratyabhijñā view, this basic self-luminosity is further analyzed into the two deeply intertwined capacities of *prakāśa* (light) and *vimarśa* (reflection). *Prakāśa* is likened to a light shining in an otherwise dark room. It is the basic capacity of consciousness to *present* any content or object. More abstractly, it is the power of sheer phenomenal presencing. Objects illuminated by *prakāśa* are said to be 'shining', that is minimally phenomenally present. Even fleeting sensations such as a flash of blue or a brief sound, insofar as they are phenomenally present, would be shining in this sense. However, on the Pratyabhijñā account, mere phenomenal presence is not sufficient for full consciousness. Utpaladeva writes:

> I.5.11 The essential nature of light [i.e. consciousness] is reflective awareness (*vimarśam*); otherwise light, though 'coloured' by objects, would be similar to an insentient reality, such as a crystal and so on.
>
> — Reflective awareness (*pratyavamarśaḥ*) constitutes the primary essence (*mukhya ātmā*) of light. In the absence of this reflective awareness, light, though objects make it assume different forms, would merely be 'limpid', but not sentient, since there is no 'savouring' (*camatkṛteḥ*).

Consciousness as *prakāśa*, then, acts as mere reflective medium like a crystal or a mirror. Objects are reflected in the medium and are thus phenomenally present. But this only means that they are thereby *available* to the conscious subject. It is the other capacity of consciousness, *vimarśa*, that accounts for the subject's grasp, reception, or "savoring" of that is made available through *prakāśa*.

We have seen this idea before in Chapters 4, 6, and 7. The basic thought is that consciousness, particularly as subjectivity, is the receptive dimension *to which* or *for which* phenomena are presented. To extend the above analogy, a light may shine in an otherwise dark room and thereby make the objects in the room visible, but the objects are only actually *seen* when a conscious subject perceives them. Thus, *prakāśa* and *vimarśa* correspond closely to what Itay Shani (already mentioned in Chapter 6) has recently called the accusative and dative aspects of consciousness. He states:

> I maintain that conscious intentional acts exhibit two complementary sides: a transeunt perceptive aspect, which provides for the grasping of intentional objects; and an immanent receptive aspect, which serves as the subjective ground for the unfolding of contentful streams of experience. Put differently, the distinction pertains to two complementary ways consciousness is, in that consciousness reaches out to grasp its objects while, at the same time, being the addressee to whom things are given and in whom they are presented. I call these two antipodes of experience the accusative mode, and the dative mode, respectively.
>
> (Shani 2024, 183)

For Utpaladeva and Abhinavagupta, the interplay between these two complementary modes of consciousness constitutes the inherent dynamism, or what Abhinava calls the *life* of consciousness. *Prakāśa* provides the basic phenomenal presence, whereas *vimarśa* provides the subjective grasp that achieves explicit awareness of any object or mental content.

Shani calls the dative aspect the "subjective ground" for the stream of experience, and Pratyabhijñā thinkers would no doubt agree. However, for them, the subjective ground is the self or subject and *vimarśa* is one of its powers. Further, the function of *vimarśa* goes beyond simply receptive subjectivity—it is the dynamic grasp, or what Staneshwar Timalsina (2020) calls the *active gaze* at the heart of a conscious life. In the Pratyabhijñā account, *vimarśa* includes the powers of representation, recognition, grasp of meaning, mental synthesis, agency, and self-representation. In short, *vimarśa* is the basic conscious *uptake* that makes basic phenomenal content available for the higher-order operations of the mind. Moreover, the connection between *vimarśa* and the sense of "I" (*ātmavimarśa*) is especially important here. Utpaladeva states:

> I.6.1 The reflective awareness 'I', which is the very essence of light [consciousness], is not a mental construct (vikalpaḥ), although it is informed by the word (vāgupaḥ). For a vikalpa is an act of ascertainment (viniścayaḥ) presenting a duality (dvayākṣepī).
>
> — The reflective awareness concerning the self, the reflective awareness 'I', which constitutes the very nature of light, cannot be called vikalpa even if it is essentially associated with a 'discourse' (sābhilāpo'pi) since the word that informs it is the supreme word. Indeed, the vikalpa is an ascertainiment (viniścayaḥ) acquired through the negative of the opposite, and, as regards pure light, there is no possibility of the existence of something that is opposite.

The first thing to note here is that I-awareness is considered the nature or essence of consciousness. It is the primitive sense of oneself as the subject of consciousness that, on this view, accompanies all mental life. In this sense it is similar to what the phenomenologist Dan Zahavi calls the first-person dimension or basic *for-me-ness* that is, he argues, an essential aspect of consciousness (Zahavi 2008). Second, Utpaladeva insists that the sense of 'I' cannot be a (mere) mental construct (*vikalpa*) because there is no duality or bifurcation between oneself as the subject and one's own mental life. Thus, third, even though it is related to what we might now call the self-concept and to the linguistic mastery of the first-person pronoun, I-awareness is more basic. For Utpaladeva, I-awareness could not be based on such mental operations as first identifying all the things that are *not-me* and then inferring that what is left over must be *me*, nor by recognizing all the mental states that are *mine* and then ascertaining that *I* am their owner.

Abhinava explains the view in this way:

> The word *citi*, derived from *cetayati*, "to make conscious," indicates the activity of consciousness, whose essential nature, its essence, is a reflexive awareness characterized by self-savouring. To explain: a pot does not have savouring with respect to itself; it does not have a reflective awareness as a self, it does not cognize with respect to itself, nor it shines as having an uninterrupted nature. This is why it is said to be unconscious. On the other hand, a person named Caitra has savouring with respect to himself, for he has the power to produce an effort towards a raised state, that is the "I"; he has reflexive awareness as a self and cognizes precisely with respect to himself.
>
> (ĪPV on ĪPK 1.5.13)

Here again we see the idea that consciousness is essentially reflexive or "self-savoring." This feature marks the difference between consciousness and unconsciousness, and it includes awareness of the self as the subject of consciousness. Since it essentially includes awareness of the self, the Pratyabhijñā account understands reflexivity or self-luminosity as a form of *self*-consciousness.[8]

Hence, in contrast to the Buddhists, the Pratyabhijñā thinkers defend an egological view of consciousness. As discussed in Chapter 7, according to Zahavi:

> an *egological* theory would claim that when I watch a movie by Bergman, I am not only intentionally directed at the *movie*, nor merely aware of the movie being *watched*, I am also aware that it is being watched by *me*, that is, that *I* am *watching* the *movie* … Thus, an egological theory would typically claim that it is a conceptual and experiential truth that any episode of experiencing necessarily includes a subject of experience.
>
> (Zahavi 2008, 99)

On an egological view of consciousness, an act of consciousness constitutively includes an awareness or sense of the subject as subject. The self (or subject) is self-manifest in its own experience. Indeed, for Pratyabhijñā, this I-awareness or first-personal subjectivity is the "very essence" of consciousness. So, we can specify the different aspects of an act of consciousness according to the Pratyabhijñā account in the following way:

Perception: <phenomenally, in this very experience[9] I now here smell coffee>

Volition: <phenomenally, I now here drink coffee>
Memory: <phenomenally, I now here remember smelling coffee this
   morning>

In each case, the act of consciousness has a phenomenal character (*camatkāra*) which is a function of how the *prakaśa* dimension presents the available ("shining") object or content. Additionally, the act includes (in Woodruff Smith's terminology) reflexive ('in this very experience'), subjective or egocentric ('I'), temporal ('now'), and spatial ('here') factors, each of which is part of the *vimarśa* dimension.

There are three further features of this account of self-consciousness worth mentioning. First, it is not actively introspective. That is, while *vimarśa* is often translated as "reflection" or "reflective awareness," this does not mean that it is a separate awareness or separate act of consciousness. It does not require active introspection, nor is it a separate cognition directed at an immediately prior cognition as in the Nyāya account of *anuvyavasāya* ("after cognition"). Rather, consistent with the general self-illuminationist (*svaprakāśavāda*) orientation, *vimarśa* is best understood as the subjective dimension that is built into each act of consciousness. Second, *ātmavimarśa* (I-awareness) is not fundamentally representational. The *I* as it appears in experience is not something *re-presented* by way of a concept or other intermediary. As Utpaladeva says, it is not a *vikalpa*. Rather, I-awareness is *presentational* or immediate. As Abhinava says, the *I* is self-manifest and *just is* the self-savoring of consciousness. Indeed, savoring (*camatkṛti*) here implies the direct experience of the flavor (*rasa*) of qualitative experience.[10] Third, self-consciousness is non-objectual or non-observational. Neither the subject nor the act of consciousness are presented as *objects*. As Zahavi explains, "[f]or something to be given as an object of experience is for it to differ from the subjective experience that takes it as an object. In other words, an object of experience is something that, per definition, stands in opposition to or over against the subject of experience" (Zahavi 2008, 64).

Here the notion of an object, or object of experience, goes beyond the thin or merely formal notion of an object as whatever one is aware of. On the thin notion of an object, if there is an awareness of x, then x is the object (target or content) of that awareness. If it is a case of reflexive awareness, then that awareness is aware of itself, and is its own (thin) object. However, the phenomenological notion of an object is thicker, where one experiences something *as an object*. Here the target of the awareness is experienced as distinct from, even "over against" the subject, as part of a deeper subject-object contrast or duality in experience. Thus, when I smell the coffee, the coffee and its aroma are experienced *as object*—that is, as distinct from me and my perceiving. In contrast, when I experience pain, I typically experience it as a state that I am in, and so not independent of me and my experiencing. Even more intimately, my sense of being a subject, on this view, is precisely *not* experiencing myself as a separate object. In this case, I experience myself *as subject*—that is, as the subjective point of view within which or for which objects may be experienced. As Isabelle Ratié comments:

> *Vimarśa* is the pre-conceptual and pre-reflexive [pre-reflective] act through which consciousness is always already grasping itself as having a specific form (whether objective or subjective), and it can only grasp itself in an objective form because all cognitive events ultimately rest on the subjective realization in which consciousness apprehends itself as a pure "I."

(Ratié 2017, 460)

This understanding of *vimarśa* as a non-objectual or non-observational subjective awareness of the flow of experience is critical the Pratyabhijñā critique of Buddhist reflexivism. As we saw in the previous section, Utpala argues that the Buddhist reflexivist view treats states of consciousness as if they were mere objects for other states of consciousness. That is, the Buddhist reflexivist view treats the relations between cognitions, including self-cognition, as representational and objectual. In contrast, the Pratyabhijñā view is that intra-mental awareness is fundamentally non-representational and non-objectual because it is grounded in the pure dynamic subjectivity of *vimarśa*. Moreover, this subjective dimension is the ground of temporal experience operating as the awareness within which different objects or experiences come and go or can be experienced in terms of past, present, or (anticipated) future. In short, the synthesis (*anusandhāna*) at the heart of consciousness includes temporal synthesis, ensuring that neither the different moments of experience nor subjectivity are temporally self-enclosed (*ātmaniṣṭha*).

8.5 Dynamic Nonduality

As mentioned in the first section of this chapter, the Pratyabhijñā school is a *nondual* branch of Tantric Śaivism. Nondualism here involves two related ideas. First, there is no ultimate ontological or phenomenological separation between subject and object in consciousness. The subject-object duality is merely apparent. Second, ultimate reality is a monistic (nondual) absolute the essence of which is pure consciousness. Thus, like the Advaita Vedānta tradition, nondual Śaivism is ultimately a form of monistic idealism. However, as we will discuss in this section, the Pratyabhijñā Śaiva thinkers sharply disagree with the Advaita Vedāntins regarding both the nature of the absolute and the ontological status of the manifest or phenomenal world of plurality.

As part of his critique of the Buddhists, Utpaladeva writes:

I 3.6-7 Thus, the functioning of the human world—which stems precisely from the unification (*anusamdhana*) of cognitions, in themselves separate from one another and incapable of knowing one another— would be destroyed if there were no Maheśvara [Supreme Lord] who contains within himself all the infinite forms, who is one, whose essence is consciousness, possessing the powers of knowledge, memory and exclusion.

— The mutual unification of all cognitions of things is [constituted by] the consciousness principle (*cittatvam*) whose form is all, since nothing distinct from it is admissible. The powers of knowledge etc. only pertain to this consciousness principle. It has been said: "From me derive memory, knowledge, exclusion."

In this passage Utpaladeva is claiming that the functioning of individual consciousness is grounded in a deeper principle of consciousness (*cittatvam*) that is unitary, has various cognitive powers, and whose form is all phenomena. This ultimate consciousness is Śiva, the Supreme Lord.

Abhinavagupta's disciple, Kṣemarāja (tenth–eleventh century CE) in his *Śivasūtravimarśinī*, summarizes the nondual view in this way:

Consciousness manifests itself both internally and externally in a variety of forms. Because objects only exist in relation to consciousness, the world has the nature of consciousness. For entities cannot be known without consciousness. So it is concluded that consciousness has assumed the forms of entities. By contemplating entities, we can rationally understand that knowable phenomena share the nature of consciousness. Consciousness and its objects have a single nature because they are experienced simultaneously.

(ŚSV 30)

Here Kṣemarāja is appealing to epistemic and phenomenological considerations in favor of idealism. It is not just that objects are known through consciousness. It is that any knowable (or cognizable) phenomenon, inner or outer, is only available by way of some relation to consciousness.

The epistemic argument then, is that "knowable phenomena" only make sense with reference to some act of consciousness through which they can be known. An object beyond the reach of consciousness, then, would be strictly unknowable.

Additionally, he appeals to the phenomenological observation that consciousness and its object appear as part of the same overall experience.[11] The object, we might say, appears in the experience *as* other than the knowing subject, while the act of consciousness manifests itself *as* an act of subjectivity. Yet, both the object and the subjective act appear within the same field of consciousness. Here again we have a version of the *horizonal* view of consciousness introduced in Chapter 6. According to this view:

> There is no way to step outside consciousness and measure it against something else. Everything we investigate, including consciousness and its relation to the brain, resides within the horizon of consciousness … Consciousness is the horizon of the world's disclosure: The world appears and is present to us from within the horizon of consciousness. Consciousness is the horizon of anything we can perceive, think about, imagine, and investigate, including when we are doing science. We can observe, imagine, and investigate things only within the horizon of consciousness, and anything that we determine to be real or factual gets its determination from within the horizon of consciousness.
>
> (Frank et al. 2024, 186)

Unlike Buddhist idealists, Pratyabhijñā philosophers do not deny the persistence of either objects or subjects. This means that an object is not reducible to its presentation in any given act of consciousness, since it can be experienced through multiple acts of consciousness by the same subject or by different subjects. Indeed, in the passage quoted above, Utpaladeva tells us that the functioning of the human world depends on various forms of synthesis between distinct cognitions. But the human world is an experientially *shared* world. We can (it seems) perceive the same objects, act in the same contexts, and communicate with one another. So, on the one hand, we have the claim that there are no knowable phenomena *outside* (the horizon of) consciousness. On the other hand, we have the claim that there is a shared world of objects and other subjects. The world of objects and other subjects, therefore, transcends the consciousness of any particular (finite) individual.

The Pratyabhijñā view is that the world transcends the consciousness of individual subjects but does not transcend consciousness as such. Generalizing from the individual case in which phenomena are presented only within the horizon of consciousness, they posit a single underlying principle of consciousness that is the ground of all phenomena. As Kṣemarāja puts it, "the world has the nature of consciousness" and "consciousness manifests itself ... in a variety of forms" (Ibid.). Thus, the phenomenological horizon of consciousness becomes the ontological ground of the world. In Western philosophical terms, Pratyabhijñā rejects subjective idealism in favor of absolute idealism. The world does not depend on *my* consciousness or *yours*, but instead the absolute ground of things is identified as a divine consciousness (*paramśiva*).

In this respect, Pratyabhijñā agrees with the absolute idealism of Advaita Vedānta. But whereas the Advaita Vedāntins treat the phenomenal world as an (ultimately) unreal (*mithyā*) appearance, Śaiva nondualists treat it as the real manifestation of the creative power and dynamism of absolute consciousness. Abhinavagupta in his *Bodhapañcadaśikā* (1–5) summarizes the view as follows:

1–2 The single principle which is both within and external, whose form is radiance unlimited in light and darkness, that is the Divinity that is the essence of all beings. Its sovereign *śakti* produces entities.

3 The *śakti* does not desire to be different from its possessor. The shared nature of the two is permanent, like that of fire and burning.

4 This is the deity Bhairava who sustains the cosmos because by his *śakti* he has made everything appear as reflected in the mirror of his own nature.

5 The *śakti* is the transcendent Goddess who delights in contemplating his essence. Her perfect state neither increases nor diminishes in relation to finite beings.

The key philosophical point here is that absolute consciousness has an inherent creative power (*śakti*) that is exercised through free will or sovereignty (*svātantrya*). The appearance of the world is not explained through *māyā* as illusion, as in Advaita Vedānta, but rather through the inherent creative dynamism of the absolute. As Utpaladeva writes, (ĪPK I.5.7) "[T]he Conscious Being, God, like the yogin, independently of material causes, in virtue of His volition alone, renders externally manifest the multitude of objects that reside within Him." Divine consciousness, therefore, is both the agentive and the material cause of the world. The difference between the insentient and sentient aspects of the world is not metaphysically fundamental. Rather, the insentient aspects of the world are explained as more limited manifestations of consciousness, whereas the sentient aspects are less limited manifestations more reflective of the true nature of divine consciousness.

The creative dynamism of consciousness (*citśakti*) is characterized by Utpaladeva in terms of freedom, meaning, and vibration. He writes:

> I 5.13 Consciousness has as its essential nature reflective awareness (*pratyavimarśa*); it is the supreme Word (*paravāk*) that arises freely. It is freedom in the absolute sense, the sovereignty (*aiśvaryam*) of the supreme Self.
>
> I 5.14 It is the luminous vibrating (*sphurattā*), the absolute being (*mahāsattā*), unmodified by space and time; it is that which is said to be the heart (*hṛdayam*) of the supreme Lord, insofar as it is his essence.

Unlike the changeless and non-agentive absolute (*brahman*) of Advaita Vedānta, the Pratyabhijñā absolute is dynamic and agentive. The Supreme Lord freely expresses himself in and as the world. This expression is accomplished through "vibration" (*spanda, sphurattā*), meaning a primordial excitation of the fundamental substance of consciousness. This vibration (which is prior to space and time) is not random but *patterned*. Like the patterns of speech, reasoning, or music, the basic patterns of the world are both intelligible and beautiful.[12]

The absolute consciousness manifests not only as the world of things, but as the plurality of the individual subjects, from animals to humans to divine beings. Utpaladeva states:

> I.5.16 The Lord, thanks to his freedom which is absence of duality, by creating a self not devoid of freedom variously representing him in the forms of Īśa etc. renders the carrying out of practical activity possible.
>
> I.5.17 The variety of notions such as 'I' etc., does not entail diversity in the nature of the self, because a self is created precisely as he who lends himself to being the object of the reflective awareness 'I' (ahaṃmṛśyataiva), like action which is expressed by personal endings (tincācyakarmavat).

Individual selves, then, are the free creation of the absolute. These distinct selves are loci of consciousness and free agency, interacting with a world of objects and other subjects that are independent of them. Yet, on the Pratyabhijñā view, the diversity of subjects does not imply that subjective consciousness is ultimately plural. Rather, the 'I' which is the deepest nature of consciousness is identical in each sentient being. There is, therefore, a contrast between two levels of subjectivity. On the first level, the I-awareness picks out the individual subject through a mode of self-consciousness called *idaṃ-parāmarśa* ('this-awareness'). It is a form of self-recognition as *this* particular being with *these* mental states, *this* body, *these* actions, and so on. It is not that one is a mere object for oneself, but rather that one is aware of oneself in and through one's body, actions, stream of experiences, and so forth. On the second, deeper level, I-awareness reflects the very principle of subjectivity itself, the universal 'I'. This mode of self-recognition is called *aham-parāmarśa* ('I-awareness'). Here the mode of self-awareness is, as we have discussed, radically non-observational—one recognizes the pure subjectivity at the heart of all experience. And this recognition (*pratyabhijñā*) is the liberating awareness of the divine within.

8.6 Comparative Connections

In Chapter 4 we discussed the "hard problem" of consciousness. As David Chalmers explains the problem:

> What makes the hard problem hard and almost unique is that it goes beyond problems about the performance of functions. To see this, note that even when we have explained the performance of all the cognitive and behavioral functions in the vicinity of experience—perceptual discrimination, categorization, internal access, verbal report—there may still remain a further unanswered question: *Why is the performance of these functions accompanied by experience?*
>
> (Chalmers 1995, 202)

There seems to be an intractable, in principle gap between the various functions of consciousness and the undeniable fact of its qualitative and subjective dimensions. Considering the persistence of the hard problem, many contemporary philosophers and scientists studying consciousness have begun to explore alternatives to physicalism as an approach to the metaphysics of consciousness. For example, theories of strong emergence, property dualism, neutral monism, and substance dualism are actively debated in the contemporary field.

Another contemporary approach—or really, family of approaches—is panpsychism. Panpsychist views hold that consciousness (or the mental in some form) is both fundamental and pervasive in the world (Goff et al. 2022). So, a physicalist may hold that consciousness is i) *not* fundamental, ii) *not* separate from the physical, and iii) localized (for example, to brains). A dualist may hold that consciousness is i) fundamental, ii) separate from the physical, iii) localized (for example, in an individual substantial self). In contrast to these, a panpsychist may hold that consciousness is i) fundamental, ii) *not* separate from the physical, and iii) ubiquitous. In this way, panpsychism might be thought of as a middle way between physicalism and dualism. On the panpsychist view, the intractability of the hard problem and the explanatory gap lends support for the idea that consciousness is a basic feature of nature. This is because it is hard to see how, even in principle, facts about conscious experience can be derived from facts about non-conscious (physical) states of affairs. The hard problem is *hard* precisely because, for any given set of facts about the non-conscious and its correlations with the conscious, it is open to ask for an account of the basis of that correlation. And further specification of the non-conscious side of things does not seem to provide such an account.

One possible response to the hard problem is to appeal to *emergence*. Perhaps consciousness is a novel, higher-level property of certain complex physical systems such as brains. In this way, consciousness might be analogous to other (purportedly) emergent properties such as the liquidity of water. However, contemporary philosophers such as Thomas Nagel and Galen Strawson have argued that, given the hard problem, a much stronger notion of emergence would be needed in the case of consciousness. As Strawson writes:

> We can easily make intuitive sense of the idea that certain sorts of molecules are so constituted that they don't bind together in a tight lattice but slide past or off each other (in accordance with van de Waals molecular interaction laws) in a way that gives rise to—is—the phenomenon of liquidity …. we move in a small set of conceptually homogeneous shape-size-mass-charge-number-position-motion-involving physics notions with no sense of puzzlement …. Using the notion of reduction in a familiar loose way, we can say that the phenomena of liquidity reduce without remainder to shape-size-mass-charge-etc.
>
> (Strawson 2024, 24)

However, in the case of consciousness, we have no such intelligible or "conceptually homogenous" bridge, and we have principled reasons to doubt we could have one. Thus, what would be needed is a kind of radical or brute emergence. And Strawson argues that brute emergence is unintelligible:

> *Emergence can't be brute.* It is built into the heart of the notion of emergence that emergence cannot be brute in the sense of there being absolutely no reason in the nature of things why the emerging thing is as it is (so that it is unintelligible even to God). For any feature Y of anything that is correctly considered to be emergent from X, there must

be something about *X* and *X* alone in virtue of which *Y* emerges, and which is sufficient for *Y*.

(Strawson 2024, 32)

So, if consciousness is real and emergence can't be brute, then perhaps we should say that consciousness is a fundamental feature of reality. We would then try to explain phenomena such as human and animal consciousness in terms of more basic forms of consciousness, not in terms of the (entirely) non-conscious.

Following this line of thought, we can then turn to the nature of this more basic form of consciousness. Here I want to highlight two dimensions along which panpsychist views might differ. The first dimension concerns the question of singularity versus plurality. According to some panpsychists (pluralists or "micropsychists"), basic consciousness is a feature of the many basic components that make up the world. For instance, if the world is made up of basic simples, these simples would be instances of basic consciousness, and we would explain more complex forms of consciousness in terms of the many simples. In contrast, other panpsychists (monists or "cosmopsychists") argue that basic consciousness is a single consciousness. As Shani explains, cosmopsychism is:

> a view according to which an omnipresent cosmic consciousness is the single ontological ultimate there is and the definitive ground of all spatiotemporally localized centres of consciousness. In broad outlines, cosmopsychism is a panpsychist theory of mind; yet, in its holistic commitments it functions as an alternative to the atomistic thinking which dominates work on panpsychism in contemporary analytic philosophy.

(Shani 2015, 390)

In the contemporary context, many cosmopsychists endorse a form of ontological monism called priority monism (Schaffer 2010). According to this view, the single ontological ultimate is the *whole* cosmos, and the plurality of individual entities are dependent parts of this whole. Thus, whole is ontologically prior (more fundamental than) the parts. Others endorse a form of existence monism (Horgan and Potrc 2011), according to which there exists only one entity, the cosmos, and this entity has no proper (or really existing) parts.

The second dimension concerns the nature the basic consciousness, in terms of its inherent qualities, powers, complexity, and so on. Is the basic consciousness the lowest or most primitive grade of consciousness? Or is it, perhaps, the highest or richest instance of consciousness? Or somewhere in between? Atomistic panpsychists tend to hold that basic entities also exhibit the lowest grade of consciousness, whereas more complex systems such as animals and humans exhibit higher or more sophisticated forms of consciousness commensurate with their organizational complexity. That is, the consciousness of an electron is very low grade compared to that of a dolphin. Indeed, *panprotopsychists* hold that the basic mental properties are pre- or sub-conscious. Likewise, some cosmopsychists (Goff 2017) hold that the fundamental macro-consciousness is primitive or low grade. As Goff writes, "It could be that the consciousness of the universe is a gigantic mess that doesn't add up to anything coherent enough to ground cognition [or agency, etc.]" (Goff et al. 2022). Other cosmopsychists posit that cosmic consciousness is the highest grade of consciousness, whereas the consciousness of "localized centers" of experience is more primitive. Here the view has similarities to pantheism (Buckareff 2022).

Returning now to the classical Indian context, we can identify several parallel views. Monima Chadha (2022) has recently argued for an atomistic panprotopsychist reading of Abhidharma and Yogācāra/Pramāṇavāda thinkers. As discussed in earlier chapters, these Buddhist philosophers held the reductionist view that apparently enduring substances, composite entities, and universals are merely conceptual constructs. What really exists are a plurality of momentary particulars (*dharmas, svalakṣaṇas*) that arise dependently on other such particulars. These simple, basic particulars are categorized as mental (*citta, caitta*) or physical (*rūpa*), though in Yogācāra the mental is primary. On Chadha's reconstruction, pervasive microphenomenal (and protopsychic) *dharmas* bundle to give rise to the macrophenomenal features of individual mind-streams (*cittasantāna*), without the need for any real self or subject. Thus, a particular macroexperience, say an individual's state of perception, will be analyzed in terms of a complex bundle of dependently arisen momentary microphenomenal *dharmas*. This bundle then conditions the arising of a distinct bundle in the next moment. The series of momentary bundles constitutes the mind-stream, which in turn gives rise to the illusion of a persisting subject. Ultimately, these microphenomenal *dharmas* are *proto*-psychic because they are more basic than the various minds (psyche, *manas*) that they may bundle together to momentarily constitute. Further, the basic, pervasive mental *dharmas* are low grade, whereas the bundled macromental phenomena can be quite rich and complex.

In contrast to Chadha's Abhidharma atomistic panprotopsychism, Miri Albahari has recently defended a form of cosmopsychism inspired by Advaita Vedānta. Like the Advaitins, Albahari's cosmopsychism is *idealist* in that universal consciousness is the ultimate reality. She writes:

[T]he most promising way forward in the mind-body problem—navigating around all the problems to date—is to renounce the pervasive panpsychist supposition that fundamental consciousness must belong to a subject. This extends the reach and scope of consciousness to ground not merely the inner nature of the cosmos, but everything we take to be the world, with its subjects and objects.

(Albahari 2019, 2)

On Albahari's view, fundamental consciousness is aperspectival. That is, the ultimate field of consciousness is not limited to the individuated perspectives of distinct sentient beings. Rather, fundamental consciousness is the ground of any (apparent) perspectives. As she puts it, "the foundational aperspectival consciousness … is the intrinsic nature of our everyday conscious field" (Albahari 2019, 31). Why does conscious experience seem perspectival? "It is," she writes, "the manifestation of objects to a subject. While objects can broadly comprise any discernible target of perception or introspection, we are always initially aware of objects via what I call 'cognisensory' imagery. These are the experiential qualities associated with different cognitive and sensory modalities: sights, sounds, thoughts, and so on" (Ibid.). Such imagery always arises within or relative to a first-person perspective. Thus, on this account, the apparent division between subjects and objects arises as a kind of illusion within a larger nondual field of consciousness. Here we have a cosmopsychism that is an idealist form of existence monism. That is, ultimately fundamental unitary nondual consciousness is all that exists. And, as in Advaita Vedānta, ultimate consciousness is radically simple and timeless. However, it would not be accurate to call this consciousness "low grade" since it is the very ground of all existence.[13]

Where Advaita Vedānta thinkers defend strict or absolute nondualism, other Vedānta thinkers defended more moderate forms of nondualism. For example, Rāmānuja critiqued Śaṅkara's nondualism and defended a *viśiṣṭādvaita* (qualified nondual) view. As Martin Ganeri describes it:

Rāmānuja argues instead that the Upaniṣads teach that Brahman is the personal God or Lord of theistic religion (Īśvara), of whom a number of distinct attributes can be predicated positively (*saguṇa* or *saviśeṣa*). The world made up of finite conscious and nonconscious entities is real and forms the body of Brahman, though these entities are wholly dependent on Brahman for their existence and activities at all times. The soteriological goal is the realization of the finite self's proper relationship with Brahman as a dependent entity independent of any connection with a material body and of the blissful experience of an eternal communion of knowledge and love with Brahman.

(Ganeri 2015, 7–8)

As Anand Vaidya (2022) has argued, Rāmānuja's qualified nondualism has important similarities to a priority monist form of cosmopsychism. While *brahman* is the nondual ground of existence, the world and individual souls or selves are also real. They are derivative, but genuine parts of the unified whole that is *brahman*. Indeed, Rāmānuja famously describes the world as God's body. And, in the case of Viśiṣṭādvaita, the fundamental cosmic consciousness is of the highest grade, since it is God.[14]

Finally, Shani has recently connected Pratyabhijñā to a distinct form of nondual cosmopsychism. In contrast to the forms of existence monism and (part-whole) priority monism so far discussed, Shani posits a form of *generative* monism, which he also attributes to nondual Śaivism and the integral (*pūrṇa*) nondualism of Śri Aurobindo.[15] According to Shani:

"generative monism" (GM) is my terminological choice for the view that the One engenders the many, that is, that it literally brings multiplicity into being. Such begetting is not, of course, the creation of a product external to the producer—as depicted in the Book of *Genesis* or in Plato's *Timaeus*—but, rather, a process of internal differentiation through which a plurality of distinct entities arises out of an originary state of undifferentiated singleness. Finally, nor is such generation akin to spawning or splintering. For while the multitude of emergent beings enjoy various forms and degrees of individuality (and in the case of subjects like us, a significant measure of personal and collective autonomy) they remain *inseparable* from their ultimate singular origin—grounded in it and pervaded by its immanent presence.

(2023, 55)

So, on Śaṅkara's existence monism, only nondual *brahman* is truly real—the world and individual selves are merely apparent. On Rāmānuja's version of priority monism, the world and selves are real parts of the organic unity of God. On the Pratyabhijñā thinker's generative monism:

[T]he entire created universe is a manifestation of, and within, Śiva. There is nothing outside of, or apart from, absolute CC [cosmic consciousness]. All lesser beings, including all other subjects, appear as internal differentiations within the cosmic playground of absolute consciousness: They can be thought of as reflections in Śiva's creative mirroring, or as moments in a spontaneous process of self-individuation… [And] the reality we identify with the familiar world of subjects, objects, and actions is an outgrowth of Śiva's pure consciousness. The cosmological picture at play is one which emphasizes a gradual outwardly movement: From the inwardness of an undifferentiated pure 'I' toward increasing levels of differentiation and absorption in particulate form, culminating in an explicit manifestation of diversity in which subjects and objects exist side by side as co-determinants.

(Shani 2023, 52)

Of course, even within the domain of panpsychist and cosmopsychist theories, each of these positions has distinctive philosophical strengths and weaknesses. But suffice it to say that classical Indian theories such a Pratyabhijñā nondualism offer philosophically rich accounts that remain underexplored in contemporary philosophy.

8.7 Questions

1. What are the two essential features of the self in Pratyabhijñā? How does their view differ from other accounts of *ātman*?
2. What is Utpaladeva's main objection to the Buddhist theory of memory and reflexive awareness? Is his objection a good one?
3. What are prakāśa and vimarśa and what role do they play in the Pratyabhijñā theory of self-awareness?
4. How is Pratyabhijñā nondualism different from Advaita Vedānta nondualism?

Notes

1 Translations are from Torella (2021).
2 "Establish" (*siddha*) here is an epistemic term denoting a correct cognitive grasp or that something is rationally evident.
3 This term is derived from *Īśvara* (Lord) and has the sense of autonomous or sovereign (lordly) freedom.
4 As Utpaladeva tells us, "Action, when it manifests itself through a body, becomes cognizable also by others. Thanks to it, knowledge in other can be guessed" (I.1.5).
5 Quoted in (Lawrence 1999, 145).

6 Quoted in (Ratié 2017, 443).

7 Quoted in (Ferrante 2021, 42).

8 Non-egological views of reflexivity—e.g. those of Buddhist reflexivists or the early Sartre—hold that consciousness is merely aware of *itself* not a *self*. In this way, reflexivity is a form of self-consciousness only in the deflationary way of a self-referential sentence or a self-cleaning oven.

9 Following Woodruff Smith, we might say that <in this very experience> is implied by <I now here smell>. However, it is worth including to show that a reflexive awareness of the experience is included in this structure.

10 Terms such as *camatkṛti* (savoring), *rasa* (flavor), and *camatkāra* (phenomenal quality, lit. 'wonder') derive from Abhinavagupta's influential work in aesthetics.

11 Kṣemarāja here appears to reference the Buddhist idealist *sahopalambaniyama* argument to the effect that the object of cognition (for example, a sensation of blue) is not different from the cognition itself because they arise simultaneously. This is another case of Pratyabhijñā thinkers drawing from Buddhist ideas or arguments for their own distinct purposes.

12 We see here a resonance with the ancient Greek ideas of *logos* and *cosmos*. However, it is important to note that Pratyabhijñā thinkers, as Tantrists, do not shy away from the destructive and frightening aspects of the absolute.

13 Indeed, fundamental consciousness is *brahman*, the ultimate divine ground characterized as being (*sat*), consciousness (*cit*), and bliss (*ānanda*).

14 For Rāmānuja, *brahman* is Viṣṇu-Nārāyaṇa who is the supreme person (*puruṣottama*), characterized by the theistic perfections such as omniscience.

15 Shani states that his generative monism is also a form of priority monism, but it differs from the standard mereological (part-whole) version of priority monism developed by Schaffer and others.

Further Reading

Abhinavagupta. 1986. *Īśvara-Pratyabhijñā-Vimarśinī of Abhinavagupta: Doctrine of Divine Recognition*. Translated by K. A. Subramania Iyer and K. C. Pandey (ed.). Motilal Banarsidass Publishing House.

Lawrence, David Peter. 1999. *Rediscovering God with Transcendental Argument: A Contemporary Interpretation of Monistic Kashmiri Śaiva Philosophy*. State University of New York Press.

Pandit, Moti Lal. 2023. *Kashmir Shaivism: A Philosophy of Being and Becoming*. Dev Publishers & Distributors.

Ratié, Isabelle. 2017. "Utpaladeva and Abhinavagupta on the Freedom of Consciousness." In *The Oxford Handbook of Indian Philosophy*. Oxford University Press. https://academic.oup.com/edited-volume/27982/chapter/211671490.
Torella, Raffaele. 2021. *The Īśvarapratyabhijñākārikā of Utpaladeva: Critical Edition and Annotated Translation*. Motilal Banarsidass Publishing House.

9

Conclusion

Through the course of this book, we have examined a wide range of theories of consciousness developed by thinkers (mostly) in the classical period of Indian philosophy. We have seen the ways that debates about the basic nature and structure of consciousness—such as those concerning the nature of luminosity—have played out across quite varied philosophical perspectives. We have also seen how debates regarding the nature and very existence of the self inform Indian views about consciousness, cognition, perception, memory, and more. And we have seen how the philosophy of consciousness intersects with fundamental questions in metaphysics such as monism, dualism, and pluralism; temporality; truth; and the status of the external world. Classical Indian thinkers offer philosophically rigorous and phenomenologically rich accounts of these (and many other) issues.

Of course, Indian philosophy didn't stop with the classical period. For instance, in the later classical period (approximately 1100–1500 CE) we see the emergence of several pivotal figures such as Śrīharṣa (twelfth century CE), Madhvācārya (1238–1317 CE), and Gaṅgeśa (c. 1325 CE). Śrīharṣa, typically construed as a proponent of Advaita Vedānta (Ram-Prasad 2013), in his *Khaṇḍanakhaṇḍanakhādya* (*Sweets of Refutation*) attacks the rational foundations of both philosophical inquiry and many commonsense categories. He argues that the philosophical method of offering rigorous definitions of, for example, knowledge or causation, fails and that even the best philosophical arguments can be met with equally persuasive counterarguments. Yet, he also argues that consciousness is undeniably real. Following the Advaita perspective discussed in Chapter 6, Śrīharṣa maintains that consciousness is self-luminous and that we have epistemically secure knowledge of its occurrence without the need of any distinct higher-order cognition. In arguing for this view, he revises and sharpens several earlier lines of argument leading to a robust defense of self-knowledge by direct epistemic acquaintance.

In contrast to Śrīharṣa's skeptical nondualism, Madhva developed a systematic defense of Dvaita (dualist) Vedānta (Sarma 2003). On Madhva's view, *brahman* is the ultimate independent (*svatantra*) reality and is none other than the supreme being, Viṣṇu. As the creator, Viṣṇu brings into existence a world (*jagat*) of souls (*jīva*) and insentient things (*jaḍa*). As created, souls and insentient things are both dependent (*asvatantra*) on and distinct from God (Viṣṇu). Madhva combines this theistic pluralism with a resolutely realist epistemology. Regarding consciousness, Madhva argues that it is an essential quality of the self, but he does not reduce the self to consciousness. Further, he argues that consciousness is both intentional (object-directed) and self-luminous. In line with his realist epistemology, he accepts the basic subject-object structure of ordinary experience. That is, the self comes to know a world of distinct objects through consciousness. Further, he argues that the self can be its own object of knowledge, just as one can take other selves and insentient things as cognitive objects.

Gaṅgeśa is a pivotal figure not just within his own Nyāya tradition, but within Indian philosophy more broadly. His innovative work aims to refine and bolster the long Nyāya tradition in logic, epistemology, philosophy of language, and metaphysics. His masterwork, the *Tattvacintāmaṇi* (*Jewel of Reflection on the Truth about Epistemology*) not only set the agenda for future work in Nyāya, but also had a wider impact on how philosophy was to be done in subsequent centuries in India. He advanced a sophisticated form of reliabilism about knowledge and justification, which he applied to the core means of knowledge: perception, inference, testimony, and analogy (Phillips 2024). He developed new lines of argument for the self as a distinctive substance, for the existence of God, and the possibility of spiritual liberation. In philosophy of mind, Gaṅgeśa argued that awareness is presumptively veridical but not intrinsically self-certifying. He also developed a rich account of the distinction between perception and apperception, and between perception and conception.

During the early modern period (c. 1500–1800 CE), philosophers working in the Sanskrit intellectual tradition, such as Raghunātha Śiromaṇi (c. 1460–1540 CE), began in earnest to engage the Persian and larger Islamic world, and to develop a more open and exploratory mode of philosophizing. As Jonardon Ganeri remarks,

> from about the middle of the sixteenth century until the middle of the eighteenth, there is a metamorphosis in epistemology, metaphysics, semantics, and philosophical logic. The works of these philosophers, many of whom lived in Raghunātha's hometown of Navadvīpa in Bengal, are full of phrases that are indicative of a newly open and exploratory attitude, phrases like "this should be considered further," "this needs to be reflected on." Openness to inquiry into the problems themselves is what drives the new work, not merely a new exegesis of the ancient texts, along with a sense that they are engaged in an ongoing project.
>
> (Ganeri 2017, 8)

Additionally, Indian philosophers grounded in the Islamic tradition began the immense project of translating philosophical texts from Sanskrit to Persian, as well as engaging in complex debates at the intersection of the Persian, Sanskrit, and Arabic philosophical traditions (Ganeri 2017).

Turning to the time of British colonial occupation (1757–1947), as Ganeri writes, Indian philosophers again developed, "new philosophical priorities, perhaps most especially the need to respond to the incompatibility between the pretensions of European claims on the values of liberty, tolerance, equality, and secularism and the multiple and manifest illiberalities, intolerances, and inequalities of colonial rule" (Ganeri 2017, 8). As the Indian independence movement grew, thinkers such as Rabindranath Tagore, Mohandus Gandhi, B. R. Ambedkar, and Jawaharlal Nehru emphasized social and political philosophy, drawing on both Indian and European sources. However, philosophical inquiry into the nature of mind, consciousness, self and related issues did not cease during this period. Here I will focus on two important thinkers active in the early twentieth century, Sri Aurobindo and K. C. Bhattacharyya.

Śri Aurobindo (Aurobindo Ghosh, 1872–1950 CE) was an Indian nationalist, poet, philosopher, and spiritual leader. In the latter half of his life, he developed both a complete system of philosophy and a novel and distinctive approach to spiritual practice, which he called integral yoga. According to Aurobindo there are two fundamental philosophical riddles: existence itself and consciousness. Why is there anything at all? Why is there consciousness? Regarding the riddle of consciousness, he writes:

> Consciousness of existence is a second insoluble miracle. It seems not to have been and now is and it may be that some day it will not be; yet it is a premier fact and without it being would not know of its own existence. Things might exist, but only as a useless encumbrance of a meaningless space,—consciousness makes being self-aware, gives it a significance. But what then is consciousness? Is it something in the very grain of being or an unstable result or fortuitous accident? To whom does it belong? to the world as a whole? or is it peculiar to individual being? Or has it come from elsewhere into this inanimate and inconscient universe? To what end this entry?
>
> (CWSA 12, 271)[1]

Aurobindo argues that fundamentally non-conscious ("inconscient") matter could not give rise to so distinct a phenomenon as consciousness. He then argues that consciousness is indeed "in the very grain of being," not as a mere adjunct to matter, but as a fundamental, pervasive, and unified reality.

As Swami Medhananda has argued recently, we can see Aurobindo's philosophy as a novel form of evolutionary cosmopsychism (Medhananda 2022). The ultimate reality is *brahman* or in Aurobindo's preferred terms *Sacchidānanda* (Being-Consciousness Force-Bliss), which is an infinite divine consciousness. *Saccidānanda* manifests through a double process of involution and evolution. As Aurobindo explains:

> There is possible a realistic as well as an illusionist Adwaita. The philosophy of *The Life Divine* is such a realistic Adwaita. The world is a manifestation of the Real and therefore is itself real. The reality is the infinite and eternal Divine, infinite and eternal Being, Consciousness-Force and Bliss [i.e., Saccidānanda]. This Divine by his power has created the world or rather manifested it in his own infinite Being. But here in the material world or at its basis he has hidden himself in what seem to be his opposites, Non-Being, Inconscience and Insentience … . The Being which is hidden in what seems to be an inconscient void emerges in the world first in Matter, then in Life, then in Mind and finally as the Spirit. The apparently inconscient Energy which creates is in fact the Consciousness-Force of the Divine and its aspect of consciousness, secret in Matter, begins to emerge in Life, finds something more of itself in Mind and finds its true self in a spiritual consciousness and finally a supramental consciousness through which we become aware of the Reality, enter into it and unite ourselves with it. This is what we call evolution which is an evolution of consciousness and an evolution of the Spirit in things and only outwardly an evolution of species.
>
> (CWSA 29, 393)

Given this view, Aurobindo's realistic or integral non-dualism (*pūrṇa-advaita*) is the first systematically evolutionary philosophy of consciousness developed in the Indian tradition (Mahapatra 2021). As part of his broader evolutionary perspective, he posits a series of levels of consciousness. At the material level, consciousness is merely implicit or unmanifest, as in certain panpsychist or panprotopsychist theories. At the level of life, consciousness manifests in the sensitivity and responsiveness of living systems. At the level of mind, consciousness manifests as perceptual, cognitive, and (in humans) rational capacities. Beyond the mind, he posits higher or supramental capacities of consciousness that include powers of intellectual intuition, spiritual insight, and non-dual consciousness. According to Aurobindo's theory, the natural universe is the evolutionary unfolding of absolute consciousness and humanity is one manifestation of this absolute slowly evolving toward higher levels of consciousness.

Krishnachandra Bhattacharyya (1875–1947 CE) was one of the most influential academic philosophers in India, active in the first half of the twentieth century. A truly cosmopolitan thinker, he specialized in both Indian philosophy—particularly Advaita Vedānta, but also Nyāya, Sāṅkhya, and Yoga—as well as the philosophy of Immanuel Kant and the post-Kantian transcendental tradition. His magnum opus, *The Subject as Freedom* (1923), is an extended philosophical engagement between Advaita Vedānta and Kant's thought, particularly *The Critique of Pure Reason*. In particular, Bhattacharyya is concerned with two closely connected issues. The first is the possibility and nature of self-knowledge, while the second is the deep connection between (transcendental) subjectivity and freedom articulated in both Kant and Vedānta (Garfield 2017).

Regarding self-knowledge, Bhattacharyya argues that "Self-knowledge is denied by Kant: the self cannot be known but can only be thought through the objective categories … there being no intuition of it" (1923, 101). That is, for Kant the self can be thought but not known. This is diametrically opposed to the Advaita Vedāntin idea that knowledge of the self (as *ātman*) is both the condition of the possibility of knowledge of objects and the highest spiritual ideal. Yet, as Jay Garfield explains, in Advaita "given that the self is never *object*, but only *subject*, and given that *thought* is always *objective*—that is, directed upon an object—the self, from the standpoint of this tradition, cannot be *thought*" (2017, 355). A main philosophical goal of *The Subject as Freedom* is to defend the Advaitin view as against Kant. He does so by developing a rigorous phenomenological account of several layers of subjectivity as forms of both freedom and self-knowledge. He writes:

> The steps … correspond to a gradation of subjective functions, of modes of freedom from the object. Identified as we are with our body, our freedom from the perceived object is actually realized only in our bodily consciousness, though even this, as well appear later, is only imperfectly realized … The next stage of freedom is suggested by the distinction of the perceived object including the body from the ghostly object in the form of the image, idea, and meaning, which may be all designated "presentation." Consciousness as undissociated from such presentation, but dissociated from the perceived and felt body, may be called presentational or psychic subjectivity. The dissociation of the subject of consciousness from this which may be called non-presentational or spiritual subjectivity. The three broad stages of subjectivity would then be the bodily, the psychical and the spiritual … Wedded as we are to our body, actual freedom is felt only in bodily subjectivity and freedom in the higher stages as suggested by psychology is believed not as what

is actual but as what has to be achieved or realized… . The elaboration of these stages of freedom in spiritual psychology would suggest the possibility of a consecutive method of realizing the subject as absolute freedom, of retracting the felt positive freedom towards the object into pure intuition of the self.

(1923, 102)[2]

The details of Bhattarcharyya's account are both philosophically rich and beyond the scope of the present work. It is worth noting, though, the resonances between his account of the layers of subjectivity and the classical Advaita (and Yoga) threefold distinction between the living body (*śarīra*), the mind (*manas*), and the self as witness (*sākṣin*) or pure subjectivity. And yet, one must also note the great originality of his attempt to integrate witness consciousness with the Kantian notion of the free spontaneity of the rational subject.

Finally, both Aurobindo and Bhattacharyya are truly global philosophers, drawing expertly on multiple traditions and methods to develop new insights into fundamental and globally significant philosophical issues. Aurobindo engaged in global philosophy through bold syncretic system-building, while Bhattarcharyya took a more rigorous interpretive and analytical route. Yet both philosophers were convinced that deep engagement with classical Indian philosophy offers profound insights and facilitates new modes of philosophizing.

As I discussed in the introduction, according to Jonardon Ganeri, cross-cultural philosophy develops a new type of philosophical skill, "the ability to attend to a conceptual terrain from a plurality of cultural perspectives, and to allow that act itself to deepen one's vision of the intellectual terrain" (Ganeri 2015, 2). The conceptual terrain of this book has been the nature of consciousness and related issues such as mind, self, and world. As we have seen, Indian thinkers developed rich, sophisticated, and rigorous philosophical accounts of these issues. It is my hope that this book has contributed to the enterprise of cross-cultural philosophy and that, through engagement with Indian thought, the reader has strengthened the philosophical skill of engaging with the deep questions about consciousness from multiple perspectives.

Notes

1   Quoted in (Medhananda 2022, 93–94).
2   Quoted in (Garfield 2017, 359–60).

References

Primary Sources

Abhinavagupta. *Bodhapañcadaśikā*. Śāstrī, Harabhaṭṭa. 1947. *Bodhapañcadaśikā*. Vol. 76. Research and Publication and Department, Jammu and Kashmir Government.

Abhinavagupta. *Īśvarapratyabhijñāvimarśinī*. Iyer, K. A. Subramania, and K. C. Pandey (ed.), trans. 1986. *Īśvara-Pratyabhijñā-Vimarśinī of Abhinavagupta: Doctrine of Divine Recognition*. Motilal Banarsidass Publishing House.

Abhinavagupta. *Īśvarapratyabhijñāvivṛtivimarśinī*. Śāstrī, Madhusūdanakaula, ed. 1938. *Īśvarapratyabhijñāvivṛtivimarśinī*. 3 vols. Kashmir Series of Texts and Studies.

Asaṅga. *Abhidharmasamuccaya*. Rahula, Walpola, and Sara Boin-Webb, trans. 2015. *Abhidharmasamuccaya: The Compendium of the Higher Teaching, Philosophy*. Jain Pub Co.

Asaṅga. *Yogācārabhūmi*. Bhattacharya, Vidhusekhara, ed. 1957. *The Yogācārabhūmi of Ācārya Asaga (Part-I)*. University of Calcutta.

Aristotle. *De Anima*. Hicks, R. D., trans. 2015. *Aristotle's De Anima: With Translation, Introduction and Notes*. Cambridge University Press.

Aristotle. *Nichomachean Ethics*. Bartlett, Robert C., and Susan D. Collins, trans. 2011. *Aristotle's Nicomachean Ethics*. University of Chicago Press.

Aurobindo, Sri. 1997. *The Complete Works of Sri Aurobindo*, vol. 12: *Essays Divine and Human: Writings from Manuscripts 1910–1950*, Pondicherry: Sri Aurobindo Ashram.

Aurobindo, Sri. 2013. *The Complete Works of Sri Aurobindo*, vol. 29: *Letters on Yoga II*, Pondicherry: Sri Aurobindo Ashram.

Bādarāyaṇa. *Brahmasūtras*. Vireswarananda, Swami, ed. 1936. *Brahma-Sūtras*. Almora, Himalayas, Advaita Ashrama.

Bhagavad Gītā. Chapple, Christopher Key, ed. 2009. *The Bhagavad Gītā: Twenty-Fifth–Anniversary Edition*. Translated by Winthrop Sargeant. State University of New York Press.

Bṛhadāraṇyaka Upaniṣad. Olivelle, Patrick, trans. 1998. *The Early Upanishads: Annotated Text and Translation*. Oxford University Press.

Buddhaghosa. *Visuddhimagga*. Bhikkhu Ñanamoli, trans. 1991. *The Path of Purification: Visuddhimagga*. Buddhist Publications Society.

Chāndogya Upaniṣad. Olivelle, Patrick, trans. 1998. *The Early Upanishads: Annotated Text and Translation*. Oxford University Press.

Citsukha. *Tattvapradīpikā*. Yogīndrānanda, Swami, ed. 1985. *Tattvapradīpikā: Citsukhī*. Caukhambhā Saṃskṛta Pratisthāna.

Dhammasaṅgaṇī. Müller, Edward, ed. 1885. *The Dhammasaṅgaṇi*. Pali Text Society.

Dharmakīrti. *Pramāṇavarttika*. Sāṅkṛtyāyana, Rahula, ed. 1937. *Dharmakīrti's Pramāṇavarttika with a Commentary by Manorathanandin*. Bihar Research Society.

Dharmakīrti. *Pramāṇaviniścaya*. Steinkellner, Ernst, ed. 2007. *Dharmakīrti's Pramāṇaviniścaya: Chapters 1 and 2*. Bilingual edition. Austrian Academy of Sciences Press.

Dharmakīrti. *Sambandha Parīkṣā*. Steinkellner, Ernst, ed. 2022. *Dharmakīrti's Sambandhaparīkṣā and Devendrabuddhi's Sambandhaparīkṣāvṛtti*. Austrian Academy of Sciences.

Dignāga. *Ālambanaparīkṣā*. Duckworth, Douglas, and Malcolm David Eckel. 2016. *Dignāga's Investigation of the Percept: A Philosophical Legacy in India and Tibet*. Translated by Jay L. Garfield, John Powers, Yeshes Thabkhas, and Sonam Thakchoe. Oxford University Press.

Dignāga. *Pramāṇasamuccaya*. Hattori, Masaaki. 1968. *Dignāga, on Perception: Being the Pratyakṣapariccheda of Dignāga's Pramāṇasamuccaya from the Sanskrit Fragments and the Tibetan Versions*. Harvard University Press.

Dignāga. *Pramāṇasamuccayavṛtti*. Pind, Ole Holten. 2015. *Dignaga's Philosophy of Language: Pramāṇasamuccayavṛtti on Anyāpoha. Part I and Part II*. Austrian Academy of Sciences Press.

Gaṅgeśa. *Tattvacintāmaṇi*. Phillips, Stephen, trans. 2020. *Jewel of Reflection on the Truth about Epistemology: A Complete and Annotated Translation of the Tattva-Cintā-Mani*. Bloomsbury Academic.

Gauḍapāda. *Māṇḍūkyakārikā*. Karmarkar, Raghunath Damodar, ed. 1953. *Gauḍapāda-Kārikā*.

Gautama. *Nyāya Sūtra*. Thakur, Anantalal. 1997. *Gautamīyanyāyadarśana with Bhāṣya of Vātsyāyana*. Munshiram Manoharlal Publishers Pvt Ltd.

Īśvarakṛṣṇa. *Sāṅkhyakārikā*. Sundara, Salatur, and Suryanarayana Sastri, eds. 1973. *The Sāṅkhyakārikā of Īśvara Kṛṣṇa*. University of Madras.

Jayanta Bhaṭṭa. *Nyāyamañjarī*. Jha, V. N., trans. 1995. *Nyāyamañjarī of Jayantabhaṭṭa*. Sri Satguru Publications.

Kṣemarāja. *Śivasūtravimarśinī*. Chatterji, J. C., ed. 1990. *Śivasūtravimarśinī*. Bibliothekā Oriyaṇṭāliyā.

Kumārila. *Ślokavārtika*. Śāstrī, Svāmī Dvārikādāsa, ed. 1978. *Ślokavārttika of Śrī Kumārila Bhaṭṭa, with the commentary Nyāyaratnākara*. Prāchyabhāratī No. 10. Tara Publications.

Kumārila. *Pratyakṣapariccheda* of ŚV. Taber, John. 2012. *A Hindu Critique of Buddhist Epistemology*. Routledge.

Majjhima Nikāya. Trenckner, Vilhelm, ed. 2002. *The Majjhima Nikāya*. Pali Text Society.

Mokṣākaragupta. *Tarkabhāṣā*. Kajiyama, Yuichi, trans. 1998. *An Introduction to Buddhist Philosophy: An Annotated Translation of the Tarkabhāṣā of Mokṣākaragupta*. Arbeitskreis f. Tibet. u. Buddhist. Studien, Univ. Wien.

Nāgārjuna. *Mūlamadhyamakakārikā*. Vaidya, P. L., ed. 1960. *Madhyamakaśāstra of Nāgārjuna*. The Mithila Institute of Post-Graduate Studies and Research in Sanskrit Learning.

Patañjali. *Yoga Sūtra*. Bryant, Edwin F. 2015. *The Yoga Sūtras of Patañjali: A New Edition, Translation, and Commentary*. Farrar, Straus and Giroux.

Saṃyutta Nikāya. Feer, Leon. 1884. *Saṃyutta Nikāya*. 6 vols. Pali Text Society.

Śaṅkara. *Upadeśasāhasrī*. Maeda, Sengaku, ed. 2006. *Śaṅkara's Upadeśasāhasrī*. Motilal Banarsidass Publishers.

Śaṅkara. *Brahmajñānāvalīmālā*. Peetam, Sri Kanchi Kamakoti, ed. 2012. *The Voice of Śaṅkara*. Adi Sankara Advaita Research Centre.

Śaṅkara. *Brahmasūtrabhāṣya*. Gambhirananda, Swami, trans. 1965. *Brahma Sūtra Bhāṣya Of Śaṅkarācārya*. Vedanta Press & Bookshop.

Śaṅkara. *Bṛhadāraṇyaka Upaniṣad Bhāṣya*. Madhavananda, trans. 2004. *The Bṛhadāraṇyaka Upaniṣad with the Commentary of Śaṅkarācārya*. Advaita Ashrama.

Śaṅkara. *Dakṣiṇāmūrtistotra*. Sastry, Alladi Mahadeva, trans. 2001. *Dakṣiṇāmūrti Stotra of Śri Śaṅkarācārya*. Gyan Publishing House.

Śaṅkara. *Dṛg Dṛśya Viveka*. Nikhilananda, Swami, ed. 2006. *Dṛg-Dṛśya-Viveka: An Inquiry into the Nature of the Seer and the Seen*. Advaita Ashrama.

Śaṅkara. *Viveka Cūḍāmaṇi*. Anubhavananda, Swami. 2009. *Viveka Cūḍāmaṇi*. Indra Publishing House.

Śākyabuddhi. *Pramāṇavarttikaṭīkā*. Inami, M., K. Matsuda, and T. Tani, eds. 1992. *A Study of the Pramāṇavārttikaṭīkā by Śākyabuddhi from the National Archives Collection, Kathmandu. Part I: Sanskrit Fragments Transcribed*. Studia Tibetica 23. Tōyō Bunko.

Somānanda. *Śivadṛṣṭi*. Śāstrī, Madhusūdanakaula, ed. 1934. *The Śivadṛṣṭi of Srisomānandanātha: with the vṛtti by Utpaladeva*. Aryabhushan Press.

Śrīharṣa. *Khaṇḍanakhaṇḍanakhādya*. Jha, Sir Ganganatha, ed. 1986. *The Khaṇḍanakhaṇḍakhādya of Shri-Harṣa, an English Translation*. Sri Satguru Publications.

Sthiramati. *Madhyāntvibhāgaṭīkā*. Yamaguchi, Susumu, ed. 1934. *Madhyāntavib hāgaṭīkā*. Librairie Hajinkaku.

Taittirīyā Upaniṣad. Olivelle, Patrick, trans. 1998. *The Early Upanishads: Annotated Text and Translation*. Oxford University Press.

Uddyotakara. *Nyāyavārttika*. Tarkatirtha, Amarendramohan, ed. 1985. *Nyāyadarśanam: with Vātsyāyana's Bhāṣya, Uddyotkara's Vārttika, Vācaspati Miśra's Tātparyaṭīkā & Viśvanātha's Vṛtti*. 2nd ed. Munshiram Manoharlal.

Utpaladeva. *Īśvarapratyabhijñākārikā* and *-vṛtti*. Torella, Raffaele. 2021. *The Īśvarapratyabhijñākārikā of Utpaladeva with the Author's Vṛtti: Critical Edition and Annotated Translation*. Motilal Banarsidass Publishing House.

Vasubandhu. *Abhidharmakośa* and -*bhāṣya*. La Vallee Poussin, Louis de. 2014. *Abhidharmakośabhāṣyam of Vasubandhu*. Translated by Leo M. Pruden. Jain Pub Co.

Vasubandhu. *Triṃśikā*. Mimaki, Katsumi, Musashi Tachikawa, and Akira Yuyuma, eds. 1989. *Three Works Of Vasubandhu in Sanskrit Manuscript: The Trisvabhāvanirdeśa, the Viṃśatikā with its Vṛtti, and the Triṃśikā with Sthiramati's Commentary*. The Center for East Asian Cultural Studies.

Vasubandhu. *Trisvabhāvanirdeśa*. Mimaki, Katsumi, Musashi Tachikawa, and Akira Yuyuma, eds. 1989. *Three Works Of Vasubandhu in Sanskrit Manuscript: The Trisvabhāvanirdeśa, the Viṃsatikā with its Vṛtti, and the Triṃśikā with Sthiramati's Commentary*. The Center for East Asian Cultural Studies.

Vasubandhu. *Viṃśatikā* and -*vṛtti*. Mimaki, Katsumi, Musashi Tachikawa, and Akira Yuyuma, eds. 1989. *Three Works Of Vasubandhu in Sanskrit Manuscript: The Trisvabhāvanirdeśa, the Viṃsatikā with its Vṛtti, and the Triṃśikā with Sthiramati's Commentary*. The Center for East Asian Cultural Studies.

Vasugupta. *Śivasūtras*. Singh, Jaideva, trans. 1979. *Śiva Sūtras*. Motilal Banarsidass Publishing House.

Vātsyāyana. *Nyāya-bhāṣya*. Tarkatirtha, Amarendramohan, ed. 1985. *Nyāyadarśanam: with Vātsyāyana's Bhāṣya, Uddyotkara's Vārttika, Vācaspati Miśra's Tātparyaṭīkā & Viśvanātha's Vṛtti*. 2nd ed. Munshiram Manoharlal.

Vijñānabhikṣu. *Yogavārttika*. Rukmani, T. S., ed. 1981. *Yogavarttika of Vijñānabhikṣu: Text, with English Translation and Critical Notes, along with the Text and English Translation of the Pātañjala Yogasūtras and Vyāsabhāṣya*. Munshiram Manoharlal Publishers.

Vyāsa. *Yogabhāṣya*. Rukmani, T. S., ed. 1981. *Yogavarttika of Vijñānabhikṣu: Text, with English Translation and Critical Notes, along with the Text and English Translation of the Pātañjala Yogasūtras and Vyāsabhāṣya*. Munshiram Manoharlal Publishers.

Secondary Sources

Ajina, Sara, and Holly Bridge. 2017. "Blindsight and Unconscious Vision: What They Teach Us about the Human Visual System." *The Neuroscientist: A Review Journal Bringing Neurobiology, Neurology and Psychiatry* 23 (5): 529–41. https://doi.org/10.1177/1073858416673817.

Albahari, Miri. 2006. *Analytical Buddhism: The Two-Tiered Illusion of Self*. 1st ed. 2006 edition. Palgrave Macmillan.

Albahari, Miri. 2019. "Perennial Idealism: A Mystical Solution to the Mind-Body Problem." *Philosopher's Imprint* 19 (44). http://hdl.handle.net/2027/spo.3521354.0019.044.

Anacker, Stefan. 2002. *Seven Works of Vasubandhu: The Buddhist Psychological Doctor*. Motilal Banarsidass.

Arnold, Dan. 2008a. "Buddhist Idealism, Epistemic and Otherwise: Thoughts on the Alternating Perspectives of Dharmakīrti." *Sophia* 47 (1): 3–28. https://doi.org/10.1007/s11841-008-0046-7.

Arnold, Dan. 2008b. *Buddhists, Brahmins, and Belief: Epistemology in South Asian Philosophy of Religion*. Columbia University Press.

Ashton, Geoffrey. 2020. "The Puzzle of Playful Matters in Non-Dual Śaivism and Sāṃkhya: Reviving Prakṛti in the Sāṃkhya Kārikā through Goethean Organics." *Religions* 11 (5): 5. https://doi.org/10.3390/rel11050221.

Balcerowicz, Piotr. 2017. "The Philosophy of Mind of Kundakunda and Umāsvāti." In *The Oxford Handbook of Indian Philosophy*, edited by Jonardon Ganeri. Oxford University Press. https://doi.org/10.1093/oxfordhb/9780199314621.013.13.

Bartley, C. J. 2013. *The Theology of Rāmānuja*. Routledge.

Bastow, David. 1995. "The First Argument for Sarvāstivāda." *Asian Philosophy* 5 (2): 109–25. https://doi.org/10.1080/09552369508575415.

Berger, Douglas L. 2015. *Encounters of Mind: Luminosity and Personhood in Indian and Chinese Thought*. SUNY Press.

Bhatt, Siddheshwar Rameshwar. 2023. *The Viśiṣṭādvaita Vedānta of Rāmānuju: A Comparative and Critical Study*. Motilal Banarsidass International.

Bhattacharya, Ramkrishna. 2002. "Cārvāka Fragments: A New Collection." *Journal of Indian Philosophy* 30 (6): 597–640. https://doi.org/10.1023/A:1023569009490.

Bhattacharyya, Krishnachandra. 1923. *Subject as Freedom: A Contemporary Translation*. Translated by Nalini Bhushan and Jay L. Garfield. Oxford University Press.

Bodhi, Bhikkhu. 2005. *In the Buddha's Words: An Anthology of Discourses from the Pali Canon*. Wisdom Publications.

Bradley, F. H. 1893. *Appearance and Reality: A Metaphysical Essay*. 1st edition. Routledge.

Brentano, Franz. 1874. *Psychology from An Empirical Standpoint*. Routledge.

Bryant, Edwin F. 2015. *The Yoga Sūtras of Patañjali: A New Edition, Translation, and Commentary*. Farrar, Straus and Giroux.

Buckareff, Andrei A. 2022. *Pantheism*. Cambridge University Press.

Buddhaghosa. 1991. *The Path of Purification: Visuddhimagga*. Buddhist Publications Society.

Burley, Mikel. 2012. *Classical Sāṃkhya and Yoga*. Routledge.

Caston, V. 2002. "Aristotle on Consciousness." *Mind* 111 (444): 751–815. https://doi.org/10.1093/mind/111.444.751.

Cermeño-Aínsa, Sergio. 2025. "Yogācāra Buddhism and the Illusion of Phenomenal Consciousness." *Asian Philosophy* 35 (2): 161–80. https://doi.org/10.1080/09552367.2024.2396746.

Chadha, Monima. 2013. "The Self in Early Nyāya: A Minimal Conclusion." *Asian Philosophy* 23 (1): 24–42. https://doi.org/10.1080/09552 367.2013.749624.

Chadha, Monima. 2015. "Time-Series of Ephemeral Impressions: The Abhidharma-Buddhist View of Conscious Experience." *Phenomenology and the Cognitive Sciences* 14 (3): 543–60. https://doi.org/10.1007/s11 097-014-9354-2.

Chadha, Monima. 2017. "Reflexive Awareness and No-Self: Dignāga Debated by Uddyotakara and Dharmakīrti." In *The Oxford Handbook of Indian Philosophy*. Oxford University Press.

Chadha, Monima. 2022. "A Buddhist Response to the Quality-Combination Problem for Panpsychism." *The Monist* 105 (1): 131–45. https://doi. org/10.1093/monist/onab027.

Chadha, Monima. 2023. *Selfless Minds: A Contemporary Perspective on Vasubandhu's Metaphysics*. Oxford University Press.

Chadha, Monima. 2024. "Perceptual Experience and Concepts in Classical Indian Philosophy." In *The Stanford Encyclopedia of Philosophy*, Summer 2024, edited by Edward N. Zalta and Uri Nodelman. Metaphysics Research Lab, Stanford University. https://plato.stanford.edu/archives/sum2024/entr ies/perception-india/.

Chakrabarti, Arindam. 1992. "I Touch What I Saw." *Philosophy and Phenomenological Research* 52 (1): 103–16. https://doi.org/10.2307/2107746.

Chakrabarti, Arindam. 2019. *Realisms Interlinked: Objects, Subjects, and Other Subjects*. Bloomsbury.

Chakrabarti, Kisor Kumar. 2024. *Classical Indian Philosophy of Mind: A Nyāya Dualist Tradition*. Motilal Banarsidass Publishing House.

Chalmers, David. 1995. "Facing Up to the Problem of Consciousness." *Journal of Consciousness Studies* 2 (3): 200–219.

Chalmers, David. 1997. *The Conscious Mind: In Search of a Fundamental Theory*. OUP USA.

Chalmers, David. 2010. *The Character of Consciousness*. Oxford University Press.

Chalmers, David J. 2010a. "Consciousness and Its Place in Nature." In *The Character of Consciousness*, edited by David J. Chalmers. Oxford University Press. https://doi.org/10.1093/acprof:oso/9780195311105.003.0005.

Chaturvedi, Amit. 2024. "Is the Mind a Magic Trick? Illusionism about Consciousness in the 'Consciousness-Only' Theory of Vasubandhu and Sthiramati." *Ergo an Open Access Journal of Philosophy* 10 (0). https://doi. org/10.3998/ergo.5189.

Coates, Paul. 2013. *Hallucinations and the Transparency of Perception*. Edited by F. Macpherson and D. Platchais. MIT Press. https://uhra.herts.ac.uk/id/epr int/13423/.

Crane, Tim, and Craig French. 2021. "The Problem of Perception." In *The Stanford Encyclopedia of Philosophy*, Fall 2021, edited by Edward N. Zalta.

Metaphysics Research Lab, Stanford University. https://plato.stanford.edu/archives/fall2021/entries/perception-problem/.

Dalal, Neil. 2020. "Contemplating Nonduality: The Method of Nididhyāsana in Śaṅkara's Advaita Vedānta." In *The Bloomsbury Research Handbook of Vedānta*, edited by Ayon Maharaj. Bloomsbury Academic.

Dasti, Matthew R. 2023. *Vātsyāyana's Commentary on the Nyāya-Sūtra: A Guide*. Oxford University Press.

Dennett, Daniel C., and Marcel Kinsbourne. 1992. "Time and the Observer: The Where and When of Consciousness in the Brain." *Behavioral and Brain Sciences* 15 (2): 183–201. https://doi.org/10.1017/s0140525x00068229.

Descartes, René. 1641. *Meditations on First Philosophy*. 2nd ed. Edited by John Cottingham. Cambridge University Press.

Dretske, Fred. 1986. *Knowledge and the Flow of Information*. MIT Press.

Dretske, Fred I. 1997. *Naturalizing the Mind*. MIT Press.

Dreyfus, Georges B. J. 1997. *Recognizing Reality: Dharmakīrti's Philosophy and Its Tibetan Interpretations*. Sri Satguru Publications.

Dreyfus, Georges, and Evan Thompson. 2007. "Asian Perspectives: Indian Theories of Mind." In *The Cambridge Handbook of Consciousness*, edited by Evan Thompson, Morris Moscovitch, and Philip David Zelazo. Cambridge Handbooks in Psychology. Cambridge University Press. https://doi.org/10.1017/CBO9780511816789.006.

Duckworth, Douglas, and Malcolm David Eckel. 2016a. *Dignāga's Investigation of the Percept: A Philosophical Legacy in India and Tibet*. Translated by Jay L. Garfield, John Powers, Yeshes Thabkhas, and Sonam Thakchoe. Oxford University Press.

Dunne, John. 2011. "Toward an Understanding of Non-Dual Mindfulness." *Contemporary Buddhism* 12 (1): 71–88. https://doi.org/10.1080/14639947.2011.564820.

Dunne, John D. 2004. *Foundations of Dharmakīrti's Philosophy*. 0512-edition eds. Wisdom Publications.

Fasching, Wolfgang. 2008. "Consciousness, Self-Consciousness, and Meditation." *Phenomenology and the Cognitive Sciences* 7 (4): 463–83. https://doi.org/10.1007/s11097-008-9090-6.

Feinberg, Todd E., and Annalena Venneri. 2014. "Somatoparaphrenia: Evolving Theories and Concepts." *Cortex; a Journal Devoted to the Study of the Nervous System and Behavior* 61 (December): 74–80. https://doi.org/10.1016/j.cortex.2014.07.004.

Ferrante, Marco. 2021. *Indian Perspectives on Consciousness, Language and Self*. Routledge.

Flanagan, Owen. 2011. *The Bodhisattva's Brain: Buddhism Naturalized*. MIT Press.

Forman, Robert K. C. 1999. *Mysticism, Mind, Consciousness*. State University of New York Press.

Frank, Adam, Marcelo Gleiser, and Evan Thompson. 2024. *The Blind Spot: Why Science Cannot Ignore Human Experience*. MIT Press.

Frankish, K. 2016. "Illusionism as a Theory of Consciousness." *Journal of Consciousness Studies* 23 (11–12): 11–39.

Frazier, Jessica. 2024. "Against Infinite Nothingness: Ultimate Ground vs Metaphysical Nihilism in Indian Philosophy." *Neue Zeitschrift Für Systematische Theologie Und Religionsphilosophie* 66 (3): 271–301. https://doi.org/10.1515/nzsth-2024-0044.

Funes Maderey, Ana Laura. 2020. "The Spaciousness of Self-Awareness: A Phenomenological Account of Self-Reflexivity in Patañjali´s Yoga Philosophy." *Asian Philosophy* 30 (4): 295–306. https://doi.org/10.1080/09552367.2020.1846845.

Gallagher, Shaun, and Dan Zahavi. 2020. *The Phenomenological Mind*. Routledge.

Ganeri, Jonardon. 2007. *The Concealed Art of the Soul: Theories of the Self and Practices of Truth in Indian Ethics and Epistemology*. 1st edition. Clarendon Press.

Ganeri, Jonardon. 2011. "Emergentisms, Ancient and Modern." *Mind* 120 (479): 671–703. https://doi.org/10.1093/mind/fzr038.

Ganeri, Jonardon. 2012. *The Self: Naturalism, Consciousness, and the First-Person Stance*. 1st edition. Oxford University Press.

Ganeri, Jonardon. 2015. "Blueprint for Cosmopoltian Philosophy in a Culturally Polycentric World." Unpublished manuscript. www.academia.edu/8434737/.

Ganeri, Jonardon. 2017a. *Attention, Not Self*. Oxford University Press.

Ganeri, Jonardon. 2017b. *The Oxford Handbook of Indian Philosophy*. Oxford University Press.

Ganeri, Martin. 2015. *Indian Thought and Western Theism: The Vedānta of Rāmānuja*. Routledge. https://doi.org/10.4324/9781315731339.

Garfield, Jay L. 2006. "The Conventional Status of Reflexive Awareness: What's at Stake in a Tibetan Debate?" *Philosophy East and West* 56 (2): 201–28.

Garfield, Jay L. 2015. *Engaging Buddhism: Why It Matters to Philosophy*. 1st edition. Oxford University Press.

Garfield, Jay L. 2017. "Solving Kant's Problem: K. C. Bhattacharyya on Self-Knowledge." In *Indian Epistemology and Metaphysics*. Bloomsbury Academic. http://www.bloomsburycollections.com/collections/encyclopedia-chapter.

Garfield, Jay L. 2022. "Cognitive Illusion and Immediate Experience: Perspectives from Buddhist Philosophy." In *Cross-Cultural Approaches to Consciousness: Mind, Nature, and Ultimate Reality*. Bloomsbury Academic.

Goff, Philip. 2017. *Consciousness and Fundamental Reality*. Oxford University Press.

Goff, Philip, William Seager, and Sean Allen-Hermanson. 2022. "Panpsychism." In *The Stanford Encyclopedia of Philosophy*, Summer 2022, edited by Edward

N. Zalta. Metaphysics Research Lab, Stanford University. https://plato.stanf
ord.edu/archives/sum2022/entries/panpsychism/.

Gold, Jonathan C. 2014. *Paving the Great Way: Vasubandhu's Unifying Buddhist Philosophy*. Columbia University Press.

Goodman, Charles. 2004. "The Treasury of Metaphysics and the Physical World." *The Philosophical Quarterly* 54 (216): 389–401. https://doi.org/10.111 1/j.0031-8094.2004.00359.x.

Goodman, Charles. 2009. "Vasubandhu's Abhidharmakósa: The Critique of the Soul." In *Buddhist Philosophy: Essential Readings*, edited by William Edelglass and Jay L Garfield. Oxford University Press. https://doi.org/10.1093/ oso/9780195328165.003.0027.

Gorisse, Marie-Hélène. 2024. "Jaina Philosophy." In *The Stanford Encyclopedia of Philosophy*, Summer 2024, edited by Edward N. Zalta and Uri Nodelman. Metaphysics Research Lab, Stanford University. https://plato.stanford.edu/ archives/sum2024/entries/jaina-philosophy/.

Grover, Sandeep, Jitender Aneja, Sonali Mahajan, and Sannidhya Varma. 2014. "Cotard's Syndrome: Two Case Reports and a Brief Review of Literature." *Journal of Neurosciences in Rural Practice* 5 (Suppl 1): S59–62. https://doi. org/10.4103/0976-3147.145206.

Gupta, Bina. 1998. *The Disinterested Witness: A Fragment of Advaita Vedanta Phenomenology*. 1st edition. Northwestern University Press.

Gupta, Bina. 2003. *CIT Consciousness*. Oxford University Press.

Gurwitsch, Aron. 1940. "A Non-Egological Conception of Consciousness." *Philosophy and Phenomenological Research* 1 (3): 325–38. https://doi. org/10.2307/2102762.

Hateren, J. H. van. 2021. "Constructing a Naturalistic Theory of Intentionality." *Philosophia* 49 (1): 473–93. https://doi.org/10.1007/s11406-020-00255-w.

Heim, Maria. 2018. *Voice of the Buddha: Buddhaghosa on the Immeasurable Words*. Oxford University Press.

Heim, Maria, and Chakravarthi Ram-Prasad. 2018. "In a Double Way: Nāmarūpa in Buddhaghosa's Phenomenology." *Philosophy East and West* 68 (4): 1085–115.

Hoffman, Donald D. 2016. "The Interface Theory of Perception." *Current Directions in Psychological Science* 25 (3): 157–61. https://doi. org/10.1177/0963721416639702.

Hoffman, Donald D., and Chetan Prakash. 2014. "Objects of Consciousness." *Frontiers in Psychology* 5 (June). https://doi.org/10.3389/fpsyg.2014.00577.

Horgan, Terry, and Matjaz Potrc. 2011. "Existence Monism Trumps Priority Monism." In *Spinoza on Monism*, edited by Philip Goff. Palgrave-Macmillan.

Hu, Chih-chiang. 2022. "The Notion of Awareness of Self-Awareness and the Problem of Infinite Regress in the Cheng Weishi Lun." *Dao* 21 (2): 299–316. https://doi.org/10.1007/s11712-022-09832-0.

Hume, David. 1739. *A Treatise of Human Nature*. Edited by Ernest C. Mossner. Penguin Classics.

Josipovic, Zoran. 2014. "Neural Correlates of Nondual Awareness in Meditation." *Annals of the New York Academy of Sciences* 1307 (1): 9–18. https://doi.org/10.1111/nyas.12261.

Josipovic, Zoran. 2021. "Implicit–Explicit Gradient of Nondual Awareness or Consciousness as Such." *Neuroscience of Consciousness* 2021 (2): niab031. https://doi.org/10.1093/nc/niab031.

Kachru, Sonam. 2021. *Other Lives: Mind and World in Indian Buddhism.* Columbia University Press.

Kammerer, François. 2021. "The Illusion of Conscious Experience." *Synthese* 198 (1): 845–66. https://doi.org/10.1007/s11229-018-02071-y.

Kant, Immanuel. 1781–84. *Critique of Pure Reason: Unified Edition.* Edited by James W. Ellington and Patricia Kitcher. Translated by Werner S. Pluhar. Hackett Publishing Company, Inc.

Kapstein, Matthew. 1988. "Mereological Considerations In Vasubandhu's 'Proof of Idealism' (Vijñaptimātratāsiddhih)." *Idealistic Studies* 18 (1): 32–54. https://doi.org/10.5840/idstudies19881815.

Kapstein, Matthew. 2001. *Reason's Traces: Identity and Interpretation in Indian and Tibetan Buddhist Thought.* Illustrated edition. Wisdom Publications.

Kaukua, Jari. 2015. *Self-Awareness in Islamic Philosophy: Avicenna and Beyond.* Cambridge University Press. https://doi.org/10.1017/CBO9781316105238.

Keating, Malcolm. 2022. "Kumārila Bhaṭṭa and Pārthasārathi Miśra on First- and Higher-Order Knowing." *Philosophy East and West* 72 (2): 396–414. https://doi.org/10.1353/pew.2022.0047.

Kellner, Birgit. 2010. "Self-Awareness (Svasaṃvedana) in Dignāga's Pramāṇasamuccaya and -Vṛtti: A Close Reading." *Journal of Indian Philosophy* 38 (3): 203–31. https://doi.org/10.1007/s10781-010-9091-y.

Kellner, Birgit. 2011a. *Dharmakīrti's Criticism of External Realism and the Sliding Scale of Analysis.* Vol. 424. Verlag der Österreichischen Akademie der Wissenschaften. https://www.austriaca.at/?arp=0x002901a3.

Kellner, Birgit. 2011b. "Self-Awareness (Svasaṃvedana) and Infinite Regresses: A Comparison of Arguments by Dignāga and Dharmakīrti." *Journal of Indian Philosophy* 39 (4): 411–26. https://doi.org/10.1007/s10 781-011-9139-7.

Kellner, Birgit. 2014. "Changing Frames in Buddhist Thought: The Concept of Ākāra in Abhidharma and in Buddhist Epistemological Analysis." *Journal of Indian Philosophy* 42 (2): 275–95. https://doi.org/10.1007/s10 781-013-9190-7.

Kitcher, Patricia. 2011. *Kant's Thinker.* Oxford University Press.

Kriegel, Uriah. 2009. *Subjective Consciousness: A Self-Representational Theory.* OUP Oxford.

Lawrence, David Peter. 1999. *Rediscovering God with Transcendental Argument: A Contemporary Interpretation of Monistic Kashmiri Śaiva Philosophy.* State University of New York Press.

Letheby, Chris. 2021. *Philosophy of Psychedelics.* Oxford University Press.

Levine, Joseph. 2001. *Purple Haze: The Puzzle of Consciousness*. Oxford University Press.

Locke, John. 1689. *An Essay Concerning Human Understanding*. Edited by Roger Woolhouse. Penguin Classics.

Maas, Philipp A. 2020. "Sarvāstivāda Buddhist Theories of Temporality and the Pātañjala Yoga Theory of Transformation (Pariṇāma)." *Journal of Indian Philosophy* 48 (5): 963–1003. https://doi.org/10.1007/s10781-020-09450-1.

MacKenzie, Matthew. 2007. "The Illumination of Consciousness: Approaches to Self-Awareness in the Indian and Western Traditions." *Philosophy East and West* 57 (1): 40–62.

MacKenzie, Matthew. 2017. "Dual-Aspect Reflexivism in Śāntarakṣita's Philosophy of Mind." *Journal of Buddhist Philosophy* 3 (3): 97–120.

MacKenzie, Matthew. 2018a. "The Yogācāra Theory of Three Natures: Internalist and Non-Dualist Interpretations." *Comparative Philosophy* 9 (1). https://doi.org/10.31979/2151-6014(2018).090105.

MacKenzie, Matthew. 2018b. "Virtue, Self-Transcendence, and Liberation in Yoga and Buddhism." In *Self-Transcendence and Virtue*. Routledge.

MacKenzie, Matthew. 2019. "Physicalism and Beyond: Flanagan, Buddhism, and Consciousness." In *Naturalism, Human Flourishing, and Asian Philosophy*. Routledge.

MacKenzie, Matthew. 2022a. *Buddhist Philosophy and the Embodied Mind: A Constructive Engagement*. Rowman & Littlefield.

MacKenzie, Matthew. 2022b. "Meditative Experience and the Plasticity of Self-Experience." In *Routledge Handbook on the Philosophy of Meditation*. Routledge.

MacKenzie, Matthew. 2024. "Minimal Subjectivity and Reflexive Awareness." *Journal of Consciousness Studies* 31 (5): 37–61. https://doi.org/10.53765/20512201.31.5.037.

MacKenzie, Matthew. 2025. "Reflexivity, Intentionality, and the Embodied Subject: A Phenomenological Reflection in Honor of J. N. Mohanty." *Philosophy East and West* 75 (3): 487–509.

Mahapatra, Debidatta Aurobinda, ed. 2021. *The Philosophy of Sri Aurobindo: Indian Philosophy and Yoga in the Contemporary World*. Bloomsbury Academic.

Matilal, Bimal Krishna. 2012. *The Central Philosophy of Jainism*. L.D. Institute of Indology.

Matthews, Gareth B. 1992. *Thought's Ego in Augustine and Descartes*. Cornell University Press.

McGinn, Colin. 1993. *The Problem of Consciousness: Essays Towards a Resolution*. New Ed edition. Wiley-Blackwell.

Medhananda, Swami. 2022. "The Playful Self-Involution of Divine Consciousness: Sri Aurobindo's Evolutionary Cosmopsychism and His Response to the Individuation Problem." *The Monist* 105 (1): 92–109. https://doi.org/10.1093/monist/onab025.

Metzinger, Thomas. 2004. *Being No One: The Self-Model Theory of Subjectivity.* MIT Press.

Metzinger, Thomas. 2009. *The Ego Tunnel: The Science of the Mind and the Myth of the Self.* Basic Books.

Metzinger, Thomas. 2011. "The No-Self Alternative." In *The Oxford Handbook of the Self,* edited by Shaun Gallagher. Oxford University Press. https://doi.org/10.1093/oxfordhb/9780199548019.003.0012.

Metzinger, Thomas. 2020. "Minimal Phenomenal Experience: Meditation, Tonic Alertness, and the Phenomenology of 'Pure' Consciousness." *Philosophy and the Mind Sciences* 1 (I): I. https://doi.org/10.33735/phimisci.2020.I.46.

Millikan, Ruth Garrett. 1987. *Language, Thought, and Other Biological Categories: New Foundations for Realism.* MIT Press.

Mohanty, J. N. 1971. *The Concept of Intentionality.* First Edition. Warren H Green, inc.

Montague, Michelle. 2016. *The Given: Experience and Its Content.* 1st edition. Oxford University Press.

Nagel, Thomas. 1974. "What Is It Like to Be a Bat?" *The Philosophical Review* 83 (4): 435–50. https://doi.org/10.2307/2183914.

O'Brien-Kop, Karen. 2023. *The Philosophy of the Yogasūtra: An Introduction.* Bloomsbury Publishing.

Pande, Govind Chandra. 1994. *Life and Thought of Śaṅkarācārya.* Motilal Banarsidass.

Pandeya, Ram Chandra, ed. 2024. *The Pramāṇavārttikam of Ācārya Dharmakīrti.* Motilal Banarsidass Publishing House.

Pandit, Moti Lal. 2023. *Kashmir Shaivism: A Philosophy of Being and Becoming.* Dev Publishers & Distributors.

Parfit, Derek. 1987. *Reasons and Persons.* Oxford University Press, USA.

Phillips, Stephen. 2009. *Yoga, Karma, and Rebirth: A Brief History and Philosophy.* Columbia University Press.

Phillips, Stephen. 2014. *Epistemology in Classical India.* 1st edition. Routledge.

Phillips, Stephen. 2024. "Gaṅgeśa." In *The Stanford Encyclopedia of Philosophy,* Summer 2024. Metaphysics Research Lab, Stanford University. https://plato.stanford.edu/archives/sum2024/entries/gangesa/.

Phillips, Stephen H., and N. S. Ramanuja Tatacharya, trans. 2004. *Epistemology of Perception: Gaṅgeśa's Tattvacintāmani.* Bilingual edition. American Institute of Buddhist Studies.

Phillips, Stephen, and Anand Vaidya. 2024. "Epistemology in Classical Indian Philosophy." In *The Stanford Encyclopedia of Philosophy,* Spring 2024, edited by Edward N. Zalta and Uri Nodelman. Metaphysics Research Lab, Stanford University. https://plato.stanford.edu/archives/spr2024/entries/epistemology-india/.

Rāmānuja. 1890. *The Vedānta-Sūtras With the Commentary by Rāmānuja.* Translated by G. Thibaut. Anson Street Press.

Rambachan, Anantanand. 2006. *The Advaita Worldview: God, World, and Humanity.* State University of New York Press.

Ram-Prasad, Chakravarthi. 2013. *Advaita Epistemology and Metaphysics: An Outline of Indian Non-Realism.* Routledge.

Ram-Prasad, Chakravarthi. 2016. *Indian Philosophy and the Consequences of Knowledge: Themes in Ethics, Metaphysics and Soteriology.* 1st edition. Routledge.

Ram-Prasad, Chakravarthi. 2022. "Buddhaghosa: Phenomenology, Hermeneutics, and Understanding." In *The Routledge Handbook of Indian Buddhist Philosophy.* Routledge.

Rao, K. Ramakrishna. 2017. *Foundations of Yoga Psychology.* 1st edition. 2017 edition. Springer.

Ratié, Isabelle. 2014. "On the Distinction Between Epistemic and Metaphysical Buddhist Idealisms: A Śaiva Perspective." *Journal of Indian Philosophy* 42 (2): 353–75. https://doi.org/10.1007/s10781-013-9191-6.

Ratié, Isabelle. 2017. "Utpaladeva and Abhinavagupta on the Freedom of Consciousness." In *The Oxford Handbook of Indian Philosophy.* Oxford University Press. https://academic.oup.com/edited-volume/27982/chapter/211671490.

Repetti, Rick, ed. 2022. *Routledge Handbook on the Philosophy of Meditation.* 1st edition. Routledge.

Robinson, Howard. 2020. "Dualism." In *The Stanford Encyclopedia of Philosophy,* Fall 2020, edited by Edward N. Zalta. Metaphysics Research Lab, Stanford University. https://plato.stanford.edu/archives/fall2020/entries/dualism/.

Roebuck, Valerie, trans. 2004. *The Upanishads.* Penguin UK.

Rohde, Marieke, Massimiliano Di Luca, and Marc O. Ernst. 2011. "The Rubber Hand Illusion: Feeling of Ownership and Proprioceptive Drift Do Not Go Hand in Hand." *PLOS ONE* 6 (6): e21659. https://doi.org/10.1371/journal.pone.0021659.

Ronkin, Noa. 2022. "Abhidharma." In *The Stanford Encyclopedia of Philosophy,* Summer 2022, edited by Edward N. Zalta. Metaphysics Research Lab, Stanford University. https://plato.stanford.edu/archives/sum2022/entries/abhidharma/.

Rosenthal, David B. 1997. "A Theory of Consciousness." /paper/A-theory-of-consciousness-Rosenthal/a5422a0d823e1b752298f26e668fa770a5b63b1d.

Rosenthal, David M. 2009. "Higher-Order Theories of Consciousness." In *The Oxford Handbook of Philosophy of Mind,* edited by Ansgar Beckermann, Brian P. McLaughlin, and Sven Walter. Oxford University Press. https://doi.org/10.1093/oxfordhb/9780199262618.003.0014.

Rowlands, Mark. 2013. "Sartre, Consciousness, and Intentionality." *Phenomenology and the Cognitive Sciences* 12 (3): 521–36. https://doi.org/10.1007/s11097-013-9333-z.

Rowlands, Mark. 2020a. "Externalism About the Mind." In *The Stanford Encyclopedia of Philosophy,* Winter 2020, edited by Edward N. Zalta. Metaphysics Research Lab, Stanford University. https://plato.stanford.edu/archives/win2020/entries/content-externalism/.

Rowlands, Mark. 2020b. "Sartre on Intentionality and Pre-Reflective Consciousness." In *The Sartrean Mind*. Routledge.

Sarma, Deepak. 2003. *An Introduction to Madhva Vedānta*. Routledge.

Sartre, Jean-Paul. 1991. *The Transcendence of the Ego: An Existentialist Theory of Consciousness*. Hill and Wang.

Sartre, Jean-Paul. 1993. *Being and Nothingness*. Original ed. edition. Translated by Hazel E. Barnes. Washington Square Press.

Śaṅkarācārya. 1965. *Brahma Sūtra Bhāṣya Of Śaṅkarācārya*. Translated by Gambhirananda. Vedanta Press & Bookshop.

Śaṅkarācārya. 1992. *A Thousand Teachings: The Upadeśasāhasrī of Śaṅkara*. Edited by Sengaku Mayeda. State University of New York Press.

Schaffer, Jonathan. 2010. "Monism: The Priority of the Whole." *The Philosophical Review* 119 (1): 31–76. https://doi.org/10.1215/00318108-2009-025.

Schweizer, Paul. 1993. "Mind/Consciousness Dualism in Sāṃkhya-Yoga Philosophy." *Philosophy and Phenomenological Research* 53 (4): 845–59. https://doi.org/10.2307/2108256.

Schweizer, Paul. 2019. "Sāṃkhya-Yoga Philosophy and the Mind-Body Problem." *Prabuddha Bharata or Awakened India* 124 (1): 232–42.

Searle, John R. 2000. "Consciousness." *Annual Review of Neuroscience* 23 (1): 557–78. https://doi.org/10.1146/annurev.neuro.23.1.557.

Shah, Nagin. 2000. *Jaina Theory of Multiple Facets of Reality and Truth*. Motilal Banarsidass.

Shani, Itay. 2015. "Cosmopsychism: A Holistic Approach to the Metaphysics of Experience." *Philosophical Papers* 44 (3): 389–437. https://doi.org/10.1080/05568641.2015.1106709.

Shani, Itay. 2023. "Cosmopsychism and Non-Śankaran Traditions of Hindu Non-Dualism: In Search of a Fertile Connection." In *Cross-Cultural Approaches to Consciousness: Mind, Nature and Ultimate Reality*, edited by Itay Shani and Susanne Kathrin Beiweis. Bloomsbury Academic. https://philarchive.org/rec/SHACAN-6.

Shani, Itay. 2024. "Pure Consciousness as the Ground of the Given: Or, Why There Is No Perception Without Background Reception." *Journal of Consciousness Studies* 31 (5): 178–205. https://doi.org/10.53765/20512201.31.5.178.

Sharma, Arvind. 2012. *Sleep as a State of Consciousness in Advaita Vedānta*. State University of New York Press.

Sharma, B. N. Krishnamurti. 2000. *History of the Dvaita School of Vedānta and Its Literature: From the Earliest Beginnings to Our Own Times*. Motilal Banarsidass Publishing House.

Shaw, Miranda. 1987. "William James and Yogācāra Philosophy: A Comparative Inquiry." *Philosophy East and West* 37 (3): 223–44. https://doi.org/10.2307/1398517.

Shear, Jonathan, and Ron Jevning. 1999. "Pure Consciousness: Scientific Exploration of Meditation Techniques." *Journal of Consciousness Studies* 6 (2–3): 189–210.

Shoemaker, Sydney. 1994. "Self-Knowledge and 'Inner Sense': Lecture I: The Object Perception Model." *Philosophy and Phenomenological Research* 54 (2): 249–69. https://doi.org/10.2307/2108488.

Siderits, Mark. 2015. *Personal Identity and Buddhist Philosophy: Empty Persons.* 2nd edition. Routledge.

Siderits, Mark. 2016. *Studies in Buddhist Philosophy.* Oxford University Press.

Siderits, Mark. 2020. "Self-Knowledge and Non-Self." In *Buddhist Philosophy of Consciousness*, edited by Mark Siderits, Ching Keng, and John Spackman. Brill. https://doi.org/10.1163/9789004440913_010.

Siderits, Mark. 2025. *Buddhist Physicalism?: Non-Self Metaphysics and Phenomenal Consciousness.* Oxford University Press.

Siderits, Mark, and Shoryu Katsura. 2013. *Nagarjuna's Middle Way: Mūlamadhyamakakārikā.* Wisdom Publications.

Siewert, Charles. 2025. "Consciousness and Intentionality." In *The Stanford Encyclopedia of Philosophy*, Spring 2025, edited by Edward N. Zalta and Uri Nodelman. Metaphysics Research Lab, Stanford University. https://plato.stanford.edu/archives/spr2025/entries/consciousness-intentionality/.

Singleton, Mark. 2010. *Yoga Body: The Origins of Modern Posture Practice.* Oxford University Press.

Smith, D. W., and R. McIntyre. 1984. *Husserl and Intentionality: A Study of Mind, Meaning, and Language.* Springer.

Smith, David Woodruff. 2016. "The Several Factors of (Self-)Consciousness." *Rivista Internazionale Di Filosofia e Psicologia* 7 (3): 3. https://doi.org/10.4453/rifp.2016.0032.

Smith, Sean. 2020. "A Pāli Buddhist Philosophy of Sentience: Reflections on Bhava\.Nga Citta." *Sophia* 59: 457–88.

Smith, Sean. 2021. "The Negation of Self in Indian Buddhist Philosophy." *Philosopher's Imprint* 21 (13). http://hdl.handle.net/2027/spo.3521354.0021.013.

Sprigge, T. L. S. 2006. *The God of Metaphysics.* Clarendon Press.

Stoljar, Daniel. 2022. "Physicalism." In *The Stanford Encyclopedia of Philosophy*, Summer 2022, edited by Edward N. Zalta. Metaphysics Research Lab, Stanford University. https://plato.stanford.edu/archives/sum2022/entries/physicalism/.

Stoltz, Jonathan. 2021. *Illuminating the Mind: An Introduction to Buddhist Epistemology.* Oxford University Press.

Strawson, Galen. 2009. *Mental Reality, Second Edition, with a New Appendix.* MIT Press.

Strawson, Galen. 2017. *The Subject of Experience.* Oxford University Press.

Strawson, Galen. 2019. "A Hundred Years of Consciousness: 'A Long Training in Absurdity.'" *Estudios de Filosofía*, no. 59 (January): 59. https://doi.org/10.17533/udea.ef.n59a02.

Strawson, Galen. 2024. *Consciousness and Its Place in Nature: Why Physicalism Entails Panpsychism (2nd Edition).* Edited by Anthony Freeman. Andrews UK Limited.

Taber, John. 2012. *A Hindu Critique of Buddhist Epistemology*. Routledge.

Taber, John A. 1990. "The Mīmāṃsā Theory of Self-Recognition." *Philosophy East and West* 40 (1): 35–57. https://doi.org/10.2307/1399548.

Thompson, Evan. 2007. *Mind in Life: Biology, Phenomenology, and the Sciences of Mind*. 1st edition. Belknap Press.

Thompson, Evan. 2011. "Self-No-Self? Memory and Reflexive Awareness." In *Self, No Self?: Perspectives from Analytical, Phenomenological, and Indian Traditions*, edited by Mark Siderits, Evan Thompson, and Dan Zahavi. Oxford University Press.

Thompson, Evan. 2014. *Waking, Dreaming, Being: Self and Consciousness in Neuroscience, Meditation, and Philosophy*. Columbia University Press.

Thompson, Evan. 2022. *Why I Am Not a Buddhist*. Yale University Press.

Tillemans, Tom. 2021. "Dharmakīrti." In *The Stanford Encyclopedia of Philosophy*, Spring 2021, edited by Edward N. Zalta. Metaphysics Research Lab, Stanford University. https://plato.stanford.edu/archives/spr2021/entries/dharmakiirti/.

Timalsina, Sthaneshwar. 2014. *Consciousness in Indian Philosophy*. Routledge.

Timalsina, Sthaneshwar. 2020. "Vimarśa: The Concept of Reflexivity in the Philosophy of Utpala and Abhinavagupta." *Acta Orientalia* 80: 98–121. https://doi.org/10.5617/ao.9395.

Torella, Raffaele. 2021. *The Īśvarapratyabhijñākārikā of Utpaladeva: Critical Edition and Annotated Translation*. Motilal Banarsidass Publishing House.

Travis, Frederick, Alarik Arenander, and David DuBois. 2004. "Psychological and Physiological Characteristics of a Proposed Object-Referral/Self-Referral Continuum of Self-Awareness." *Consciousness and Cognition* 13 (2): 401–20. https://doi.org/10.1016/j.concog.2004.03.001.

Tye, Michael. 1999. *Ten Problems of Consciousness: A Representational Theory of the Phenomenal Mind*. MIT Press.

Vaidya, Anand Jayprakash. 2022. "Analytic Panpsychism and the Metaphysics of Rāmānuja's Viśiṣṭādvaita Vedānta." *The Monist* 105 (1): 110–30. https://doi.org/10.1093/monist/onab026.

Valberg, J. J. 1992. *The Puzzle of Experience*. Clarendon Press.

Waldron, William S. 2003. *The Buddhist Unconscious: The Ālaya-Vijñāna in the Context of Indian Buddhist Thought*. 1st edition. Routledge.

Waldron, William S. 2023. *Making Sense of Mind Only: Why Yogācāra Buddhism Matters*. Simon and Schuster.

Watson, Alex. 2006. *The Self's Awareness of Itself: Bhaṭṭa Rāmakaṇṭha's Arguments Against the Buddhist Doctrine of No-Self*. Wien.

Watson, Alex. 2020. "Four Mīmāṃsā Views Concerning the Self's Perception of Itself." *Journal of Indian Philosophy* 48 (5): 889–914. https://doi.org/10.1007/s10781-020-09446-x.

Westerhoff, Jan. 2009. *Nāgārjuna's Madhyamaka: A Philosophical Introduction*. Oxford University Press.

Westerhoff, Jan. 2016. "What It Means to Live in a Virtual World Generated by Our Brain." *Erkenntnis* 81 (3): 507–28. https://doi.org/10.1007/s10 670-015-9752-z.

Westerhoff, Jan. 2017. "Nāgārjuna on Emptiness: A Comprehensive Critique of Foundationalism." In *The Oxford Handbook of Indian Philosophy*, edited by Jonardon Ganeri. Oxford University Press.

Westerhoff, Jan. 2020. *The Non-Existence of the Real World*. Oxford University Press.

Westerhoff, Jan. 2024. *Candrakīrti's Introduction to the Middle Way: A Guide*. Oxford University Press.

Williams, Donald C. 2018. *The Elements and Patterns of Being: Essays in Metaphysics*. Illustrated edition. Edited by A. R. J. Fisher. Oxford University Press.

Windt, Jennifer Michelle, and Thomas Metzinger. 2007. "The Philosophy of Dreaming and Self-Consciousness: What Happens to the Experiential Subject During the Dream State?" In *The New Science of Dreaming Vol 3: Cultural and Theoretical Perspectives*, edited by Deirdre Barrett and Patrick McNamara. Praeger Publishers/Greenwood Publishing Group.

Zahavi, Dan. 2003. "Inner Time-Consciousness and Pre-Reflective Self-Awareness." In *The New Husserl: A Critical Reader*, edited by Donn Welton. Indiana University Press.

Zahavi, Dan. 2008. *Subjectivity and Selfhood: Investigating the First-Person Perspective*. MIT Press.

Zahavi, Dan. 2014. *Self and Other: Exploring Subjectivity, Empathy, and Shame*. Oxford University Press.

Zahavi, Dan. 2020. *Self-Awareness and Alterity: A Phenomenological Investigation*. 2nd edition. Northwestern University Press.

Zimmerman, Dean. 2010. "I—Dean Zimmerman: From Property Dualism to Substance Dualism." *Aristotelian Society Supplementary Volume* 84 (1): 119–50. https://doi.org/10.1111/j.1467-8349.2010.00189.x.

Index